HOUSE OF SAUD

SAUDI ARABIA'S ROYAL DYNASTY

THRONES, OIL, AND VISION 2030

4 BOOKS IN 1

BOOK 1
THE RISE OF THE HOUSE OF SAUD: FROM DESERT CHIEFTAINS TO SAUDI MONARCHS (1700S-1900S)

BOOK 2
OIL, POWER, AND INFLUENCE: HOUSE OF SAUD IN THE 20TH CENTURY (1900S-2000S)

BOOK 3
MODERNIZATION AND TRADITION: HOUSE OF SAUD'S VISION 2030 (2000S-PRESENT)

BOOK 4
DISSIDENCE AND THE HOUSE OF SAUD: A HISTORY OF OPPOSITION (20TH-21ST CENTURY)

BY A.J. KINGSTON

Copyright © 2023 by A. J. Kingston
All rights reserved. No part of this book may be reproduced or transmitted in any form or by any means, electronic or mechanical, including photocopying, recording, or by any information storage and retrieval system, without permission in writing from the publisher.

Published by A. J. Kingston
Library of Congress Cataloging-in-Publication Data
ISBN 978-1-83938-483-7
Cover design by Rizzo

Disclaimer

The contents of this book are based on extensive research and the best available historical sources. However, the author and publisher make no claims, promises, or guarantees about the accuracy, completeness, or adequacy of the information contained herein. The information in this book is provided on an "as is" basis, and the author and publisher disclaim any and all liability for any errors, omissions, or inaccuracies in the information or for any actions taken in reliance on such information.

The opinions and views expressed in this book are those of the author and do not necessarily reflect the official policy or position of any organization or individual mentioned in this book. Any reference to specific people, places, or events is intended only to provide historical context and is not intended to defame or malign any group, individual, or entity.

The information in this book is intended for educational and entertainment purposes only. It is not intended to be a substitute for professional advice or judgment. Readers are encouraged to conduct their own research and to seek professional advice where appropriate.

Every effort has been made to obtain necessary permissions and acknowledgments for all images and other copyrighted material used in this book. Any errors or omissions in this regard are unintentional, and the author and publisher will correct them in future editions.

Join Our Productivity Group and Access your Bonus

If you're passionate about history books and want to connect with others who share your love of the subject, joining our Facebook group (search for "History Books by A.J.Kingston") can be a great way to do so. By joining a group dedicated to history books, you'll have the opportunity to connect with like-minded individuals, share your thoughts and ideas, and even discover new books that you might not have come across otherwise. You can also access your FREE BONUS once you joined our Facebook group called "History Books by A.J.Kingston".

One of the biggest advantages of joining our Facebook group is the sense of community it provides. You'll be able to interact with other history book enthusiasts, ask questions, and share your own knowledge and expertise. This can be especially valuable if you're a student or someone who is just starting to explore the world of history books.

If you love audiobooks, then joining our YouTube channel that offers free audiobooks on a weekly basis can be a great way to stay entertained and engaged. By subscribing to our channel, you'll have access to a range of audiobooks across different genres, all for free. Not only this is a great opportunity to enjoy some new audiobooks, but it's also a chance to discover new authors and titles that you might not have come across otherwise.

>> Click Here to Join our YouTube Channel <<

Lastly, don't forget to follow us on Facebook and YouTube by searching for A.J. Kingston.

TABLE OF CONTENTS – BOOK 1 - THE RISE OF THE HOUSE OF SAUD: FROM DESERT CHIEFTAINS TO SAUDI MONARCHS (1700S-1900S)

Introduction 7
Chapter 1: The Bedouin Beginnings: Tracing the Origins of the House of Saud (1700s) 9
Chapter 2: Desert Warriors and Tribal Alliances: Early Years of Saud Dominance (18th Century) 20
Chapter 3: The First Saudi State: Consolidation and Expansion (Late 18th Century) 30
Chapter 4: Turmoil and Exile: Decline of the First Saudi State (Early 19th Century) 38
Chapter 5: From the Ashes: Rebirth of the Saud Dynasty (Late 19th Century) 48
Chapter 6: Rivalries and Reconquests: The Second Saudi State (Mid-19th Century) 56
Chapter 7: Lawrence of Arabia and the House of Saud: World War I and the Arabian Peninsula 63
Chapter 8: Ibn Saud's Ascendance: Birth of the Modern Saudi State (Early 20th Century) 73
Chapter 9: Oil, Power, and the House of Saud: Shaping the Kingdom (Mid-20th Century) 84
Chapter 10: Changing of the Guard: The House of Saud in the Late 20th Century 94

TABLE OF CONTENTS – BOOK 2 - OIL, POWER, AND INFLUENCE: HOUSE OF SAUD IN THE 20TH CENTURY (1900S-2000S)

Chapter 1: The Black Gold Rush: Saudi Arabia's Oil Revolution (Early 1900s) 106
Chapter 2: Petrodollars and Political Power: Oil Wealth and Influence (Mid-20th Century) 116
Chapter 3: The OPEC Era: Saudi Arabia's Role in Global Energy Markets (1970s) 125
Chapter 4: Royal Intrigues and Succession Struggles: The House of Saud's Internal Dynamics (1980s) 136
Chapter 5: Desert Storm and Regional Realignment: Saudi Arabia in the Gulf War (1990s) 142
Chapter 6: Islam, Extremism, and the House of Saud: Challenges and Responses (Late 20th Century) 150
Chapter 7: Modernization and Globalization: Saudi Arabia in a Changing World (Late 20th Century) 158
Chapter 8: The 21st Century Awakening: Saudi Arabia's Quest for Economic Diversification (Early 2000s) ... 167
Chapter 9: Leadership Transition: The Post-9/11 Era and Beyond (2000s) 176
Chapter 10: Vision 2030 and Beyond: Saudi Arabia's Ambitious Transformation (21st Century) 186

TABLE OF CONTENTS – BOOK 3 - MODERNIZATION AND TRADITION: HOUSE OF SAUD'S VISION 2030 (2000S-PRESENT)

Chapter 1: The Visionary Roadmap: Unveiling Vision 2030 (Early 2000s) 200
Chapter 2: Economic Transformation: Diversifying Beyond Oil (2000s-2010s) 210
Chapter 3: Societal Reforms: Women's Rights, Entertainment, and Social Change (2010s) 216
Chapter 4: Megaprojects and Modern Infrastructure: Redefining Urban Landscapes (2010s-Present) 222
Chapter 5: Investment and International Relations: Saudi Arabia's Global Outreach (2010s-Present) 228
Chapter 6: Challenges and Criticisms: Vision 2030's Hurdles and Controversies (2010s-Present) 234
Chapter 7: Cultural Heritage and Identity: Balancing Tradition with Modernization (2010s-Present) 239
Chapter 8: Leadership and Succession: The Crown Prince's Role in Shaping the Vision (2010s-Present) 244
Chapter 9: Green Initiatives and Sustainability: Saudi Arabia's Environmental Commitments (2010s-Present) 249
Chapter 10: The Road Ahead: Prospects and Possibilities for Vision 2030 (Present and Beyond) 254

TABLE OF CONTENTS – BOOK 4 - DISSIDENCE AND THE HOUSE OF SAUD: A HISTORY OF OPPOSITION (20TH-21ST CENTURY)

Chapter 1: Seeds of Discontent: Early Opposition Movements (20th Century) 260
Chapter 2: Islamist Challenges: Radicalism and the House of Saud (Late 20th Century) 264
Chapter 3: Regional Tensions: Saudi Arabia and Its Neighbors (20th Century) 269
Chapter 4: The Arab Spring and Unrest: Saudi Arabia's Response to Regional Upheavals (2010s) 274
Chapter 5: The Reformist Wave: Intellectuals, Activists, and Calls for Change (21st Century) 279
Chapter 6: The Role of the Shia Minority: Marginalization and Discontent (21st Century) 284
Chapter 7: International Criticism and Human Rights: Saudi Arabia in the Global Spotlight (21st Century) 288
Chapter 8: The Khashoggi Affair: Murder and International Fallout (2018) 293
Chapter 9: Online Dissent and Social Media: Challenges to State Control (21st Century) 298
Chapter 10: The Future of Dissidence: Prospects for Change and Stability (Present and Beyond) 303
Conclusion 308
About A. J. Kingston 310

**BOOK 1
THE RISE OF THE HOUSE OF SAUD
FROM DESERT CHIEFTAINS TO SAUDI MONARCHS (1700S-1900S)

BY A.J. KINGSTON**

Introduction

In the heart of the Arabian Peninsula, a saga unfolds—a tale of power, tradition, ambition, and change. Welcome to "House of Saud: Saudi Arabia's Royal Dynasty - Thrones, Oil, and Vision 2030," an extraordinary journey through the corridors of history and the complexities of modernity. This compelling four-book bundle offers an unprecedented glimpse into the epic story of the House of Saud and the Kingdom of Saudi Arabia.

Book 1, "The Rise of the House of Saud: From Desert Chieftains to Saudi Monarchs (1700s-1900s)," unravels the enigmatic origins of the Saudi dynasty. We travel back in time to the nomadic beginnings of a family that would rise from the desert sands to establish a legacy that reverberates through the ages.

In Book 2, "Oil, Power, and Influence: House of Saud in the 20th Century (1900s-2000s)," we delve into the transformative impact of the discovery of oil on Saudi Arabia and the world. The House of Saud emerges as a global player, navigating the shifting tides of geopolitics and economics.

The third installment, "Modernization and Tradition: House of Saud's Vision 2030 (2000s-Present)," propels us into the 21st century, where Saudi Arabia stands at a crossroads. Vision 2030, a bold and ambitious plan, aims to usher in a new era of diversification and societal change. Yet, it is a vision that teeters on the precipice of tradition and modernity.

Lastly, Book 4, "Dissidence and the House of Saud: A History of Opposition (20th-21st Century)," brings to light the voices of dissent that have echoed through the annals of Saudi history. From religious scholars challenging authority to women advocating for their rights, this is a narrative of resilience and resistance.

Together, these four volumes paint a panoramic portrait of the House of Saud—a dynasty that has weathered storms, harnessed the power of oil, embarked on a modernization journey, and faced the complexities of dissent. It is a story that spans centuries, continents, and cultures—a story that continues to shape not only the destiny of Saudi Arabia but also the dynamics of the Middle East and the world.

Join us on this illuminating odyssey through time, where tradition meets transformation, where thrones rise and fall, where oil flows like black gold, and where the vision of a nation hangs in the balance. "House of Saud: Saudi Arabia's Royal Dynasty - Thrones, Oil, and Vision 2030" invites you to explore the past, present, and future of a kingdom that remains a fascinating enigma on the world stage.

Chapter 1: The Bedouin Beginnings: Tracing the Origins of the House of Saud (1700s)

Nomadic roots are an integral part of the history and identity of the Arabian Peninsula, a vast and arid region that has been home to various nomadic tribes and communities for centuries. These nomadic roots extend to the House of Saud, the ruling dynasty of Saudi Arabia. The House of Saud's journey from its early Bedouin beginnings in the 18th century to its establishment as a modern monarchy in the 20th century is intertwined with the nomadic traditions and lifestyle of the Arabian desert.

The Arabian Peninsula, with its harsh desert terrain and limited resources, fostered a nomadic way of life for many of its inhabitants. Nomadic tribes roamed the vast deserts, relying on their deep knowledge of the land and their herds of camels and sheep for survival. These tribes were organized along tribal lines, with each tribe led by a chieftain who held authority and made decisions for the group. Among these tribes was the Al Saud clan, which would later become the House of Saud.

The emergence of the Al Saud clan as a prominent force within the Arabian Peninsula can be traced back to the 18th century. At this time, the Arabian Peninsula was characterized by a fragmented and often turbulent landscape, with various tribes vying for power and resources. The Al Saud clan, led by its founder, Muhammad bin Saud, entered the political scene and began forming alliances with religious leaders, particularly with the religious reformer Muhammad ibn Abd al-Wahhab.

This alliance between the Al Saud and Ibn Abd al-Wahhab laid the foundation for the First Saudi State, a state that sought to establish a strict interpretation of Islam and unify the Arabian Peninsula under its banner. The nomadic roots of the Al Saud played a pivotal role during this period, as the tribe's mobility and knowledge of the desert allowed them to wage successful campaigns and expand their territory.

As the First Saudi State consolidated its power and expanded its influence, it faced resistance from regional powers, particularly the Ottoman Empire. This resistance culminated in military campaigns against the Saudi state in the early 19th century, resulting in the fall of the First Saudi State and the exile of the Al Saud clan. It was a period marked by turmoil and challenges, but it did not mark the end of the House of Saud's journey.

From the ashes of defeat and exile, the House of Saud would experience a rebirth in the late 19th century. During this time, a charismatic leader named Abdulaziz Ibn Saud emerged as a unifying force. He led a series of campaigns to reconquer territory and reestablish the authority of the Al Saud clan. Ibn Saud's leadership and military prowess allowed the House of Saud to regain control over Riyadh, the future capital of Saudi Arabia, and surrounding areas.

The late 19th century and early 20th century saw the House of Saud gradually expand its territory and influence across the Arabian Peninsula. It was a period of rivalries and reconquests, as the House of Saud clashed with other tribes and regional powers. This expansion set the stage for Ibn Saud's ascendance and the birth of the modern Saudi state.

Ibn Saud's leadership was characterized by a combination of military conquests and strategic alliances. He skillfully navigated the complex web of tribal politics and regional rivalries, forging partnerships that would later prove instrumental in the formation of the Kingdom of Saudi Arabia. It was during this time that the discovery of vast oil reserves in the region would dramatically alter the course of Saudi history.

The emergence of oil as a valuable resource in the early 20th century presented both opportunities and challenges for the House of Saud. Oil wealth had the potential to transform the kingdom's economy and provide the means to modernize the nation. However, it also brought the attention of international powers seeking access to Saudi Arabia's vast oil reserves.

As Saudi Arabia entered the mid-20th century, it faced the complex task of managing its newfound oil wealth while navigating the shifting sands of global politics. Oil revenues brought unprecedented prosperity to the kingdom, allowing for the development of infrastructure, education, and healthcare. However, the influence of foreign powers in the region, particularly during the era of decolonization and the Cold War, presented geopolitical challenges for Saudi Arabia.

Throughout this period, the House of Saud faced internal dynamics related to leadership succession and power consolidation. The process of passing the mantle of leadership from one generation to the next was carefully managed within the royal family. Succession struggles and rivalries within the family occasionally flared up but were largely managed behind closed doors.

The late 20th century saw Saudi Arabia assume a more prominent role in regional and international affairs. The kingdom played a key role in the oil embargo of the 1970s, using its influence as a major oil producer to respond to geopolitical events in the Middle East. Saudi Arabia's involvement in regional conflicts and its support for conservative Islamic movements also garnered attention and scrutiny.

The late 20th century marked a period of tension and change, both domestically and internationally. Saudi Arabia faced challenges from within, as conservative religious elements clashed with those advocating for social and economic reforms. The country's leadership grappled with how to balance traditional Islamic values with the demands of modernization and globalization.

The turn of the 21st century brought a new set of challenges and opportunities for Saudi Arabia. The rise of extremist ideologies, including Al Qaeda and its affiliates, posed a threat to the kingdom's security and stability. Saudi Arabia embarked on a concerted effort to combat extremism and terrorism, both within its borders and through international cooperation.

At the same time, the kingdom initiated a series of socio-economic reforms aimed at modernizing Saudi society. These reforms included efforts to expand women's rights, promote cultural and entertainment events, and diversify the economy away from its heavy reliance on oil.

The emergence of the Al Saud clan is a foundational element in the history of Saudi Arabia, intricately tied to the nomadic roots and tribal dynamics of the Arabian Peninsula. In the 18th century, when the Arabian

Peninsula was a patchwork of tribal communities and shifting alliances, the Al Saud clan began to rise to prominence, marking the early stages of their journey toward becoming the ruling dynasty of Saudi Arabia.

This emergence was led by Muhammad bin Saud, the founder of the Al Saud dynasty, whose leadership and vision played a pivotal role in shaping the clan's destiny. The Arabian Peninsula at the time was characterized by its arid desert landscapes, where nomadic tribes roamed, each led by a chieftain who held sway over their respective territories.

Muhammad bin Saud hailed from this Bedouin tradition, and his leadership began to unite various Bedouin tribes under the banner of the Al Saud clan. This unification was not just based on tribal loyalties but was deeply intertwined with religious developments in the region. It was during this period that Muhammad bin Saud forged an alliance with Muhammad ibn Abd al-Wahhab, a religious reformer and scholar.

The alliance between the Al Saud and Ibn Abd al-Wahhab laid the ideological foundation for the First Saudi State. It was a unique partnership that blended tribal power with a strict interpretation of Islam, emphasizing the purity of monotheism and denouncing practices that were seen as deviating from this belief. This religious fervor not only provided a cohesive ideology for the emerging state but also fueled its expansion.

Muhammad bin Saud and Ibn Abd al-Wahhab jointly embarked on a campaign to promote their version of Islam and establish their authority over the Arabian Peninsula. This campaign included not only military conquests but also a call to purify Islamic practices and eliminate perceived heresies.

One of the defining moments in the emergence of the Al Saud clan as a regional power was the capture of the city of Riyadh in 1773. Riyadh would later become the capital of Saudi Arabia. The capture of Riyadh marked a significant step in the Al Saud clan's journey toward consolidating power and expanding their influence across the region.

The First Saudi State, established under the leadership of Muhammad bin Saud and inspired by the teachings of Ibn Abd al-Wahhab, aimed to unify the Arabian Peninsula under a strict interpretation of Islam. This state-building effort was characterized by a strong sense of religious mission, as the leaders sought to root out practices they viewed as contrary to their interpretation of Islamic monotheism.

The emergence of the Al Saud clan and the establishment of the First Saudi State were not without challenges. The region was marked by competing tribal interests and rivalries, and the Al Saud's expansionist policies sometimes led to conflicts with neighboring tribes and powers.

One of the key challenges was the opposition from the Ottoman Empire, which sought to maintain its influence over the Arabian Peninsula. The Ottomans viewed the rise of the First Saudi State as a threat to their imperial interests and launched military campaigns to suppress it. This resistance from the Ottoman Empire would ultimately lead to the downfall of the First Saudi State in the early 19th century.

The decline and subsequent exile of the Al Saud clan marked a period of turmoil and uncertainty. The emergence of the Al Saud as a regional power had been met with resistance, and the Ottoman Empire's campaigns had taken a toll on the nascent state. The leaders of the Al Saud clan were forced into exile, leaving Riyadh and their ambitions behind.

However, the story of the Al Saud clan did not end with exile. From the ashes of defeat, a resurgence would take shape in the late 19th century. The House of Saud would experience a rebirth, led by a charismatic and determined leader, Abdulaziz Ibn Saud.

Abdulaziz Ibn Saud would play a pivotal role in the clan's history, leading a series of campaigns to reconquer territory and reestablish the authority of the Al Saud clan. His leadership and military prowess allowed the House of Saud to regain control over Riyadh and surrounding areas.

The late 19th century and early 20th century witnessed the gradual expansion of the House of Saud's territory and influence across the Arabian Peninsula. This period was marked by rivalries and reconquests, as the House of Saud clashed with other tribes and regional powers.

Ibn Saud's leadership style was a blend of military conquests and strategic alliances. He skillfully navigated the complex web of tribal politics and regional rivalries, forging partnerships that would later prove instrumental in the formation of the Kingdom of Saudi Arabia.

The emergence of oil as a valuable resource in the early 20th century brought both opportunities and challenges for the House of Saud. Oil wealth had the potential to transform the kingdom's economy and provide the means to modernize the nation. However, it also brought the attention of international powers seeking access to Saudi Arabia's vast oil reserves.

The emergence of the Al Saud clan from its early Bedouin beginnings to its eventual establishment as the ruling dynasty of Saudi Arabia is a testament to the clan's resilience, adaptability, and ability to navigate the complexities of the Arabian Peninsula's history and politics. From tribal alliances to religious alliances, from conflicts to conquests, the emergence of the Al Saud clan is a story of determination and destiny that would shape the modern kingdom of Saudi Arabia.

Early Bedouin traditions are an essential aspect of the rich and diverse cultural heritage of the Arabian Peninsula, influencing the way of life, social structures, and values of the nomadic tribes that inhabited the region for centuries. These traditions, deeply rooted in the arid desert landscapes, played a fundamental role in shaping the identity of the Arabian Bedouins and continue to hold significance in the broader context of the Arab world.

At the heart of early Bedouin traditions lies the nomadic lifestyle, characterized by mobility, self-sufficiency, and a deep connection to the desert environment. Bedouin communities were traditionally organized into tribes, each with its own distinct lineage, customs, and territory. The tribe was the central social unit, and it provided a sense of belonging and protection to its members.

In the vast and challenging terrain of the Arabian Peninsula, the ability to navigate the desert was a fundamental skill for Bedouin nomads. They developed an intricate knowledge of the desert's geography, including water sources, oases, and trade routes. This expertise allowed them to survive in an environment where resources were scarce and the climate was harsh.

The camel, often referred to as the "ship of the desert," played a crucial role in Bedouin life. Camels served as a means of transportation, a source of milk, and a valuable commodity for trade. Bedouins were known for their expert camel husbandry, and the animals were highly prized for their adaptability to desert conditions.

The traditional Bedouin diet consisted primarily of dairy products, dates, and meat from livestock such as goats and camels. Dates, in particular, held great importance as a staple food, providing a valuable source of energy in the desert. The ability to preserve and store dates was a vital skill, allowing Bedouins to sustain themselves during long journeys across the arid landscape.

One of the key elements of early Bedouin traditions was the concept of hospitality. In a harsh and unforgiving environment, the practice of offering food, water, and shelter to travelers and guests was not only a matter of courtesy but also a survival strategy. Bedouin tribes would go to great lengths to ensure the well-being of their guests, and the bonds formed through hospitality were highly valued.

The social structure within Bedouin tribes was hierarchical, with a tribal leader or chieftain holding authority and making decisions for the group. Leadership was often hereditary, passed down through family lines, but it was also influenced by a leader's ability to provide for and protect the tribe. Tribes had their own systems of justice and dispute resolution, often relying on the wisdom of respected elders.

Early Bedouin traditions also encompassed a rich oral tradition of storytelling and poetry. Bedouin poets, known as "sha'irs," played a significant role in preserving and transmitting the cultural heritage of their tribes. Through poetry, they recounted the heroic deeds of their ancestors, celebrated tribal history, and expressed the values and virtues of Bedouin life.

Religion held a central place in Bedouin traditions. Before the advent of Islam, Arabian Bedouins practiced various forms of polytheism, worshiping a pantheon of deities associated with natural elements. The Kaaba in Mecca, an ancient religious sanctuary, was a focal point of pilgrimage and religious significance for Bedouins and other Arabian tribes.

With the arrival of Islam in the 7th century, many Bedouin tribes embraced the new monotheistic faith. Islam's message of monotheism and social justice resonated with the Bedouin ethos, and it brought about significant changes in their religious practices and way of life. The pilgrimage to Mecca, known as the Hajj, became one of the Five Pillars of Islam and drew Bedouin pilgrims from across the Arabian Peninsula.

The Bedouin ethos also emphasized values such as honor, loyalty, and courage. Honor, in particular, was highly regarded, and any affront to a tribe's honor could lead to conflicts and feuds. Tribes would defend their honor fiercely and were known for their code of chivalry.

The concept of "diyya," or blood money, was another important aspect of Bedouin traditions. It was a means of compensating victims or their families in cases of injury or death caused by disputes or conflicts. Diyya served as a way to restore balance and prevent long-standing vendettas.

The early Bedouin traditions left an indelible mark on the cultural fabric of the Arabian Peninsula. While the modernization and urbanization of the region have transformed many aspects of Bedouin life, these traditions continue to be celebrated and preserved as a vital part of Arab heritage. Today, Bedouin communities and their descendants maintain a connection to their cultural roots, often sharing their traditions with the world through art, music, and storytelling, offering a glimpse into the enduring legacy of early Bedouin traditions.

Chapter 2: Desert Warriors and Tribal Alliances: Early Years of Saud Dominance (18th Century)

The rise of the Saud leadership is a remarkable chapter in the history of Saudi Arabia and the Arabian Peninsula, marked by strategic alliances, territorial conquests, and the establishment of the House of Saud as the ruling dynasty of the modern Kingdom of Saudi Arabia. This rise to power began in the 18th century and unfolded over several generations, ultimately culminating in the formation of a unified Saudi state.

At the heart of this rise to leadership was the charismatic and visionary founder of the House of Saud, Muhammad bin Saud. In the 18th century, the Arabian Peninsula was a region characterized by fragmented tribal communities, shifting alliances, and a complex web of tribal politics. Muhammad bin Saud emerged as a formidable leader, known for his ability to navigate these intricate tribal dynamics.

One of the pivotal moments in the rise of Saud leadership occurred when Muhammad bin Saud forged a historic alliance with a religious scholar named Muhammad ibn Abd al-Wahhab. This alliance, often referred to as the "Saud-Wahhabi alliance," laid the ideological foundation for the First Saudi State.

Muhammad ibn Abd al-Wahhab was a prominent Islamic reformer who advocated for a strict interpretation of Islam based on the principles of monotheism. His teachings emphasized the rejection of practices he viewed as deviating from the pure monotheistic faith. This strict interpretation of Islam served as a unifying ideology for the emerging Saudi state and played a central role in the expansion of Saud authority.

The alliance between Muhammad bin Saud and Muhammad ibn Abd al-Wahhab was not solely motivated by religious convictions but also served practical purposes. It provided a sense of legitimacy to the Saud leadership and allowed them to rally tribes under the banner of their religious mission.

Under this alliance, the Saud-Wahhabi forces embarked on a campaign to promote their version of Islam and establish their authority over the Arabian Peninsula. They sought to unify the region under their interpretation of Islam, emphasizing strict adherence to the principles of monotheism and the rejection of what they perceived as religious deviations.

Riyadh, the present-day capital of Saudi Arabia, played a pivotal role in this rise to leadership. In 1773, Muhammad bin Saud and his forces captured Riyadh, marking a significant milestone in their quest for territorial control. Riyadh would later become the central stronghold of the emerging Saudi state.

The First Saudi State, established under the leadership of Muhammad bin Saud and inspired by the teachings of Muhammad ibn Abd al-Wahhab, aimed to unite the Arabian Peninsula under their strict interpretation of Islam. This state-building effort was characterized by a strong sense of religious mission, as the leaders sought to root out practices they viewed as contrary to their interpretation of Islamic monotheism.

However, the rise of the Saud leadership was not without its challenges. The expansion of the First Saudi State brought it into conflict with the Ottoman Empire, which sought to maintain its influence over the Arabian Peninsula. The Ottoman Empire viewed the rising influence of the Saud-Wahhabi alliance as a threat to its imperial interests.

This resistance from the Ottoman Empire led to a series of military campaigns against the First Saudi State, culminating in the fall of the state and the exile of the Al Saud clan in the early 19th century. It was a period marked by turmoil and challenges, as the Al Saud clan faced defeat and the loss of territory.

The decline and exile of the Al Saud clan did not mark the end of their journey. From the ashes of defeat, a resurgence would take shape in the late 19th century, led by Abdulaziz Ibn Saud, the great-grandson of Muhammad bin Saud. Ibn Saud's leadership would prove pivotal in the clan's rise to power.

Abdulaziz Ibn Saud emerged as a charismatic and determined leader, leading a series of campaigns to reconquer territory and reestablish the authority of the Al Saud clan. His leadership and military prowess allowed the House of Saud to regain control over Riyadh and surrounding areas.

The late 19th century and early 20th century witnessed the gradual expansion of the House of Saud's territory and influence across the Arabian Peninsula. This period was marked by rivalries and reconquests, as the House of Saud clashed with other tribes and regional powers.

Ibn Saud's leadership style was a blend of military conquests and strategic alliances. He skillfully navigated the complex web of tribal politics and regional rivalries, forging partnerships that would later prove instrumental in the formation of the Kingdom of Saudi Arabia.

The emergence of oil as a valuable resource in the early 20th century brought both opportunities and challenges for the House of Saud. Oil wealth had the potential to transform the kingdom's economy and provide the means to modernize the nation. However, it also brought the attention of international powers seeking access to Saudi Arabia's vast oil reserves.

The rise of Saud leadership, from its early Bedouin beginnings in the 18th century to the establishment of the House of Saud as the ruling dynasty of Saudi Arabia, is a testament to the clan's resilience, adaptability, and ability to navigate the complexities of the Arabian Peninsula's history and politics. It is a story of determination and destiny that would shape the modern kingdom of Saudi Arabia.

Tribal alliances and conflicts have played a pivotal role in shaping the history, politics, and social dynamics of the Arabian Peninsula, particularly during the era of Bedouin and tribal societies. These alliances and conflicts were characterized by intricate tribal politics, shifting loyalties, and territorial rivalries, and they continue to influence the region's dynamics to this day.

In the arid and challenging terrain of the Arabian Peninsula, where resources were often scarce and the environment harsh, tribal communities formed the basis of social organization. These tribes were organized along clan and familial lines, each led by a chieftain or tribal leader who held authority and made decisions for the group.

Tribal alliances were forged through a variety of mechanisms, often driven by shared interests, kinship ties, or strategic considerations. These alliances served as a means of protection and support in a challenging environment where cooperation and unity were essential for survival.

One of the key elements in tribal alliances was the concept of "diyya," or blood money. This concept provided a framework for resolving disputes and conflicts within and between tribes. Diyya allowed tribes to compensate victims or their families in cases of injury or death caused by disputes, serving as a means to restore balance and prevent long-standing vendettas.

Territorial rivalries and disputes were common among tribes in the Arabian Peninsula. Control over water sources, pastures, and trade routes was often a source of contention. Tribes would vie for control of valuable territories, and conflicts could escalate into protracted feuds if left unresolved.

The nomadic way of life in the Arabian Peninsula meant that tribes were often on the move in search of water and pasture for their livestock. This mobility added complexity to tribal alliances and conflicts, as tribal boundaries were not fixed, and alliances could shift as tribes moved in search of resources.

Tribal leaders, known as chieftains or sheikhs, played a central role in negotiating alliances and mediating conflicts. These leaders were often respected for their wisdom, experience, and ability to maintain order within their tribes. They also served as representatives of their tribes in intertribal negotiations.

The arrival of Islam in the 7th century brought significant changes to tribal alliances and conflicts in the Arabian Peninsula. Islam emphasized the importance of unity and brotherhood among Muslims, transcending tribal loyalties. The concept of the "ummah," or the Muslim community, became a unifying force that challenged traditional tribal divisions.

During the time of the Prophet Muhammad, the Islamic community in Medina, known as the "Ansar," provided a model of cooperation and solidarity among different tribes. This model emphasized the importance of cooperation and unity for the greater good of the Muslim community.

However, even with the emergence of Islam, tribal identities and alliances persisted. The early Islamic period saw a series of tribal conflicts and alliances, particularly during the Ridda Wars (Apostasy Wars), when various tribes and leaders rebelled against the central Islamic authority.

Tribalism and alliances continued to shape the politics of the Arabian Peninsula throughout history. The emergence of powerful tribal confederations, such as the Qarmatians and Banu Hilal, had a significant impact on the region's history and contributed to both regional stability and conflicts.

In the 18th century, the rise of the House of Saud and the formation of the First Saudi State marked a period when tribal alliances and conflicts played a critical role. The Saud-Wahhabi alliance, which brought together the House of Saud and the religious reformer Muhammad ibn Abd al-Wahhab, was instrumental in consolidating authority and expanding territory.

The alliance with religious scholars provided the House of Saud with religious legitimacy and support for their territorial ambitions. Together, they waged campaigns to promote their interpretation of Islam and establish their authority over the Arabian Peninsula.

The consolidation of the First Saudi State and the expansion of Saud authority were met with resistance from other tribes and regional powers. The Ottoman Empire, in particular, viewed the rise of the Saud-Wahhabi alliance as a threat to its influence in the region and launched military campaigns against the First Saudi State.

These conflicts and rivalries culminated in the fall of the First Saudi State and the exile of the Al Saud clan in the early 19th century. It was a period marked by territorial losses and challenges to the authority of the House of Saud.

However, the exile of the Al Saud clan did not mark the end of their journey. From the ashes of defeat, a resurgence would take shape in the late 19th century, led by Abdulaziz Ibn Saud. His leadership and military campaigns would ultimately lead to the reconquest of territory and the establishment of the modern Kingdom of Saudi Arabia.

In the modern era, tribal identities and alliances continue to hold significance in Saudi Arabia and the broader Arabian Peninsula. While the central government has worked to foster national identity and unity, tribal affiliations remain important in social and political contexts.

Tribal conflicts, though less frequent, still occur and are often mediated by tribal leaders and authorities. The Saudi Arabian government has sought to strike a balance between maintaining tribal traditions and promoting national unity.

In summary, tribal alliances and conflicts have been a fundamental aspect of the Arabian Peninsula's history, shaping the region's social fabric and politics for centuries. These alliances and rivalries continue to be a dynamic force in the region, reflecting the complex interplay between tradition, identity, and modernization.

The expansion across the Arabian Peninsula by the House of Saud is a remarkable chapter in the history of Saudi Arabia, marked by strategic conquests, territorial expansion, and the eventual unification of the Arabian Peninsula under the banner of the Saudi state. This expansion, which unfolded over several generations, played a pivotal role in establishing the House of Saud as the ruling dynasty of the modern Kingdom of Saudi Arabia. The early expansion of the House of Saud was characterized by a blend of military campaigns and strategic alliances with various tribes and communities across the Arabian Peninsula. Abdulaziz Ibn Saud, the great-grandson of the founder of the House of Saud, emerged as a charismatic and determined leader in the late 19th century, leading the efforts to regain control over territory that had been lost during the decline of the First Saudi State.

One of the key aspects of the House of Saud's expansion strategy was its ability to navigate the complex web of tribal politics and regional rivalries. Abdulaziz Ibn Saud skillfully forged partnerships with tribal leaders, often using diplomacy and alliances to avoid protracted conflicts. This approach allowed the House of Saud to gradually extend its influence and authority.

Riyadh, the present-day capital of Saudi Arabia, played a central role in the House of Saud's expansion. In 1902,

Abdulaziz Ibn Saud recaptured Riyadh from rival tribal forces, marking a significant milestone in the House of Saud's journey toward territorial control. Riyadh would later become the stronghold of the emerging Saudi state.

The late 19th century and early 20th century witnessed a series of campaigns led by Abdulaziz Ibn Saud to reestablish control over territories that had once been part of the First Saudi State. These campaigns often involved battles, negotiations, and alliances with tribal leaders, as the House of Saud sought to consolidate its authority.

One of the notable achievements of Abdulaziz Ibn Saud was the recapture of the city of Mecca in 1925, a significant religious and political center in the Arabian Peninsula. This achievement bolstered the House of Saud's legitimacy and influence, as Mecca held immense religious significance for Muslims worldwide.

The emergence of oil as a valuable resource in the early 20th century added a new dimension to the House of Saud's expansion. Saudi Arabia's vast oil reserves brought economic opportunities and international attention. Abdulaziz Ibn Saud skillfully managed relationships with foreign powers seeking access to Saudi Arabia's oil wealth, while also using oil revenue to modernize the nation.

The House of Saud's expansion across the Arabian Peninsula culminated in the formation of the modern Kingdom of Saudi Arabia in 1932. Abdulaziz Ibn Saud, now known as King Abdulaziz, declared himself the ruler of the newly established kingdom. This marked the unification of various tribal regions, communities, and territories under a centralized Saudi state.

The expansion of the House of Saud across the Arabian Peninsula was a complex and multifaceted process, driven by a combination of military campaigns, strategic alliances, and diplomatic efforts. It required adept leadership, a deep understanding of tribal dynamics, and the ability to balance regional interests.

The establishment of the Kingdom of Saudi Arabia represented a turning point in the region's history. It brought about a centralized government, modern infrastructure, and economic development. Saudi Arabia's oil wealth would later transform the nation's economy and position it as a major player on the global stage.

The expansion of the House of Saud across the Arabian Peninsula reflects the enduring legacy of the Bedouin traditions of adaptability, resilience, and tribal diplomacy. It also serves as a testament to the determination of the House of Saud to unify the Arabian Peninsula and establish the modern nation of Saudi Arabia. Today, the kingdom stands as a regional powerhouse with a unique blend of tradition and modernity.

Chapter 3: The First Saudi State: Consolidation and Expansion (Late 18th Century)

The foundations of the First Saudi State are rooted in the emergence of the House of Saud as a significant political and religious force in the Arabian Peninsula during the late 18th century. This period marked the beginning of a series of events that would lead to the establishment of the First Saudi State and lay the groundwork for the modern Kingdom of Saudi Arabia.

1. Rise of Muhammad bin Saud: The foundation of the First Saudi State can be traced back to the leadership of Muhammad bin Saud, the founder of the House of Saud. In the 18th century, the Arabian Peninsula was characterized by fragmented tribal communities, shifting alliances, and a complex web of tribal politics. Muhammad bin Saud emerged as a charismatic and influential leader, known for his ability to navigate the intricate tribal dynamics of the region.

2. Alliance with Muhammad ibn Abd al-Wahhab: One of the pivotal moments in the establishment of the First Saudi State was the alliance forged between Muhammad bin Saud and Muhammad ibn Abd al-Wahhab, a prominent religious scholar and reformer. This alliance, often referred to as the "Saud-Wahhabi alliance," was not only political but also deeply religious. It laid the ideological foundation for the First Saudi State.

3. Ideological Foundation: Muhammad ibn Abd al-Wahhab's teachings emphasized a strict interpretation of Islam based on the principles of monotheism. His teachings rejected practices he viewed as deviating from the pure monotheistic faith, including various traditional customs and rituals. This religious ideology served as a unifying force for the emerging Saudi state, providing it with a cohesive and powerful narrative.

4. Territorial Expansion: With the backing of religious legitimacy and a sense of mission to purify Islam, the Saud-Wahhabi alliance embarked on a campaign to expand their territory and influence across the Arabian Peninsula. Their expansion efforts were characterized by both military conquests and religious reforms aimed at promoting their interpretation of Islam.

5. Capture of Riyadh: In 1773, Muhammad bin Saud's forces captured the city of Riyadh, which would later become the capital of the First Saudi State. This event marked a significant milestone in their quest for territorial control and the establishment of a centralized authority.

6. Consolidation and Expansion: Over the following years, the First Saudi State continued to consolidate its power and expand its territory. The leaders of the state sought to unify the Arabian Peninsula under their strict interpretation of Islam, emphasizing the rejection of practices they viewed as contrary to their version of Islamic monotheism.

7. Ottoman Resistance: The rise of the First Saudi State was met with resistance from the Ottoman Empire, which sought to maintain its influence over the Arabian Peninsula. The Ottomans viewed the expanding Saud-Wahhabi authority as a threat to their imperial interests and launched military campaigns against the First Saudi State.

8. Decline and Exile: Despite its initial successes, the First Saudi State faced challenges from both external and internal sources. Conflict with the Ottoman Empire, tribal rivalries, and power struggles led to the decline of the state. The leaders of the Al Saud clan were forced into exile, leaving Riyadh and their ambitions behind.

9. Legacy and Resurgence: While the First Saudi State may have experienced a period of decline and exile, it left a lasting legacy. The House of Saud would experience a resurgence in the late 19th century, led by charismatic leaders like Abdulaziz Ibn Saud. This resurgence would ultimately lead to the reconquest of territory and the establishment of the modern Kingdom of Saudi Arabia.

The foundations of the First Saudi State reflect a unique blend of religious zeal, political ambition, and strategic leadership. It set the stage for the House of Saud's enduring influence in the Arabian Peninsula and the establishment of a modern nation-state built on the principles of Islamic monotheism and cultural heritage.

The concept of "regional ascendancy" refers to the rise of a particular nation, state, or power to a position of dominance or preeminence within a specific geographical region. Regional ascendancy can occur through a combination of political, economic, military, and diplomatic means, and it often has significant implications for the balance of power within the region and beyond. This phenomenon has been observed throughout history and continues to shape the dynamics of various regions around the world. Here are some key examples of regional ascendancy:

1. Roman Empire in Ancient Europe: The Roman Empire, at its height, achieved regional ascendancy in Europe, controlling vast territories encompassing modern-day Italy, Spain, France, and parts of England, Germany, and North Africa. Roman influence extended far beyond military conquests, encompassing culture, governance, and law.

2. Ottoman Empire in the Middle East and Southeast Europe: The Ottoman Empire, centered in present-day Turkey, achieved regional ascendancy during the late medieval and early modern periods. At its zenith, it controlled large parts of the Middle East, Southeast Europe, and North Africa, exerting significant cultural, political, and military influence.

3. British Empire in the 19th Century: The British Empire was a prime example of a global power achieving regional ascendancy. In the 19th century, it dominated regions such as South Asia, Africa, and the Pacific, spreading its influence through colonization, trade, and diplomacy.

4. Soviet Union in Eastern Europe: Following World War II, the Soviet Union emerged as a dominant power in Eastern Europe through its military and political influence. The Eastern Bloc, comprising countries under Soviet control, demonstrated the concept of regional ascendancy during the Cold War.

5. China's Rise in East Asia: In recent decades, China has experienced significant regional ascendancy in East Asia. Its economic growth, military modernization, and diplomatic initiatives have established it as a major player in the region, challenging the traditional dominance of the United States.

6. Brazil in South America: Brazil has asserted regional ascendancy in South America, both economically and politically. With its large economy, Brazil has played a central role in organizations like Mercosur and has sought to assert itself as a regional leader.

7. Gulf States in the Middle East: Gulf states such as Saudi Arabia, the United Arab Emirates, and Qatar have achieved regional ascendancy through their economic and political influence. They play pivotal roles in regional conflicts, diplomacy, and energy markets.

8. India's Influence in South Asia: India's size and growing economy have led to regional ascendancy in South Asia. It maintains strong diplomatic and economic ties with its neighbors, although regional dynamics are often complex due to historical tensions.

9. African Regional Powers: Countries like Nigeria and South Africa have sought to assert themselves as regional leaders in Africa due to their economic and demographic significance. They play roles in regional organizations like the African Union.

10. European Union: The European Union, while not a nation-state, represents a regional bloc that has achieved ascendancy in Europe through its economic integration and diplomatic efforts. It has played a crucial role in shaping European politics and economics.

Regional ascendancy is a dynamic process influenced by shifting geopolitical, economic, and social factors. It can lead to power struggles, cooperation, and realignments within a given region. Understanding regional ascendancy is essential for analyzing international relations and global politics as it provides insights into the distribution of power and influence in specific areas of the world.

Saudi sovereignty, like that of many other nations, has faced various challenges over the years. These challenges can take many forms, including external pressures, internal dissent, regional conflicts, and economic fluctuations. Here are some of the key challenges to Saudi sovereignty:

1. Regional Conflict and Geopolitical Tensions: Saudi Arabia is situated in a volatile region with ongoing conflicts, such as the Yemeni Civil War and tensions with Iran. These regional conflicts can spill over and pose a direct threat to Saudi sovereignty, leading to security concerns and the need for military intervention.

2. Iran-Saudi Rivalry: Saudi Arabia and Iran have a long-standing rivalry in the Middle East. This rivalry is characterized by proxy conflicts, support for opposing factions, and a struggle for influence in the region. It poses a significant challenge to Saudi sovereignty and regional stability.

3. Terrorism and Extremism: Saudi Arabia has faced internal and external threats from terrorist groups, including Al-Qaeda and ISIS. These groups have sought to undermine Saudi sovereignty through acts of terrorism and extremism, targeting both the government and civilians.

4. Internal Dissent: Dissent and opposition to the Saudi government, whether in the form of political activism, human rights advocacy, or religious dissent, have at times challenged the kingdom's authority and sovereignty. The government has responded with varying degrees of repression.

5. Oil Price Volatility: Saudi Arabia's economy is heavily reliant on oil exports. Fluctuations in oil prices can significantly impact the country's financial stability and sovereignty. The government has implemented economic diversification efforts, such as Vision 2030, to reduce this dependence.

6. Regional Dynamics: The dynamics within the Gulf Cooperation Council (GCC) can impact Saudi sovereignty. Disputes and tensions among GCC member states, such as the 2017 Qatar crisis, can strain the unity and influence of the council, which is important for Saudi Arabia's regional objectives.

7. Social and Cultural Change: Saudi society is undergoing significant social and cultural changes, including reforms aimed at increasing personal freedoms, especially for women. These changes, while positive for many, can also lead to social tensions and challenges to traditional norms.

8. Economic Challenges: The Saudi government faces the challenge of diversifying its economy away from oil, reducing unemployment, and ensuring sustainable economic growth. Economic challenges can impact the government's ability to provide services and maintain stability.

9. Human Rights Concerns: Saudi Arabia has faced international criticism and scrutiny over its human rights record, particularly concerning issues such as freedom of expression, treatment of dissidents, and the rule of law. These concerns can affect the kingdom's international reputation and relationships.

10. Yemen Conflict: Saudi Arabia's military involvement in the Yemeni Civil War has been a significant challenge, both in terms of security and international perception.

The conflict has strained Saudi resources and led to criticism from human rights organizations.

Navigating these challenges to sovereignty requires a delicate balancing act for the Saudi government. It must maintain internal stability while managing regional conflicts, economic reforms, and social changes. The kingdom's response to these challenges plays a crucial role in shaping its domestic and international standing.

Chapter 4: Turmoil and Exile: Decline of the First Saudi State (Early 19th Century)

Internal struggles and power shifts have been recurring themes in the history of Saudi Arabia, reflecting the complex dynamics of governance, royal succession, and political influence within the kingdom. These internal challenges have shaped the evolution of Saudi leadership and had significant implications for the country's domestic and foreign policies.

Throughout Saudi Arabia's history, the power structure has largely revolved around the Al Saud royal family, which has ruled the country since its inception. However, the Al Saud family is vast, with numerous princes and factions vying for influence and control. This internal competition has often led to power struggles and shifts within the royal family.

One of the most prominent internal struggles in Saudi Arabia's history occurred in the early 1960s, when King Saud bin Abdulaziz Al Saud faced mounting economic and political challenges. King Saud's lavish spending and fiscal mismanagement strained the kingdom's finances, leading to economic instability. His leadership was also criticized for its perceived inefficiency and corruption.

This internal crisis prompted senior members of the Al Saud family, including Crown Prince Faisal bin Abdulaziz Al Saud, to take action. In 1964, King Saud was deposed by a royal decree, and Crown Prince Faisal assumed the throne. This power shift marked a significant turning point in Saudi Arabia's history and governance.

Under King Faisal's leadership, Saudi Arabia underwent a series of reforms and modernization efforts aimed at stabilizing the country's economy and government. Faisal implemented strict fiscal discipline, reduced government spending, and sought to diversify the economy away from its heavy reliance on oil revenues. His leadership was characterized by a more pragmatic and disciplined approach to governance.

Another internal challenge to Saudi leadership emerged in the late 1970s and early 1980s when a group of Islamic militants, inspired by a strict interpretation of Wahhabi Islam, opposed the monarchy's policies and called for a more conservative and puritanical form of governance. This movement, known as the Sahwa or Islamic Awakening, challenged the royal family's authority and sought to impose its vision of Islamic rule.

The Sahwa movement posed a significant internal threat to the Saudi government, leading to a crackdown on its leaders and supporters. The government's response to this challenge involved a combination of repression and accommodation, as it sought to maintain its grip on power while addressing some of the movement's concerns.

In the late 20th century, Saudi Arabia faced internal power struggles related to the issue of royal succession. The Al Saud family had to navigate a complex system of determining who would become the next king. The Saudi monarchy did not follow a strict hereditary line of succession, and decisions about the next king were made through a consensus among senior princes.

This process led to competition among different branches of the Al Saud family, with each branch seeking to have its candidate ascend to the throne. These succession disputes often involved intense negotiations, family rivalries, and power struggles behind closed doors. The need to maintain unity within the royal family and ensure a smooth transition of power remained paramount.

In 2015, King Salman bin Abdulaziz Al Saud ascended to the throne, and he initiated a significant reshuffling of the country's leadership positions. He appointed his son, Mohammed bin Salman (commonly referred to as MbS), as the crown prince and deputy prime minister. This move consolidated power within the younger generation of the Al Saud family and marked a notable power shift within the royal family.

MbS has played a prominent role in Saudi Arabia's domestic and foreign policies. He has implemented a series of ambitious reforms, including the Vision 2030 plan aimed at diversifying the economy and reducing the kingdom's dependence on oil. However, these reforms have also been accompanied by a more centralized style of governance and a crackdown on dissent.

One of the most significant internal challenges of MbS's leadership was the controversy surrounding the murder of journalist Jamal Khashoggi in 2018. The international outcry and criticism that followed strained Saudi Arabia's relationships with Western allies and raised questions about the kingdom's human rights record.

Internal power dynamics continue to shape Saudi Arabia's leadership and governance. The Al Saud family remains at the core of the country's political system, but power struggles, generational shifts, and the need to address economic and social challenges create an ever-evolving landscape of internal dynamics.

Navigating these internal challenges while maintaining stability and unity remains a central challenge for Saudi leadership. The country's ability to address these issues will have implications not only for its domestic governance but also for its role in the broader Middle East and on the international stage. As Saudi Arabia continues to face a changing world, its leadership will need to adapt to internal shifts while managing external pressures and opportunities.

The history of Saudi Arabia is marked by various intrusions and incursions by neighboring powers, with the Ottoman Empire and Egypt being two prominent examples of external forces that sought to exert control or influence over the Arabian Peninsula. These intrusions played a significant role in shaping the region's history, politics, and relations with external powers.

One of the most notable episodes in Saudi Arabia's history involving external intrusions occurred during the expansionist policies of the Ottoman Empire in the 18th and 19th centuries. The Ottoman Empire, a vast and powerful empire with its center in Istanbul, sought to extend its influence over various parts of the Arabian Peninsula, including the regions controlled by the House of Saud.

The House of Saud, led by its founder, Muhammad bin Saud, and the religious reformer Muhammad ibn Abd al-Wahhab, had established the first Saudi state in the mid-18th century. This state was characterized by its strict interpretation of Islam and its efforts to unify various tribal communities under its authority.

The expansion of the Saudi state posed a perceived threat to the Ottoman Empire's interests in the region. As a result, the Ottomans launched a series of military campaigns against the nascent Saudi state, seeking to curb its influence and reassert Ottoman control.

These conflicts, often referred to as the "Wahhabi Wars," were characterized by a series of battles and campaigns between the Ottoman forces and the Saudi-Wahhabi alliance. The battles were marked by fierce fighting and shifting alliances among various tribal groups in the region.

Despite facing significant military pressure from the Ottomans, the Saudi-Wahhabi alliance, known for its determination and guerrilla tactics, managed to maintain control over parts of the Arabian Peninsula. The conflict persisted for several decades, with both sides experiencing victories and setbacks.

However, the tide of the Wahhabi Wars began to turn in the early 19th century when the Ottoman Empire, under the leadership of Muhammad Ali Pasha, the governor of Egypt, intervened decisively in the Arabian Peninsula. Muhammad Ali Pasha saw an opportunity to expand Egyptian influence and control over the region.

The Egyptian forces, well-organized and equipped, launched a campaign in the early 1810s to crush the Saudi-Wahhabi alliance. The conflict culminated in the capture of the Saudi capital, Diriyah, in 1818. This marked a turning point in the region's history, as the Saudi state was significantly weakened, and its leaders were exiled.

The Egyptian occupation of parts of the Arabian Peninsula brought about a period of significant change. Under Muhammad Ali Pasha's rule, the region experienced administrative reforms, infrastructure development, and efforts to modernize governance. However, this period of

Egyptian rule also faced resistance from local tribes and communities.

The Ottoman Empire formally recognized Egyptian control over the region, effectively ceding authority to Muhammad Ali Pasha. This marked a shift in the balance of power in the Arabian Peninsula, as the Ottomans had struggled to exert direct control over the region.

The Egyptian intrusion into the Arabian Peninsula continued for several decades, with varying degrees of stability and resistance. It wasn't until the mid-19th century that the Al Saud family, under the leadership of Faisal bin Turki, launched a successful campaign to reclaim territory and reestablish their authority.

Faisal bin Turki's leadership marked the resurgence of the House of Saud and the decline of Egyptian influence in the region. The Saudi forces, with the support of tribal allies, managed to recapture Riyadh and reestablish their rule in the central Najd region.

The decline of Egyptian influence in the Arabian Peninsula was further accelerated by international developments, including the intervention of the European great powers, particularly Britain, which sought to limit Muhammad Ali Pasha's expansionism.

By the late 19th century, Egyptian influence in the region had waned, and the House of Saud had reestablished its control over a significant portion of the Arabian Peninsula. However, the legacy of these intrusions and conflicts continued to shape the region's politics and relationships with external powers.

In the 20th century, the Arabian Peninsula witnessed the emergence of new geopolitical dynamics, including the decline of the Ottoman Empire and the establishment of the modern state of Saudi Arabia in 1932. Saudi Arabia, under the leadership of King Abdulaziz Ibn Saud, embarked on a path of nation-building and modernization. The legacy of Ottoman and Egyptian intrusions served as a backdrop to the evolving regional dynamics. Saudi Arabia's efforts to consolidate its sovereignty and establish a centralized state were influenced by its historical experiences with external powers.

Today, Saudi Arabia is a prominent regional player in the Middle East, with its own set of challenges and opportunities. The historical intrusions and conflicts, whether with the Ottoman Empire or Egypt, have contributed to the kingdom's sense of identity, its approach to governance, and its interactions with the broader Arab world.

The retreat and exile of the Saud family from their ancestral homeland in the early 19th century is a significant chapter in the history of Saudi Arabia. This period marked a period of upheaval and hardship for the House of Saud, but it also laid the groundwork for the family's eventual return and the establishment of the modern Kingdom of Saudi Arabia.

The roots of the Sauds' retreat and exile can be traced back to the tumultuous period of the Wahhabi Wars, which were fought against the backdrop of the expanding Ottoman Empire's efforts to exert control over the Arabian Peninsula. The House of Saud, led by its founder Muhammad bin Saud and the religious reformer Muhammad ibn Abd al-Wahhab, had established the first Saudi state with a strict interpretation of Islam in the 18th century.

This state posed a perceived threat to the Ottoman Empire's interests in the region, leading to a series of military campaigns, often referred to as the "Wahhabi Wars," to suppress the Saudi-Wahhabi alliance. These conflicts involved fierce battles and shifting alliances among various tribal groups.

Despite facing significant military pressure from the Ottomans, the Saudi-Wahhabi alliance, known for its determination and guerrilla tactics, managed to maintain control over parts of the Arabian Peninsula for several decades. The conflict led to a state of instability and insecurity, with tribal rivalries and regional politics playing a significant role.

The tide began to turn against the House of Saud in the early 19th century when the Egyptian forces, led by Muhammad Ali Pasha, the governor of Egypt, intervened decisively in the Arabian Peninsula. Muhammad Ali Pasha sought to expand Egyptian influence and control over the region, viewing it as an opportunity for territorial gain.

The Egyptian forces launched a campaign to crush the Saudi-Wahhabi alliance, and the conflict culminated in the capture of the Saudi capital, Diriyah, in 1818. This marked a turning point in the region's history, as the Saudi state was significantly weakened, and its leaders, including members of the Saud family, were exiled.

The exile of the Saud family and the fall of Diriyah marked a period of hardship and displacement for the House of Saud. The family and its supporters scattered across the Arabian Peninsula, seeking refuge among various tribes and communities. The years of exile were marked by economic and social challenges, as the family struggled to maintain its authority and influence.

During this period, the House of Saud faced internal divisions and power struggles, as different branches of the family vied for leadership and control. The family's survival and prospects for a return to power appeared uncertain.

However, the resilience of the Saud family and their determination to reclaim their homeland eventually led to a resurgence in the mid-19th century. Faisal bin Turki, a member of the House of Saud, emerged as a charismatic leader who sought to reunify the family and regain control over the central Najd region.

Under Faisal bin Turki's leadership, the Saud family launched a successful campaign to reclaim territory and reestablish their authority. Riyadh, the future capital of Saudi Arabia, was recaptured, marking a symbolic victory for the Sauds.

The decline of Egyptian influence in the region, international developments, and shifting alliances contributed to the Sauds' ability to regain control. By the late 19th century, the Saud family had reestablished its authority over a significant portion of the Arabian Peninsula.

The eventual return and resurgence of the House of Saud in their homeland laid the groundwork for the establishment of the modern Kingdom of Saudi Arabia in 1932. King Abdulaziz Ibn Saud, the great-grandson of the founder of the House of Saud, unified various tribal regions, communities, and territories under a centralized Saudi state.

The Sauds' retreat and exile, while a period of hardship and displacement, ultimately contributed to the family's determination and resilience. It shaped their approach to governance and leadership, emphasizing the importance of unity and centralization in a diverse and tribal society.

Today, Saudi Arabia stands as a prominent regional player in the Middle East, with its own unique set of challenges and opportunities. The historical experiences of the Saud family, including their exile and eventual return, continue to influence the kingdom's sense of identity, its approach to governance, and its interactions with the broader Arab world. The story of the Sauds' retreat and exile serves as a testament to their enduring legacy and the establishment of the modern Saudi state.

Chapter 5: From the Ashes: Rebirth of the Saud Dynasty (Late 19th Century)

The resurgence and changes in leadership within the House of Saud have been pivotal in shaping the modern history of Saudi Arabia. This period witnessed the rise of King Abdulaziz Ibn Saud, the founder of the modern Saudi state, and the subsequent leadership transitions within the royal family.

King Abdulaziz Ibn Saud, often referred to as Ibn Saud, played a central role in the resurgence of the House of Saud. Born in the late 19th century, Ibn Saud was a member of the Al Saud family and the great-grandson of the dynasty's founder, Muhammad bin Saud. In the early 20th century, he embarked on a mission to reunify the fragmented Arabian Peninsula under the banner of the House of Saud.

Ibn Saud's journey to power began in the early 1900s, when he launched a series of military campaigns to retake territory and consolidate power. His leadership was characterized by a combination of military strategy, diplomacy, and tribal alliances. Over the course of several decades, he successfully expanded the territory controlled by the House of Saud.

One of Ibn Saud's most significant achievements was the capture of Riyadh in 1902, which served as the foundation for the modern Saudi state. Riyadh later became the capital of Saudi Arabia. Throughout his campaigns, Ibn Saud demonstrated a keen ability to navigate the complex tribal dynamics of the Arabian Peninsula and forge alliances with various tribal leaders.

By the 1920s, Ibn Saud had managed to unify much of the Arabian Peninsula, including regions that are now part of modern-day Saudi Arabia. In 1932, he officially proclaimed the Kingdom of Saudi Arabia, consolidating his rule over the newly formed nation.

Ibn Saud's leadership was marked by a commitment to conservative Islamic values and the principles of Wahhabism, a strict interpretation of Sunni Islam. This approach to governance played a significant role in shaping Saudi Arabia's domestic policies and societal norms.

Upon Ibn Saud's death in 1953, his sons and brothers faced the challenge of transitioning leadership within the Al Saud family. One of his sons, Saud bin Abdulaziz Al Saud, succeeded him as king. However, King Saud's reign faced numerous challenges, including economic difficulties and a lack of political stability.

The period of King Saud's rule was marked by financial mismanagement and a growing dissatisfaction among members of the royal family and the broader Saudi society. In 1964, a group of senior princes, including Crown Prince Faisal bin Abdulaziz Al Saud, took action to address these challenges.

In a historic move, King Saud was deposed by royal decree in 1964, and Crown Prince Faisal assumed the throne. This leadership transition marked a significant turning point in Saudi Arabia's history. King Faisal's reign was characterized by a more pragmatic and disciplined approach to governance.

Under King Faisal's leadership, Saudi Arabia implemented a series of economic and administrative reforms. These reforms included efforts to stabilize the kingdom's finances, reduce government spending, and diversify the economy away from its heavy dependence on oil revenues.

King Faisal also played a prominent role in international affairs, advocating for Arab and Muslim causes on the global stage. His leadership contributed to Saudi Arabia's growing influence in regional and international politics.

The changes in leadership within the House of Saud during this period demonstrated the family's commitment to maintaining stability and addressing the kingdom's challenges. Successive kings and leaders of Saudi Arabia sought to modernize the country's infrastructure, education system, and economy while upholding the conservative values of Wahhabism.

The leadership transitions within the House of Saud continued into the late 20th century and early 21st century, with each new king facing unique challenges and opportunities. The family's ability to navigate these transitions while maintaining the unity of the kingdom has been a central aspect of Saudi Arabia's political landscape.

Today, Saudi Arabia is a prominent regional player in the Middle East, with its own set of challenges and opportunities. The historical experiences of the House of Saud, including the resurgence of the dynasty under King Abdulaziz Ibn Saud and subsequent leadership transitions, continue to shape the kingdom's sense of identity, its approach to governance, and its role in the broader Arab world.

The reconquering of Riyadh is a significant chapter in the history of Saudi Arabia, marking a pivotal moment in the rise of the House of Saud and the establishment of the modern Saudi state. This historical event, which occurred in the early 20th century, laid the foundation for Riyadh's status as the capital of Saudi Arabia and marked a turning point in the House of Saud's quest for unification and sovereignty.

The House of Saud, led by its founder, King Abdulaziz Ibn Saud (often referred to as Ibn Saud), had embarked on a mission to unify the fragmented Arabian Peninsula under its rule. The House of Saud's ancestral home was in the Najd region of central Arabia, and Riyadh was a significant center of power within the Najd.

In the late 19th and early 20th centuries, the Arabian Peninsula was characterized by a patchwork of tribal territories and regions controlled by various tribal leaders and emirates. The House of Saud sought to assert its authority and expand its territorial control beyond its traditional Najdi heartland.

Riyadh, a strategic and symbolic city in the Najd, was of particular importance to Ibn Saud's unification efforts. It was seen as a key step in the House of Saud's quest to establish a centralized and sovereign state.

In 1902, Ibn Saud launched a daring and successful campaign to recapture Riyadh from the Rashidi Emirate, which had controlled the city. This event, known as the "Recapture of Riyadh," marked a significant moment in the history of the Arabian Peninsula.

The campaign involved a combination of military strategy, tribal alliances, and determination on the part of the House of Saud. Ibn Saud's forces employed guerrilla warfare tactics and leveraged tribal support to achieve victory. After a protracted battle, Riyadh was liberated, and Ibn Saud established himself as its ruler.

The recapture of Riyadh not only solidified Ibn Saud's control over the city but also served as a symbol of the House of Saud's resurgence and determination to unify the Arabian Peninsula. It marked the beginning of a series of military campaigns and diplomatic efforts that would eventually lead to the unification of much of the Arabian Peninsula.

Ibn Saud's leadership was characterized by his ability to navigate the complex tribal dynamics of the region and forge alliances with various tribal leaders. He recognized the importance of tribal support in his quest for unification and sovereignty.

Over the following decades, Ibn Saud continued to expand the territory under his control, forming alliances with tribes and emirates and incorporating them into the growing Saudi state. This process of territorial expansion and consolidation laid the groundwork for the establishment of the modern Kingdom of Saudi Arabia.

In 1932, Ibn Saud officially proclaimed the Kingdom of Saudi Arabia, unifying the various tribal regions and territories under a centralized government. Riyadh was designated as the capital of the new kingdom, a status it continues to hold to this day.

The reconquering of Riyadh is not only a historical milestone but also a symbol of the House of Saud's determination to establish a modern and sovereign state in the Arabian Peninsula. It underscores the significance of Riyadh as a political and cultural center and reflects the complex and dynamic history of Saudi Arabia's unification process.

Today, Riyadh stands as a vibrant and rapidly growing city, serving as the political, economic, and cultural heart of

Saudi Arabia. The events of the early 20th century, including the reconquering of Riyadh, continue to shape the kingdom's sense of identity and its role in the broader Middle East. Reestablishing Al Saud's authority was a pivotal chapter in the history of Saudi Arabia, marking a period of resurgence and consolidation of power for the ruling family. This historical period, which unfolded in the 19th century and continued into the early 20th century, laid the foundation for the eventual establishment of the modern Saudi state under King Abdulaziz Ibn Saud.

The Al Saud family, descended from its founder, Muhammad bin Saud, had established the first Saudi state in the mid-18th century in the Najd region of central Arabia. This state was characterized by its strict adherence to Wahhabi Islam, a conservative and puritanical interpretation of Sunni Islam, and its efforts to unify various tribal communities under its authority.

However, the rise of the Saudi state posed a perceived threat to the interests of external powers, particularly the Ottoman Empire, which sought to exert control over the Arabian Peninsula. The ensuing conflicts, known as the "Wahhabi Wars," were characterized by a series of battles and campaigns between the Saudi-Wahhabi alliance and the Ottoman forces.

Despite facing significant military pressure from the Ottomans and their allies, the Saudi-Wahhabi alliance, known for its determination and guerrilla tactics, managed to maintain control over parts of the Arabian Peninsula for several decades. The conflicts resulted in a state of instability and insecurity, with shifting alliances among various tribal groups and regional rivalries.

The tide began to turn against the Al Saud family in the early 19th century when the Egyptian forces, under the leadership of Muhammad Ali Pasha, the governor of Egypt, intervened decisively in the Arabian Peninsula. Muhammad Ali Pasha saw an opportunity to expand Egyptian influence and control over the region.

The Egyptian forces launched a campaign to crush the Saudi-Wahhabi alliance, leading to the capture of the Saudi capital, Diriyah, in 1818. This marked a significant turning point as the Saudi state was weakened, and its leaders, including members of the Al Saud family, were exiled.

The exile of the Al Saud family marked a period of hardship and displacement. Members of the family and their supporters scattered across the Arabian Peninsula, seeking refuge among various tribes and communities. The years of exile were marked by economic and social challenges as the family struggled to maintain its authority and influence.

During this period, the Al Saud family faced internal divisions and power struggles as different branches of the family vied for leadership and control. The family's survival and prospects for a return to power appeared uncertain.

However, the resilience of the Al Saud family and their determination to reclaim their homeland eventually led to a resurgence in the mid-19th century. Faisal bin Turki, a member of the Al Saud family, emerged as a charismatic leader who sought to reunify the family and regain control over the central Najd region.

Under Faisal bin Turki's leadership, the Al Saud family launched a successful campaign to reclaim territory and reestablish their authority. Riyadh, the future capital of

Saudi Arabia, was recaptured, marking a symbolic victory for the family.

The decline of Egyptian influence in the region, international developments, and shifting alliances contributed to the Al Saud family's ability to regain control. By the late 19th century, the Al Saud family had reestablished its authority over a significant portion of the Arabian Peninsula.

The eventual return and resurgence of the Al Saud family in their homeland laid the groundwork for the establishment of the modern Kingdom of Saudi Arabia in 1932. King Abdulaziz Ibn Saud, the great-grandson of the founder of the Al Saud family, unified various tribal regions, communities, and territories under a centralized Saudi state.

Reestablishing Al Saud's authority was not only a testament to the family's determination but also a reflection of their ability to navigate the complex tribal dynamics of the region and forge alliances with various tribal leaders. The family's vision for a unified and sovereign state played a central role in shaping the modern Saudi state.

Today, Saudi Arabia is a prominent regional player in the Middle East, with its own unique set of challenges and opportunities. The historical experiences of the Al Saud family, including their exile and eventual return, continue to influence the kingdom's sense of identity, its approach to governance, and its interactions with the broader Arab world. The story of reestablishing Al Saud's authority serves as a testament to their enduring legacy and the establishment of the modern Saudi state.

Chapter 6: Rivalries and Reconquests: The Second Saudi State (Mid-19th Century)

The formation of the Second Saudi State is a significant chapter in the history of Saudi Arabia, characterized by the House of Saud's resurgence and the reestablishment of their authority in the Arabian Peninsula. This period, spanning the mid-19th century, marked the family's determination to rebuild after their initial exile and laid the foundation for the modern Saudi state.

The decline of the First Saudi State, which had been established in the 18th century by the founder of the House of Saud, Muhammad bin Saud, and the religious reformer Muhammad ibn Abd al-Wahhab, began in the early 19th century. The First Saudi State faced external pressures, particularly from the Ottoman Empire, which sought to exert control over the Arabian Peninsula and perceived the First Saudi State as a threat to its interests.

The First Saudi State's decline culminated in the capture of the Saudi capital, Diriyah, by Egyptian forces under Muhammad Ali Pasha in 1818. This marked the end of the First Saudi State and the exile of members of the House of Saud.

Following their exile, the Saud family scattered across the Arabian Peninsula, seeking refuge among various tribes and communities. It was a period marked by economic hardships and social challenges as the family struggled to maintain its authority and influence.

However, the resilience of the Saud family and their determination to reclaim their homeland set the stage for the formation of the Second Saudi State. The emergence of Faisal bin Turki, a member of the Saud family, as a charismatic leader was a turning point.

Under Faisal bin Turki's leadership, the Saud family began to regroup and rebuild their strength. They aimed to reclaim territory in central Arabia, which had historically been their stronghold. Faisal bin Turki launched a campaign to retake Riyadh, a city of great significance to the Saud family.

The campaign to retake Riyadh, which began in the mid-19th century, was characterized by a combination of military strategy, tribal alliances, and determination on the part of the Saud family. Faisal bin Turki's forces employed guerrilla warfare tactics and leveraged tribal support to achieve their goal.

After a period of conflict and battles, Riyadh was successfully recaptured by the Saud family in 1865. This marked a symbolic and strategic victory for the Sauds and marked the foundation of the Second Saudi State.

With the recapture of Riyadh, the Saud family began the process of rebuilding and consolidating their authority in central Arabia. They sought to reunify various tribal regions and communities that had been fragmented during their exile.

Faisal bin Turki's leadership was instrumental in this process, and he worked to establish a central authority in Riyadh. The formation of the Second Saudi State was characterized by efforts to forge alliances with tribal leaders and communities, emphasizing the importance of unity and stability.

The Second Saudi State continued to expand its territorial control in central Arabia, incorporating various tribal regions into its domain. This period laid the groundwork for the eventual unification of much of the Arabian Peninsula under the leadership of King Abdulaziz Ibn Saud in the early 20th century.

The formation of the Second Saudi State not only demonstrated the resilience and determination of the Saud family but also underscored their vision for a unified and sovereign Arabian Peninsula. It represented a significant step in the House of Saud's journey toward reestablishing their authority and laying the foundation for the modern Kingdom of Saudi Arabia.

Today, Riyadh, the city that played a pivotal role in the formation of the Second Saudi State, stands as the capital of Saudi Arabia and serves as a symbol of the kingdom's history and identity. The historical experiences of the Saud family during this period continue to influence Saudi Arabia's approach to governance, unity, and sovereignty in the modern era.

Regional competitors and conflicts have been a recurring theme in the history of Saudi Arabia, shaping the geopolitical landscape of the Arabian Peninsula and the broader Middle East. Throughout different periods, Saudi Arabia has encountered regional rivals and engaged in conflicts that have influenced its foreign policy and regional dynamics.

Ottoman Empire: During the 19th century, the Ottoman Empire was a major regional competitor for control over the Arabian Peninsula. The Ottomans sought to assert their authority over the region, including parts of present-day Saudi Arabia. This competition led to conflicts, including the Wahhabi Wars, in which the Ottomans and their allies sought to suppress the First Saudi State. These conflicts marked a struggle for territorial control and influence in the Arabian Peninsula.

Egyptian Expansion: In the early 19th century, Muhammad Ali Pasha of Egypt launched a campaign to extend Egyptian influence into the Arabian Peninsula. This expansion brought Egyptian forces into direct conflict with the Saudi-Wahhabi alliance and resulted in the capture of Riyadh and the decline of the First Saudi State.

Rival Arab States: Throughout the 20th century, Saudi Arabia has had regional competitors among other Arab states. Egypt, under leaders like Gamal Abdel Nasser, vied for leadership and influence in the Arab world, leading to political rivalries and differing visions for the region's future. Additionally, Iraq, under Saddam Hussein, pursued its regional ambitions, leading to conflicts such as the Gulf War.

Iran: Saudi Arabia and Iran have been regional competitors for influence in the Middle East, with both countries representing different branches of Islam (Sunni and Shia, respectively). Their competition has played out in various ways, including through proxy conflicts in countries like Yemen, where Saudi Arabia supports the Yemeni government, while Iran backs Houthi rebels. The sectarian dimension of this rivalry has had far-reaching implications for regional conflicts.

Gulf Cooperation Council (GCC) Rivalries: Within the GCC, Saudi Arabia has sometimes encountered rivalries with fellow member states, such as Qatar and the United Arab Emirates (UAE). These conflicts have centered on differing regional policies, alliances, and approaches to regional issues. Diplomatic and economic disputes have at times strained relations within the GCC.

Yemen Conflict: The ongoing conflict in Yemen has drawn Saudi Arabia into a protracted regional conflict. The Saudi-led coalition, which includes other Arab states, has been involved in the Yemeni civil war against Houthi rebels since 2015. This conflict represents a complex regional rivalry with geopolitical implications.

Syrian Civil War: Saudi Arabia has been involved in the Syrian civil war, supporting various rebel groups in their bid to overthrow the Assad regime. This conflict has brought Saudi Arabia into competition with regional powers like Iran, which supports the Syrian government.

Israeli-Palestinian Conflict: Saudi Arabia, like many other Arab states, has a vested interest in the Israeli-Palestinian conflict. The competition for influence and leadership in addressing this long-standing conflict has been a part of regional dynamics for decades.

These examples highlight the complex web of regional competitors and conflicts that have shaped Saudi Arabia's foreign policy and regional role. The kingdom has sought to navigate these challenges while maintaining its regional influence and addressing its own domestic priorities. The evolving dynamics of the Middle East continue to present Saudi Arabia with both opportunities and challenges in the pursuit of its regional interests.

The demise of the Second Saudi State marked a critical juncture in the history of Saudi Arabia, characterized by external pressures, internal divisions, and a temporary setback for the House of Saud. This period, which unfolded in the late 19th century, represents a challenging chapter in the family's quest for reunification and sovereignty.

Expansion and Internal Challenges: Following the successful reconquest of Riyadh and the formation of the Second Saudi State, the Saud family continued their efforts to consolidate power and extend their authority. However, the expansion brought new challenges, including the need to manage diverse tribal territories and communities with varying interests and loyalties.

Ottoman Threat: The Second Saudi State faced renewed threats from the Ottoman Empire, which sought to reassert control over the Arabian Peninsula. The Ottomans viewed the Saudi-Wahhabi alliance as a threat to their interests in the region and launched a series of campaigns to suppress the Saudis. The most significant of these campaigns was the Ottoman reconquest of Riyadh in 1871.

Internal Divisions: The Second Saudi State experienced internal divisions and rivalries among different branches of the Saud family. These divisions weakened the family's ability to respond effectively to external threats and posed challenges to the unity of the state.

Treaty of Rawdat Muhanna: In 1891, the Saudi ruler, Abdul Rahman bin Faisal, signed the Treaty of Rawdat Muhanna with the Ottoman Empire. This treaty, which recognized Ottoman suzerainty over the Second Saudi State, marked a significant concession by the Saud family. It temporarily ended hostilities but left the Saudis in a weakened position.

Revival of the Rashidis: The decline of the Second Saudi State allowed the Rashidi emirate, a rival power, to regain strength and expand its influence in central Arabia. The Rashidis became a formidable competitor, further challenging the stability and territorial integrity of the Second Saudi State.

Continued Struggles: The Second Saudi State continued to face external pressures and internal strife. The rivalry with the Rashidis persisted, and the Ottomans maintained a watchful eye over the region. This period of uncertainty and instability strained the resources and capabilities of the Saud family.

Final Conquest by the Rashidis: In 1902, the Rashidis launched a successful campaign against the Second Saudi State, culminating in the capture of Riyadh. This event marked the end of the Second Saudi State and the temporary exile of members of the Saud family.

The demise of the Second Saudi State was a challenging and turbulent period for the Saud family. It represented a setback in their quest for sovereignty and reunification of the Arabian Peninsula. However, the story does not end here, as it set the stage for the eventual resurgence of the House of Saud and the establishment of the modern Kingdom of Saudi Arabia.

The subsequent chapter in Saudi history, led by King Abdulaziz Ibn Saud, saw the reunification of various tribal territories and communities under a centralized Saudi state. This period laid the foundation for the modern Saudi Arabia we know today.

The demise of the Second Saudi State serves as a reminder of the resilience and determination of the Saud family, who would go on to overcome these challenges and reassert their authority in the Arabian Peninsula, ultimately realizing their vision of a unified and sovereign Saudi state.

Chapter 7: Lawrence of Arabia and the House of Saud: World War I and the Arabian Peninsula

T.E. Lawrence, famously known as Lawrence of Arabia, played a pivotal role in the Arab Revolt during World War I. His actions and influence in the Arabian Peninsula had far-reaching consequences, shaping the course of history in the region and leaving an indelible mark on the Arab world.

Born in Wales in 1888, Thomas Edward Lawrence was a British archaeologist, military officer, diplomat, and writer. He first arrived in the Arabian Peninsula in 1916 as an intelligence officer with the British Army, stationed in Cairo, Egypt. It was in this role that Lawrence would become deeply involved in the Arab Revolt, a military campaign aimed at ending Ottoman rule in the Arabian Peninsula.

Lawrence's involvement in the Arab Revolt was not limited to his military duties; he also became an advisor and confidant to key Arab leaders, most notably Emir Faisal, who would later become King Faisal I of Iraq. Lawrence's unique blend of skills, including his knowledge of Arab culture and language, his military acumen, and his charismatic personality, made him a crucial figure in the unfolding events of the Arab Revolt.

One of Lawrence's most significant contributions was his role in uniting the various Arab tribes and factions under a common cause. The Arabian Peninsula was a mosaic of tribal loyalties and rivalries, making coordination and cooperation a formidable challenge. Lawrence's ability to bridge these divides and foster a sense of unity among the Arab leaders was instrumental in the success of the revolt. Lawrence's deep understanding of guerrilla warfare and irregular tactics also proved invaluable during the Arab Revolt. He organized and led Arab forces in hit-and-run attacks, ambushes, and sabotage operations against the Ottoman military, effectively disrupting their control over key territories. His military strategy emphasized mobility, surprise, and the use of local knowledge to gain advantages over the enemy.

Perhaps one of Lawrence's most iconic achievements during the Arab Revolt was his leadership in the capture of the port city of Aqaba in 1917. Aqaba was a heavily fortified Ottoman stronghold that was considered impregnable from the land, but Lawrence conceived a daring plan to attack it from the desert, catching the Ottomans off guard. The successful capture of Aqaba marked a turning point in the Arab Revolt and opened up new supply routes for the Arab forces.

Lawrence's fame as "Lawrence of Arabia" began to spread internationally, largely due to the efforts of war correspondents and journalists who were captivated by his exploits in the Arabian desert. His charisma, distinctive attire, and enigmatic persona added to his mystique, turning him into a symbol of resistance against Ottoman rule and an advocate for Arab self-determination.

Beyond his military contributions, Lawrence played a crucial diplomatic role in advocating for Arab interests on the international stage. He accompanied Emir Faisal to the Paris Peace Conference in 1919, where he lobbied for the recognition of Arab independence and territorial sovereignty. His efforts resulted in the issuance of the

McMahon–Hussein Correspondence, a series of letters exchanged between the British High Commissioner in Egypt, Sir Henry McMahon, and Sharif Hussein of Mecca, which promised Arab independence in exchange for their support against the Ottomans.

However, the promises made in the McMahon–Hussein Correspondence would later be overshadowed by the secret Sykes-Picot Agreement, a separate agreement between Britain and France to divide the Middle East into spheres of influence. Lawrence was deeply disillusioned by this betrayal, and it fueled his determination to see Arab self-determination realized.

Lawrence's influence extended beyond the battlefield and the negotiating table. He became an advocate for Arab culture and heritage, recognizing the importance of preserving Arab identity in the face of colonialism. He penned "Seven Pillars of Wisdom," an autobiographical account of his experiences during the Arab Revolt, which also served as a literary celebration of Arab culture and history.

After the war, Lawrence's life took on a complex trajectory. He struggled with the conflicting interests and promises made by the Allied powers and faced personal challenges related to his wartime experiences. He attempted to distance himself from his own legend but remained a symbol of inspiration for many in the Arab world and beyond.

The legacy of T.E. Lawrence in the Arab world is a complex one. While he is celebrated for his role in the Arab Revolt and his advocacy for Arab independence, his involvement also raises questions about the impact of Western intervention in the Middle East and the consequences of colonialism. Lawrence himself grappled with these complexities, and his life continues to be a subject of historical and literary exploration.

In summary, T.E. Lawrence's role in the Arab Revolt was multi-faceted and influential. He combined military expertise, diplomatic finesse, and a deep respect for Arab culture to contribute significantly to the success of the Arab Revolt. His legacy is both celebrated and scrutinized, reflecting the intricate tapestry of history and the enduring impact of his actions on the Arab world and the broader geopolitical landscape of the Middle East.

The Arab Revolt, which took place during World War I, was a pivotal event in the history of the Middle East, with far-reaching political, social, and geopolitical consequences that continue to shape the region to this day. This revolt, led by Arab leaders and supported by the British and French, aimed to end Ottoman rule in the Arab lands and achieve Arab independence. Its impact can be examined through several key dimensions.

1. Ottoman Rule and Arab Discontent: Before delving into the revolt itself, it is essential to understand the backdrop of Ottoman rule in the Arab world. The Ottoman Empire, which had ruled over various Arab territories for centuries, was seen by many Arabs as oppressive and exploitative. This discontent sowed the seeds for future resistance.

2. The Role of Arab Nationalism: Arab nationalism was a driving force behind the Arab Revolt. Prominent Arab intellectuals and leaders, such as Sharif Hussein of Mecca and his sons, Emir Faisal and Abdullah, championed the idea of Arab self-determination and unity. They sought to break free from Ottoman control and establish independent Arab states.

3. The McMahon-Hussein Correspondence: The McMahon-Hussein Correspondence played a crucial role in the lead-up to the revolt. In these letters exchanged between the British government and Sharif Hussein, the British promised support for Arab independence in exchange for Arab assistance in fighting against the Ottoman Empire. This promise was a catalyst for the Arab Revolt.

4. T.E. Lawrence and Guerrilla Warfare: T.E. Lawrence, also known as Lawrence of Arabia, emerged as a central figure in the Arab Revolt. His expertise in guerrilla warfare and his ability to unite disparate Arab tribes were instrumental in the revolt's military successes. Lawrence's leadership and tactical genius helped Arab forces achieve remarkable victories against the Ottomans.

5. The Capture of Aqaba: One of the most significant early victories of the Arab Revolt was the capture of the heavily fortified port city of Aqaba in 1917. This success opened up a new supply route for the Arab forces and demonstrated their ability to challenge Ottoman dominance.

6. The Balfour Declaration: While the Arab Revolt was underway, the British government issued the Balfour Declaration in 1917, expressing support for the establishment of a "national home for the Jewish people" in Palestine. This declaration created tension and mistrust among Arab leaders, who felt that their aspirations were being undermined.

7. The Sykes-Picot Agreement: Another factor that complicated the Arab Revolt's goals was the secret Sykes-

Picot Agreement between Britain and France. This agreement, which divided the Middle East into zones of influence, contradicted the promises of Arab independence made in the McMahon-Hussein Correspondence.

8. The Paris Peace Conference: After World War I, Arab leaders, including Emir Faisal, attended the Paris Peace Conference in 1919 to advocate for Arab self-determination and territorial sovereignty. Their efforts resulted in some recognition of Arab independence, but the realities on the ground often did not align with their aspirations.

9. Legacy of the Arab Revolt: The immediate impact of the Arab Revolt was mixed. While it contributed to the weakening of the Ottoman Empire and laid the groundwork for the dissolution of Ottoman rule in the Arab lands, it also exposed the complexities of international politics and the challenges of securing Arab independence.

10. Borders and Modern Nation-States: The aftermath of World War I led to the redrawing of borders in the Middle East and the establishment of modern nation-states. Some Arab territories gained independence, while others came under the mandates of colonial powers. These borders and divisions continue to influence regional conflicts and dynamics.

11. Arab Nationalism and Identity: The Arab Revolt helped foster a sense of Arab identity and nationalism among the peoples of the region. It was a catalyst for political movements that aimed to unify Arab nations and assert their collective identity in the face of external influence.

12. Geopolitical Complexities: The legacy of the Arab Revolt also underscores the enduring geopolitical complexities of the Middle East. The region remains a focal point of global attention and is marked by conflicts, alliances, and interventions by various powers.

13. Lessons and Controversies: The Arab Revolt remains a subject of historical debate and controversy. It raises questions about the promises and commitments made to Arab leaders, the impact of external interventions in the Middle East, and the ongoing struggles for self-determination and sovereignty in the region.

In summary, the Arab Revolt of World War I was a multifaceted and transformative event that left a lasting imprint on the Middle East. It was driven by the aspirations of Arab leaders for independence and self-determination but also influenced by the geopolitical complexities of the era. Its impact continues to reverberate in the modern Middle East, shaping the region's political landscape and the dynamics of Arab nationalism and identity. The legacy of the revolt serves as a reminder of the complexities of history and the enduring quest for autonomy and sovereignty in the Arab world.

The aftermath of World War I witnessed significant geopolitical realignments that reshaped the global order, redrew borders, and laid the groundwork for the turbulent 20th century. These realignments were driven by a complex interplay of factors, including the consequences of the war, the collapse of empires, the emergence of new ideologies, and the pursuit of national self-determination. Examining the post-World War I realignments reveals a nuanced and intricate tapestry of historical events and their lasting impact.

1. The Treaty of Versailles: The Treaty of Versailles, signed in 1919, officially ended World War I and imposed significant penalties on Germany. It not only redrew the map of Europe but also sought to address the issue of war guilt and reparations. The treaty's terms, which included territorial losses for Germany and restrictions on its military, were seen as punitive and contributed to future instability.

2. The Dissolution of Empires: World War I marked the demise of several powerful empires, including the Ottoman Empire, the Austro-Hungarian Empire, and the Russian Empire. The collapse of these empires created a power vacuum in Eastern Europe and the Middle East, leading to struggles for independence and territorial realignments.

3. Redrawing the Map of Europe: The dissolution of empires in Europe prompted the redrawing of national borders and the creation of new states. Nations like Poland, Czechoslovakia, and Yugoslavia emerged as independent entities, while regions such as Alsace-Lorraine were returned to France. These changes sought to address national aspirations but also generated ethnic and territorial conflicts.

4. The League of Nations: In the aftermath of World War I, the League of Nations was established as a precursor to the United Nations. The League aimed to promote international cooperation, prevent future conflicts, and facilitate diplomatic solutions to disputes. However, its effectiveness was limited, and it struggled to prevent the outbreak of World War II.

5. The Russian Revolution and the Soviet Union: The Russian Revolution of 1917 led to the rise of the

Bolsheviks and the establishment of the Soviet Union in 1922. This communist state transformed Russia into a major world power and initiated a new ideological and geopolitical struggle between communism and capitalism.

6. The Middle East and the Mandate System: The collapse of the Ottoman Empire resulted in the redrawing of borders in the Middle East. The mandate system, established by the League of Nations, divided the region into zones of influence administered by colonial powers. This system sowed the seeds for future conflicts and struggles for self-determination in the Middle East.

7. The Arab Revolt and Nationalism: The Arab Revolt during World War I was driven by Arab nationalism and the desire for independence from Ottoman rule. However, the promises made to Arab leaders, such as those in the McMahon-Hussein Correspondence, were often contradicted by the secret Sykes-Picot Agreement and the Balfour Declaration.

8. Economic Realities: The economic consequences of World War I, including the destruction of infrastructure and the disruption of trade, played a role in shaping post-war realignments. Economic hardships and the need for reconstruction influenced political decisions and alliances.

9. Rise of Totalitarian Regimes: The interwar period saw the rise of totalitarian regimes, including Adolf Hitler's Nazi Germany and Joseph Stalin's Soviet Union. These regimes pursued expansionist agendas and contributed to the tensions that would lead to World War II.

10. The Great Depression: The global economic downturn of the Great Depression in the 1930s had a profound impact on international relations. Economic hardships fueled protectionism, nationalism, and militarism, further destabilizing the world order.

11. Legacy and Lessons: The post-World War I realignments serve as a critical historical lesson on the complexities of forging peace and stability after a global conflict. The unresolved issues, territorial disputes, and geopolitical rivalries of the post-war period set the stage for future conflicts and continue to shape the world today.

12. Lessons for Diplomacy: The diplomatic failures and unintended consequences of post-World War I realignments underscore the importance of effective diplomacy, the need for addressing root causes of conflict, and the imperative of fostering international cooperation.

In summary, the post-World War I realignments were a complex and multifaceted process that redrew borders, reshaped states, and set the stage for the geopolitical dynamics of the 20th century. These realignments were marked by a delicate balance between addressing national aspirations and managing the consequences of war, and they hold valuable lessons for understanding the challenges of forging peace and stability in a rapidly changing world. The interplay of political, economic, and ideological factors in the post-war era underscores the intricacies of global history and its enduring impact on the present.

Chapter 8: Ibn Saud's Ascendance: Birth of the Modern Saudi State (Early 20th Century)

The story of Ibn Saud, the founder of modern Saudi Arabia, is a tale of ambition, leadership, and perseverance that shaped the destiny of a nation and the broader Middle East. Born in 1875 in the desert region of Najd, which is now part of Saudi Arabia, Ibn Saud's early years and rise to leadership are a fascinating chapter in history.

Early Life and Tribal Roots: Ibn Saud was born into the Al Saud family, a prominent tribal group in Najd. His family had a history of tribal leadership but had seen a decline in fortunes over the years. Ibn Saud's early years were marked by the harsh realities of desert life, including tribal rivalries, a nomadic existence, and the struggle for resources in a harsh environment.

Education and Exposure: Despite the challenging conditions of his upbringing, Ibn Saud received some education in Islamic studies and tribal traditions. His early exposure to the complexities of tribal politics and the shifting alliances in the Arabian Peninsula would later prove invaluable in his leadership journey.

Conflict and Displacement: In the late 19th century, the Arabian Peninsula was a turbulent region marked by tribal conflicts and power struggles. Ibn Saud's early experiences included witnessing the turmoil of tribal warfare, which sometimes forced his family into exile. These hardships served as formative experiences that would shape his leadership style and determination.

Emergence as a Leader: Ibn Saud's path to leadership began to crystallize in the early 20th century. With a combination of military prowess, political acumen, and diplomacy, he embarked on a mission to reunify the disparate tribal communities of Najd and reestablish the authority of the Al Saud family.

Alliances and Military Campaigns: One of Ibn Saud's key strengths was his ability to forge strategic alliances with other tribal leaders. He recognized the importance of building a coalition of tribes to strengthen his position. These alliances allowed him to launch successful military campaigns against rival clans and tribes in Najd, gradually expanding his influence.

Rise to Power: By 1902, Ibn Saud had achieved a significant milestone in his journey when he captured Riyadh, a major city in Najd. This marked the beginning of his ascendancy as a regional leader. He continued to consolidate his power, forging alliances when possible and engaging in battles when necessary to secure his position.

Conflict with the Rashidis: One of the defining moments in Ibn Saud's early leadership was his conflict with the Rashidi emirate, a rival power in the region. The struggle between the Al Saud and Rashidi forces would shape the balance of power in central Arabia and test Ibn Saud's leadership and determination.

Tribal Reunification: Ibn Saud's leadership was characterized by his efforts to unify the tribes of Najd under a common banner. He recognized that a united front was essential for achieving his vision of a unified Arabian state. Through diplomacy, military campaigns, and the skillful management of tribal dynamics, he succeeded in bringing many tribes under his leadership.

The First Saudi State: By 1921, Ibn Saud had achieved his goal of reunifying much of Najd and had declared the establishment of the First Saudi State. This marked a significant milestone in his leadership journey. However, his ambitions extended beyond Najd, and he set his sights on the broader Arabian Peninsula.

Vision for Arabia: Ibn Saud's vision for Arabia went beyond tribal unification. He sought to establish a stable and prosperous nation that could provide security and leadership in a turbulent region. His leadership was guided by a commitment to Islamic principles, tribal traditions, and the welfare of his people.

Relationship with the British: Throughout his rise to power, Ibn Saud maintained diplomatic ties with the British government. These ties were strategic, as the British sought regional stability and influence in the Arabian Peninsula. The Anglo-Saudi Treaty of 1915 and subsequent agreements secured British support for Ibn Saud's leadership.

Challenges and Adversaries: Ibn Saud's leadership was not without challenges and adversaries. He faced resistance from rival tribal leaders, including those aligned with the Rashidis and other regional powers. The shifting sands of tribal politics and the complexities of Arabian diplomacy tested his leadership skills.

Consolidation and Expansion: In the years following the establishment of the First Saudi State, Ibn Saud continued to consolidate his authority and expand his territory. His military campaigns extended into parts of the Hejaz region, including the holy cities of Mecca and Medina, solidifying his position as a key leader in the Arabian Peninsula.

Legacy and Modern Saudi Arabia: Ibn Saud's leadership laid the foundation for modern Saudi Arabia. His determination, political savvy, and ability to navigate the complexities of tribal and regional dynamics were instrumental in the formation of a unified nation. His vision and leadership continue to influence Saudi Arabia's political landscape and its role in the Middle East.

In summary, Ibn Saud's early years and rise to leadership represent a remarkable journey from the harsh desert conditions of Najd to the founding of a modern nation-state. His leadership was marked by a combination of military strategy, diplomatic skill, and a commitment to his vision for Arabia. His legacy as the founder of Saudi Arabia endures, shaping the nation's identity and its role in the wider Middle East.

The consolidation of the Saudi territories represents a pivotal chapter in the history of Saudi Arabia and the broader Middle East. This period, which followed the establishment of the First Saudi State by Ibn Saud, marked a phase of state-building, expansion, and the solidification of Saudi authority across the Arabian Peninsula. The consolidation of the Saudi territories was marked by a series of significant developments, challenges, and achievements that shaped the trajectory of the young nation.

1. Expansion into the Hejaz: One of the most notable aspects of the consolidation of Saudi territories was the expansion of Saudi rule into the Hejaz region. This included the capture of the holy cities of Mecca and Medina, a milestone that carried immense religious and symbolic significance. Ibn Saud's forces gradually extended their control over the Hejazi territories, culminating in the capture of Mecca in 1924.

2. Political and Religious Authority: The capture of Mecca and Medina solidified Ibn Saud's position as a political and religious leader. His role as the guardian of Islam's holiest sites bolstered his legitimacy and provided him with a unique standing in the Muslim world. It also presented a significant challenge in terms of managing the religious responsibilities associated with these cities.

3. Diplomacy and Alliances: The consolidation of Saudi territories required a delicate balancing act of diplomacy and alliances. Ibn Saud cultivated relationships with tribal leaders, regional powers, and international actors. These diplomatic efforts were essential in securing support, managing rivalries, and ensuring the stability of the expanding Saudi state.

4. The Role of Ikhwan: The Ikhwan, or "Brotherhood," was a crucial element in the consolidation of Saudi territories. Comprising Bedouin warriors, the Ikhwan played a central role in Ibn Saud's military campaigns. Their loyalty and fighting prowess contributed significantly to the expansion of Saudi rule. However, managing the Ikhwan and their ambitions posed challenges, leading to internal tensions.

5. Tribal Dynamics: Tribal dynamics were a fundamental aspect of the consolidation process. Ibn Saud's leadership was marked by his ability to navigate the intricate web of tribal loyalties and rivalries. By securing the loyalty of influential tribal leaders and incorporating them into the Saudi state, he strengthened the unity of the territories under his rule.

6. The Unification of Law and Governance: As the Saudi territories expanded, Ibn Saud faced the task of unifying law and governance across diverse regions and tribal groups. He worked to establish a legal framework that combined Islamic law (Sharia) with tribal customs, seeking to strike a balance that would be accepted by the diverse populations of the kingdom.

7. Economic Development: Economic development was integral to the consolidation of Saudi territories. The Saudi state sought to diversify its economy beyond traditional activities like agriculture and herding. Initiatives were launched to tap into the region's natural resources, including oil exploration, which would later become a significant source of wealth.

8. Infrastructure and Connectivity: Building infrastructure and improving connectivity between regions were vital components of the consolidation process. Roads, railways, and telecommunication networks were developed to facilitate trade, travel, and communication, fostering a sense of national unity.

9. Administrative Reforms: Ibn Saud introduced administrative reforms aimed at creating a functional bureaucracy capable of managing the expanding Saudi territories. This included the establishment of government ministries, the formalization of administrative processes, and the appointment of qualified officials.

10. Challenges of Governance: Governing the vast and diverse Saudi territories presented ongoing challenges. These included addressing the needs of a growing population, providing essential services, and balancing the interests of various regions and communities. The Saudi state grappled with issues of education, healthcare, and infrastructure development.

11. Role in Regional Stability: The consolidation of Saudi territories had broader implications for regional stability. The emergence of a unified Saudi Arabia altered the geopolitical landscape of the Arabian Peninsula. It created a more stable and cohesive entity that could exert influence in regional affairs.

12. The Legacy of Ibn Saud: The consolidation of the Saudi territories stands as a testament to the leadership and vision of Ibn Saud. His ability to unite disparate tribal groups, navigate the challenges of governance, and expand Saudi rule over a vast expanse of land left a lasting legacy. His name is synonymous with the founding of modern Saudi Arabia.

13. Contemporary Saudi Arabia: The process of consolidation initiated by Ibn Saud continues to influence the character and governance of contemporary Saudi Arabia. The kingdom, which bears his name, remains a key player in regional and international politics, shaped by the historical foundations laid during this period.

In summary, the consolidation of the Saudi territories represented a complex and transformative phase in the history of Saudi Arabia. It involved the expansion of Saudi rule into the Hejaz, the management of tribal dynamics, the establishment of governance structures, and the pursuit of economic development. Ibn Saud's leadership and the challenges he navigated during this period continue to shape the identity and role of modern Saudi Arabia on the world stage.

The establishment of the foundations of modern Saudi Arabia was a monumental historical process that transformed a vast and diverse territory into a unified nation-state under the leadership of King Abdulaziz Ibn Saud, often referred to as Ibn Saud. This period, which spanned the early to mid-20th century, was marked by a series of significant political, social, economic, and cultural developments that laid the groundwork for the modern Saudi state.

The Role of King Abdulaziz Ibn Saud: At the center of this transformative era was King Abdulaziz Ibn Saud himself. His visionary leadership, military prowess, and diplomatic skill were instrumental in uniting the various tribal factions and regions under the banner of a single Saudi state.

Consolidation of Territory: One of the primary objectives during this period was the consolidation of territory. King Abdulaziz embarked on a series of military campaigns to bring disparate regions and tribal groups under Saudi control. The capture of Riyadh in 1902 marked the beginning of this process, and it continued with the capture of other key cities and regions, including the Hejaz, Asir, and Najran.

Capture of the Hejaz: The capture of the Hejaz, which included the holy cities of Mecca and Medina, was a watershed moment in the consolidation of the Saudi state. It not only solidified the kingdom's control over important religious sites but also elevated King Abdulaziz's standing as the Custodian of the Two Holy Mosques, a position of immense religious authority and responsibility.

The Ikhwan Movement: The Ikhwan, or "Brotherhood," played a crucial role during this period. Comprising Bedouin warriors, the Ikhwan were fiercely loyal to King Abdulaziz and served as the backbone of the Saudi military. Their disciplined and highly effective fighting force contributed significantly to the unification of the kingdom.

Religious Authority: The religious dimension was integral to the establishment of modern Saudi Arabia. King Abdulaziz's role as the Custodian of the Two Holy Mosques carried immense religious authority, and he sought to govern the kingdom in accordance with Islamic principles. This emphasis on religion would shape the character of the Saudi state.

Political Structure and Governance: The foundations of modern Saudi Arabia also included the establishment of political structures and governance mechanisms. King Abdulaziz worked to formalize administrative processes, create government ministries, and appoint qualified officials to oversee various aspects of state affairs.

Economic Development: Economic development was a key component of the nation-building process. King Abdulaziz recognized the importance of diversifying the Saudi economy beyond traditional activities like agriculture and herding. Initiatives were launched to harness the region's natural resources, including the exploration and extraction of oil.

Infrastructure and Connectivity: Building infrastructure and improving connectivity were essential for fostering national unity. Roads, railways, and telecommunication networks were developed to facilitate trade, travel, and communication across the vast expanse of the kingdom.

Social and Cultural Transformations: The establishment of modern Saudi Arabia also brought about social and cultural transformations. Efforts were made to modernize education and healthcare systems, and reforms were introduced in areas such as women's education. These changes aimed to bring the kingdom in line with the evolving global landscape.

Regional and International Relations: Managing regional and international relations was a significant challenge. King Abdulaziz navigated a complex geopolitical environment, balancing relationships with neighboring states, tribal leaders, and international powers. Diplomacy played a crucial role in safeguarding the interests of the nascent Saudi state.

Challenges and Conflicts: The establishment of modern Saudi Arabia was not without challenges and conflicts. King Abdulaziz had to manage the sometimes competing interests of tribal leaders, address regional rivalries, and quell internal dissent. The transition from a fragmented tribal society to a centralized state was fraught with difficulties.

The Discovery of Oil: One of the most transformative events during this period was the discovery of oil. Oil exploration in the 1930s and the subsequent establishment of the Arabian American Oil Company (ARAMCO) marked the beginning of Saudi Arabia's emergence as a major player in the global energy market. The revenue generated from oil exports would have profound implications for the kingdom's development.

Legacy of King Abdulaziz: The legacy of King Abdulaziz Ibn Saud as the founder of modern Saudi Arabia endures to this day. His leadership, vision, and determination left an indelible mark on the nation's identity and its role in the Middle East and the world. The kingdom bears his name as a testament to his pivotal role in its establishment.

Contemporary Saudi Arabia: The foundations established during this era continue to shape contemporary Saudi Arabia. The kingdom's political structure, religious authority, economic policies, and regional prominence can be traced back to the nation-building efforts of this period.

In summary, the establishment of the foundations of modern Saudi Arabia was a complex and multifaceted process that encompassed political, social, economic, and cultural dimensions. It was a transformative era marked by visionary leadership, territorial consolidation, economic development, and the integration of diverse regions and tribal groups into a unified state. The legacy of King Abdulaziz Ibn Saud, the Custodian of the Two Holy Mosques, remains central to the identity and governance of the modern Saudi state.

Chapter 9: Oil, Power, and the House of Saud: Shaping the Kingdom (Mid-20th Century)

The discovery of oil reserves in Saudi Arabia marked a turning point in the nation's history, reshaping its economy, society, and global significance. This transformative event, which unfolded in the 1930s, had far-reaching consequences that continue to impact Saudi Arabia and the world today.

Early Exploration: The journey to discover oil in Saudi Arabia was a result of collaboration between the Saudi government and international oil companies. The Arabian American Oil Company (ARAMCO), a consortium of American oil companies, was granted the rights to explore and extract oil in the kingdom.

First Commercial Discovery: In 1938, ARAMCO made its first commercial oil discovery in the Dammam Well No. 7, located in what is now the Eastern Province of Saudi Arabia. This discovery, known as the "Prosperity Well," revealed significant oil reserves beneath the desert sands.

Transformational Impact: The discovery of oil reserves had a transformational impact on Saudi Arabia. It led to the rapid development of the country's oil industry and the establishment of a thriving petroleum sector. Oil revenues soon became the lifeblood of the Saudi economy.

Economic Boom: Oil exports brought immense wealth to Saudi Arabia, fueling an economic boom that funded ambitious development projects and modernization efforts. The revenue generated from oil exports allowed the government to invest in infrastructure, education, healthcare, and other essential sectors.

Infrastructure Development: The newfound wealth enabled Saudi Arabia to embark on a massive infrastructure development program. Roads, ports, airports, and telecommunications networks were built, connecting previously isolated regions and facilitating economic growth.

Social and Cultural Changes: The oil boom also triggered significant social and cultural changes. Urbanization accelerated as people moved to cities in search of employment opportunities. This shift from a predominantly rural society to an increasingly urban one brought about changes in lifestyle, education, and employment.

Education and Healthcare: The government invested heavily in education and healthcare. Schools, universities, and hospitals were built, and efforts were made to improve the overall standard of living. This investment in human capital contributed to the development of a skilled workforce.

Global Energy Player: Saudi Arabia's oil reserves elevated the kingdom to a position of global importance in the energy sector. The country became a leading player in the global oil market, with its production capacity and reserves influencing global oil prices and geopolitics.

OPEC Membership: Saudi Arabia's role in the oil industry was further solidified when it became a founding member of the Organization of the Petroleum Exporting Countries (OPEC) in 1960. OPEC allowed oil-producing countries to collectively manage oil production and pricing, giving

Saudi Arabia significant influence in shaping global oil policies.

Diversification Efforts: While oil remains central to the Saudi economy, the government has recognized the importance of economic diversification. Initiatives like Vision 2030, launched in 2016, aim to reduce the kingdom's dependence on oil by developing other sectors such as tourism, entertainment, and technology.

Environmental Concerns: The discovery and extraction of oil reserves have raised environmental concerns. The oil industry's impact on the environment, including issues related to pollution and climate change, is a subject of global debate and scrutiny.

Global Energy Security: Saudi Arabia's oil reserves also make it a key player in global energy security. The kingdom's ability to maintain stable oil production and supply has a significant impact on global energy markets and the stability of the world economy.

Geopolitical Influence: Saudi Arabia's oil reserves have contributed to its geopolitical influence. The kingdom's strategic importance has made it a key player in regional and international politics, and its relationship with major powers, particularly the United States, has been a cornerstone of its foreign policy.

Sustainable Development: Saudi Arabia faces the challenge of managing its oil wealth for sustainable development. Balancing economic growth with environmental preservation and societal needs is an ongoing concern.

In summary, the discovery of oil reserves in Saudi Arabia was a historic event that transformed the nation and its role on the global stage. It brought unprecedented wealth and development opportunities while also presenting challenges related to sustainability, environmental responsibility, and diversification. Saudi Arabia's oil reserves continue to be a defining feature of its identity and its place in the world.

Oil diplomacy and economic transformation are intertwined facets of Saudi Arabia's modern history, reflecting the nation's strategic use of its vast oil reserves to shape its domestic economy and international relations. The nexus between oil, diplomacy, and economic development has played a pivotal role in defining Saudi Arabia's role in the global arena and the trajectory of its domestic prosperity.

Oil as a Diplomatic Tool: Saudi Arabia's substantial oil reserves have endowed the nation with significant diplomatic leverage. The kingdom's ability to control and influence oil production and pricing has allowed it to wield considerable power in international negotiations and alliances. By adjusting oil output, Saudi Arabia can affect global oil prices and, consequently, the economies of oil-importing nations.

The Oil Embargo of 1973: A landmark moment in oil diplomacy was the oil embargo imposed by Saudi Arabia and other Arab nations in response to Western support for Israel during the Yom Kippur War of 1973. The embargo demonstrated Saudi Arabia's capacity to use oil as a geopolitical weapon and highlighted the interconnectedness of global energy markets.

Oil Production and OPEC: Saudi Arabia has been a leading member of the Organization of the Petroleum Exporting Countries (OPEC) since its inception in 1960. As a key player within OPEC, Saudi Arabia has participated in coordinating oil production levels to stabilize global oil prices and protect the interests of oil-producing nations. Its willingness to adjust production has often been instrumental in managing oil market dynamics.

Economic Transformation: The revenue generated from oil exports has been the linchpin of Saudi Arabia's economic transformation. The nation's rulers recognized the need to diversify the economy to reduce its dependency on oil, which was susceptible to price fluctuations.

Investment in Infrastructure: Oil revenues have funded massive infrastructure projects, including roads, airports, ports, and telecommunications networks. These developments have facilitated economic growth, trade, and connectivity within the kingdom and with the wider world.

Industrialization: Saudi Arabia has invested in industrialization, seeking to create a more diverse and self-reliant economy. This effort has led to the establishment of industrial cities, petrochemical complexes, and manufacturing facilities that produce a wide range of goods.

Economic Diversification: Recognizing the vulnerability of an oil-dependent economy, Saudi Arabia has embarked on ambitious economic diversification initiatives. Vision 2030, launched in 2016, outlines a comprehensive roadmap for diversifying the Saudi economy. It includes plans to develop sectors such as tourism, entertainment, technology, and renewable energy.

Foreign Direct Investment (FDI): Saudi Arabia has sought to attract foreign direct investment (FDI) to stimulate economic growth and create job opportunities for its burgeoning population. The nation has taken steps to improve its business environment, reduce bureaucratic hurdles, and provide incentives for foreign investors.

Sovereign Wealth Fund: The establishment of the Public Investment Fund (PIF) represents a critical aspect of Saudi Arabia's economic transformation. PIF is one of the world's largest sovereign wealth funds and plays a central role in financing strategic investments and diversification projects.

Social and Cultural Changes: Economic transformation has brought about social and cultural changes in Saudi Arabia. Efforts to modernize the nation include initiatives to promote entertainment, tourism, and women's participation in the workforce. These changes aim to align Saudi society with evolving global norms.

Sustainable Development: Saudi Arabia faces the challenge of managing its economic transformation in a sustainable manner. Balancing economic growth with environmental preservation, resource management, and social equity is a paramount concern.

Global Economic Integration: Saudi Arabia's economic transformation has driven the nation's integration into the global economy. It seeks to play a role in international economic forums, encourage trade and investment, and diversify its international economic partnerships.

Challenges and Opportunities: While economic transformation presents opportunities, it also poses challenges. Ensuring that economic benefits are distributed equitably, fostering innovation, and adapting to a changing global economy are ongoing challenges.

In summary, the nexus between oil diplomacy and economic transformation has been instrumental in shaping Saudi Arabia's modern history. The strategic use of oil reserves in diplomacy has allowed the nation to exert influence on the global stage, while the economic windfall from oil exports has underpinned domestic development and diversification efforts. Saudi Arabia's continued pursuit of sustainable economic transformation and its role in the global energy landscape remain pivotal aspects of its contemporary identity and aspirations.

The era of the oil boom in Saudi Arabia, which began with the discovery of significant oil reserves in the 1930s, ushered in a period of profound political and social changes that transformed the kingdom in numerous ways. As vast oil wealth flowed into the country, it not only fueled economic development but also reshaped the political landscape, social structures, and cultural norms.

Political Changes:

Centralization of Power: The newfound oil wealth allowed the Saudi monarchy, under King Abdulaziz Ibn Saud, to centralize power. The government strengthened its authority and control over various regions and tribes, resulting in a more centralized state structure.

Establishment of Government Ministries: To manage the complexities of a rapidly developing nation, various government ministries were established. These ministries oversaw sectors such as finance, education, health, and infrastructure, contributing to the professionalization of government administration.

Modern Legal Framework: The need for a modern legal framework to govern the nation's affairs became evident. Efforts were made to codify laws and regulations, blending Islamic Sharia law with contemporary legal principles to create a legal system that could accommodate the demands of a modern state.

Foreign Diplomacy: The political changes were not confined to domestic affairs. Saudi Arabia began to play a more prominent role in international diplomacy, leveraging its oil resources to forge alliances and influence regional and global politics.

OPEC Membership: Saudi Arabia's participation in the formation of the Organization of the Petroleum Exporting Countries (OPEC) in 1960 marked a significant political move. As one of OPEC's founding members, Saudi Arabia exercised its influence in the global energy market, contributing to the kingdom's political clout.

Geopolitical Significance: The kingdom's strategic location and oil wealth elevated its geopolitical significance. Saudi Arabia became a crucial ally for Western powers, particularly the United States, during the Cold War, and it played a pivotal role in maintaining regional stability.

Social Changes:

Urbanization: The oil boom era saw a rapid influx of people from rural areas to urban centers in search of employment and better living conditions. This led to significant urbanization, with cities like Riyadh, Jeddah, and Dhahran experiencing exponential growth.

Education Reform: Investment in education became a priority. New schools and universities were established, and scholarships were offered to students for higher education abroad. This educational reform aimed to develop a skilled workforce and facilitate modernization.

Healthcare Improvement: Access to healthcare services improved as the government invested in building hospitals and clinics. This contributed to better healthcare outcomes and an increase in life expectancy.

Changing Role of Women: The role of women in Saudi society began to evolve. While traditional gender roles persisted in many areas, women gained increased access to education and employment opportunities. Over the years, there have been gradual reforms to expand women's rights.

Social Welfare Programs: Oil revenues enabled the government to introduce social welfare programs, including subsidies for basic necessities like food, fuel, and housing. These programs aimed to improve the standard of living for all citizens.

Cultural Shifts: The exposure to global influences and the influx of expatriates working in the oil industry contributed to cultural shifts. Saudi society saw an integration of Western cultural elements, which sometimes led to debates about preserving cultural traditions.

Youth Empowerment: With a young population, the government recognized the importance of empowering the youth through education, employment opportunities, and youth centers. Engaging the youth became crucial for the nation's future development.

Emergence of a Middle Class: The oil boom era saw the emergence of a middle class in Saudi Arabia. This burgeoning middle class enjoyed increased access to consumer goods, leisure activities, and travel opportunities.

Social Challenges: The rapid changes brought about by the oil boom also posed social challenges. Traditional values sometimes clashed with modernization, leading to debates about cultural identity and societal norms.

Social Cohesion: Maintaining social cohesion and unity in a rapidly changing society became a priority. The government worked to balance the demands of a modern economy with the preservation of Saudi cultural values and traditions.

In summary, the era of the oil boom in Saudi Arabia was marked by significant political and social changes. The vast oil wealth transformed the nation's political landscape, leading to centralization of power, modernization of legal systems, and a more prominent role in international diplomacy. On the social front, urbanization, education reform, changes in gender roles, and the emergence of a middle class reshaped Saudi society. These changes, while bringing economic prosperity, also posed challenges as the nation sought to navigate the complexities of modernization while preserving its cultural identity.

Chapter 10: Changing of the Guard: The House of Saud in the Late 20th Century

Leadership transitions and succession have been critical aspects of Saudi Arabia's political landscape, shaping the trajectory of the nation and its governance. Throughout its history, Saudi Arabia has experienced a series of leadership transitions, each with its unique dynamics and implications for the country's domestic and international affairs.

Founding of the Modern Saudi State: The foundational transition in Saudi Arabia's history occurred with the establishment of the modern Saudi state by King Abdulaziz Ibn Saud, often referred to as Ibn Saud. His leadership and vision were instrumental in unifying the Arabian Peninsula and laying the foundations of the contemporary Saudi state. The transition from fragmented tribal entities to a centralized nation under his rule was a defining moment.

Ibn Saud's Legacy: King Abdulaziz Ibn Saud's death in 1953 marked a significant transition. His passing raised questions about the succession process and the stability of the newly established kingdom. The subsequent leadership transition saw his eldest son, Saud bin Abdulaziz Al Saud, ascend to the throne.

King Saud's Rule: King Saud's reign faced challenges related to governance and financial mismanagement. These difficulties culminated in his deposition in 1964 by a council of senior princes, led by his half-brother, Crown Prince Faisal. This transition marked the first instance of the kingdom's leaders intervening to remove a sitting monarch.

Crown Prince Faisal's Ascension: Crown Prince Faisal's ascension to the throne marked a return to more stable and effective governance. His reign was marked by modernization efforts, economic development, and a continued commitment to the principles laid down by King Abdulaziz. Faisal's leadership was also characterized by a balanced foreign policy and strengthening of Saudi Arabia's position on the global stage.

King Faisal's Assassination: Tragically, King Faisal's reign came to an end with his assassination in 1975. His nephew, King Khalid bin Abdulaziz Al Saud, succeeded him. The transition following Faisal's death demonstrated the stability of the Saudi monarchy and its ability to manage leadership changes.

King Khalid's Rule: King Khalid's reign was marked by economic prosperity and further modernization efforts. His leadership saw the expansion of social welfare programs, infrastructure development, and efforts to improve the quality of life for Saudi citizens.

King Fahd's Leadership: Following King Khalid's death in 1982, King Fahd bin Abdulaziz Al Saud ascended to the throne. His rule was characterized by a focus on regional stability, a commitment to the Palestinian cause, and the expansion of the oil sector. King Fahd's leadership also witnessed Saudi Arabia's response to the Gulf War in 1990-1991 when the kingdom hosted coalition forces in the conflict against Iraq.

Succession Dynamics: The question of succession and the process of determining the next king has been a critical aspect of Saudi leadership transitions. Traditionally, the king has been selected from among the sons of King Abdulaziz, and this process has been guided by consensus among senior princes of the Al Saud family. This approach has ensured stability and continuity.

King Abdullah's Reign: King Fahd's death in 2005 marked another transition, with King Abdullah bin Abdulaziz Al Saud taking the throne. King Abdullah's reign was characterized by an emphasis on modernization, social development, and efforts to enhance Saudi Arabia's global image. He also played a diplomatic role in the Middle East and advocated for peace.

Challenges and Regional Turbulence: King Abdullah's reign coincided with a period of regional turbulence, including the Arab Spring and conflicts in neighboring countries. Managing these challenges while ensuring domestic stability was a significant aspect of his leadership.

King Salman's Ascension: King Abdullah's death in 2015 saw the ascension of King Salman bin Abdulaziz Al Saud. His leadership has focused on consolidating economic reforms, promoting the Saudi Vision 2030 initiative, and confronting regional security challenges.

Crown Prince Mohammad bin Salman: An important development in recent years has been the rise of Crown Prince Mohammad bin Salman, often referred to as MbS. As the heir apparent, he has played a central role in shaping Saudi Arabia's domestic and foreign policies. His Vision 2030 initiative aims to diversify the economy, reduce dependency on oil, and promote social reforms.

Continuity and Change: Leadership transitions in Saudi Arabia have been marked by a balance between continuity and change. While the core principles of the state have remained intact, each new leader has brought their own vision and priorities to the forefront.

The Role of the Al Saud Family: The Al Saud family, through the Allegiance Council, has played a crucial role in ensuring a smooth succession process. The council, established in 2006, formalizes the process of selecting the king and crown prince, enhancing transparency and stability.

In summary, leadership transitions and succession have been pivotal moments in Saudi Arabia's history, shaping the nation's governance, policies, and international relations. The ability of the Saudi monarchy to manage these transitions while maintaining stability and continuity has been a hallmark of the kingdom's political system. As Saudi Arabia continues to navigate domestic and global challenges, leadership transitions will remain a significant aspect of its evolving political landscape.

Saudi Arabia's position in a globalized world has evolved significantly over the years, reflecting the kingdom's efforts to adapt to the challenges and opportunities presented by globalization. As one of the world's leading oil producers and a key player in the Middle East, Saudi Arabia's engagement with the global community has profound implications for the nation's economy, politics, culture, and society.

Economic Globalization:

Saudi Arabia's economy is deeply intertwined with the global economy, primarily due to its vast reserves of oil. The kingdom is a major player in the global energy market, with oil exports accounting for a substantial portion of its revenue. As such, fluctuations in global oil prices have a direct impact on the Saudi economy, making it highly sensitive to global economic trends.

The government has recognized the need to diversify the economy and reduce its reliance on oil exports. Vision 2030, launched in 2016, is a comprehensive blueprint for economic transformation. It aims to promote sectors such as tourism, entertainment, technology, and renewable energy, fostering greater economic diversity and resilience to global economic shocks.

Political Diplomacy and Alliances:

Saudi Arabia's diplomatic engagement in a globalized world is characterized by a multifaceted approach. The kingdom maintains strategic alliances with various countries, particularly the United States, which has been a long-standing partner in the areas of security, energy, and trade. These alliances serve as pillars of Saudi foreign policy, ensuring the kingdom's security and stability.

Saudi Arabia has also played a significant role in regional diplomacy, addressing conflicts and crises in the Middle East. The kingdom's involvement in initiatives like the Gulf Cooperation Council (GCC) and its leadership in regional organizations reflects its commitment to addressing regional challenges and fostering cooperation.

In recent years, Saudi Arabia has pursued a more assertive foreign policy, seeking to diversify its international partnerships and strengthen its global influence. The kingdom has forged economic and diplomatic ties with emerging powers like China and India, recognizing the shifting dynamics of global geopolitics.

Cultural Exchange and Global Influence:

Globalization has facilitated cultural exchange and the dissemination of Saudi culture and heritage on a global scale. The kingdom has made efforts to promote its cultural identity and values, including initiatives to showcase Saudi art, music, and cuisine internationally.

Saudi Arabia's efforts to modernize and open up to the world have included cultural reforms. Initiatives such as allowing cinemas, hosting international entertainment events, and easing restrictions on women's participation in public life reflect a desire to engage with global cultural norms while preserving Saudi traditions.

Economic Integration:

Saudi Arabia actively seeks economic integration with the global community. The kingdom is a member of various international organizations and institutions, including the World Trade Organization (WTO) and the International Monetary Fund (IMF). These memberships promote economic cooperation, trade, and investment opportunities.

Additionally, Saudi Arabia has attracted foreign investment through initiatives like the Saudi Arabian General Investment Authority (SAGIA), which streamlines the process for businesses to establish a presence in the kingdom. The government's efforts to enhance the ease of doing business have positioned Saudi Arabia as an attractive destination for foreign capital.

Technology and Innovation:

Globalization has accelerated the adoption of technology and innovation in Saudi Arabia. The kingdom has invested heavily in technology infrastructure and digitalization. Initiatives to develop smart cities, promote entrepreneurship, and foster a digital economy align with global trends in technology and innovation.

Saudi Arabia has also sought to position itself as a hub for technology and innovation in the Middle East. The establishment of the NEOM megaproject, a futuristic city in the northwest of the country, exemplifies the kingdom's ambition to leverage technology and innovation for economic growth and development.

Global Challenges and Responsibilities:
Saudi Arabia's engagement with the globalized world brings with it a set of challenges and responsibilities. As a major oil producer, the kingdom faces the dual challenge of meeting global energy demands while addressing environmental concerns and the transition to renewable energy sources.

Additionally, Saudi Arabia has a role to play in addressing regional conflicts and security challenges in the Middle East. The kingdom's diplomatic initiatives, such as the Yemen peace process and efforts to counter extremism, underscore its commitment to regional stability and global security.

Sustainable Development and Environmental Concerns:
Saudi Arabia's vision for the future includes a commitment to sustainable development. As part of Vision 2030, the kingdom has set goals for environmental conservation, renewable energy adoption, and the reduction of carbon emissions. These efforts align with global efforts to combat climate change and environmental degradation.

Global Health and Humanitarian Initiatives:
The kingdom has also engaged with global health and humanitarian challenges. Saudi Arabia has contributed to international efforts to address humanitarian crises and provide aid to countries in need. Additionally, the kingdom has played a role in promoting global health initiatives and research.

In summary, Saudi Arabia's position in a globalized world is marked by its economic interdependence, diplomatic engagement, cultural exchange, and commitment to addressing global challenges. The kingdom's efforts to diversify its economy, promote cultural openness, and adopt technology reflect its recognition of the changing dynamics of the globalized era. As Saudi Arabia continues to navigate the complexities of globalization, it remains a key player in regional and international affairs, with a role that extends beyond its borders.

The late 20th century was a period of significant challenges and transformations for Saudi Arabia, with profound impacts on its society, economy, and political landscape. During this era, the kingdom faced both internal and external pressures that forced it to adapt and evolve in various ways.

Oil Price Volatility:
One of the central challenges faced by Saudi Arabia in the late 20th century was the volatility of oil prices. The kingdom's economy was heavily dependent on oil exports, and fluctuations in global oil prices could have a direct impact on government revenues and economic stability. The 1970s and 1980s witnessed dramatic fluctuations in oil prices, including the oil price shocks of the 1970s and the subsequent price collapse in the 1980s. These events forced Saudi Arabia to reassess its economic strategy.

Economic Diversification:
In response to the vulnerability posed by its oil-dependent economy, Saudi Arabia embarked on efforts to diversify its economic base. This diversification included investments in sectors such as petrochemicals, manufacturing, and

infrastructure development. The goal was to reduce reliance on oil exports and create a more balanced and resilient economy.

The Gulf War and Regional Stability:

The invasion of Kuwait by Iraq in 1990, leading to the Gulf War in 1990-1991, had significant implications for Saudi Arabia and the region. Saudi Arabia played a central role in hosting coalition forces and was at the forefront of the international effort to expel Iraqi forces from Kuwait. The conflict highlighted the kingdom's importance in regional security and its commitment to maintaining stability.

Islamic Extremism and Security Concerns:

The late 20th century also saw the rise of extremist ideologies in the Muslim world, including Saudi Arabia. The kingdom faced internal challenges from Islamist militants who sought to undermine the government and establish a more conservative form of Islamic rule. Acts of terrorism, such as the 1996 bombing of the Khobar Towers in Dhahran, underscored the security threats faced by Saudi Arabia.

Social and Cultural Changes:

Saudi Arabia underwent significant social and cultural changes in the late 20th century. While traditional customs and religious conservatism remained influential, there were efforts to modernize and open up the society. Initiatives included expanding educational opportunities, including for women, and introducing limited entertainment options.

Gender Rights and Women's Participation:

During this period, there were limited but noteworthy steps taken to expand women's rights and participation in public life. These included access to education and employment opportunities for women. However, Saudi women still faced significant gender-related challenges and restrictions.

Political Stability and Leadership Changes:
Saudi Arabia maintained political stability despite regional and internal challenges. Leadership transitions occurred smoothly, and the kingdom continued to be ruled by members of the Al Saud family. King Fahd's reign (1982-2005) and King Abdullah's reign (2005-2015) were marked by a focus on economic development, social reform, and regional diplomacy.

Regional Relations and Foreign Policy:
Saudi Arabia played an active role in regional diplomacy during the late 20th century. The kingdom sought to balance its relationships with regional and global powers while navigating complex regional dynamics. Its role in initiatives like the Gulf Cooperation Council (GCC) and efforts to mediate regional conflicts reflected its commitment to regional stability.

Globalization and Technological Advancements:
Globalization and technological advancements began to have a noticeable impact on Saudi society. Increased access to information, communication technologies, and global media exposed Saudis to international influences and trends. This exposure contributed to discussions about cultural identity and societal norms.

Vision for the Future:
The late 20th century laid the groundwork for Saudi Arabia's vision for the future. Economic diversification, social reform, and efforts to address security challenges were all part of the kingdom's evolving strategy. Vision 2030, launched in 2016, builds on these foundations,

outlining a comprehensive roadmap for the kingdom's transformation in the 21st century.

In summary, the late 20th century was a period of significant challenges and transformations for Saudi Arabia. The kingdom faced economic volatility, security threats, and social changes, all of which contributed to its evolving identity and vision for the future. As Saudi Arabia moved into the 21st century, it continued to navigate these complexities while striving to balance tradition and modernization.

BOOK 2
OIL, POWER, AND INFLUENCE
HOUSE OF SAUD IN THE 20TH CENTURY (1900S-2000S)

BY A.J. KINGSTON

Chapter 1: The Black Gold Rush: Saudi Arabia's Oil Revolution (Early 1900s)

Early explorations and drilling efforts marked the beginning of Saudi Arabia's journey as a major player in the global oil industry. These endeavors laid the foundation for the kingdom's economic transformation, political influence, and geopolitical significance. Here, we delve into the early history of oil exploration and drilling in Saudi Arabia.

Discovery of Oil: The exploration of oil in Saudi Arabia began in the early 20th century when the kingdom was still a relatively young nation. In 1933, a momentous event occurred when American geologists working for the Standard Oil Company of California (now Chevron) discovered commercial quantities of oil in the Eastern Province of Saudi Arabia. This discovery, which came to be known as the Dammam No. 7 well, was a game-changer for the region and the world.

Concession Agreements: Following the discovery, negotiations between the Saudi government and foreign oil companies led to the signing of concession agreements that granted these companies exclusive rights to explore, extract, and market Saudi Arabia's oil reserves. The first of these agreements was signed with the Arabian American Oil Company (ARAMCO), a consortium of American companies, in 1933. These agreements would shape the oil industry in Saudi Arabia for decades to come.

Early Drilling Efforts: With the concession agreements in place, drilling operations commenced in earnest. The first commercial oil well, Dammam No. 7, was soon followed by the drilling of other successful wells, including Dhahran No. 1. These early drilling efforts confirmed the vastness of Saudi Arabia's oil reserves.

Infrastructure Development: To support oil exploration and production, significant infrastructure development was required. This included the construction of pipelines, storage facilities, refineries, and export terminals. Dhahran, in the Eastern Province, became a hub for the emerging oil industry, hosting the headquarters of ARAMCO and serving as the base for exploration and drilling operations.

World War II and Geopolitical Significance: World War II had a profound impact on the global oil industry, and Saudi Arabia's oil resources became strategically vital. The kingdom's oil played a critical role in supplying the Allied forces with the energy needed to win the war. This geopolitical significance would continue to shape Saudi Arabia's relations with foreign powers.

Expansion and Modernization: In the post-World War II period, Saudi Arabia's oil industry expanded rapidly. Production facilities were modernized, and drilling technologies improved. This expansion allowed Saudi Arabia to increase its oil production and export capacity, solidifying its position as a major oil exporter.

Nationalization of Oil: The question of control and ownership of Saudi Arabia's oil resources became a central issue in the 1950s and 1960s. Saudi Arabia, along with other oil-producing nations, sought a greater share of the revenues generated from their oil reserves. This led to negotiations between the Saudi government and the foreign oil companies operating in the kingdom.

Formation of Saudi Aramco: In 1988, the Saudi government acquired full ownership of ARAMCO, marking a historic milestone in the kingdom's oil industry. The company was renamed Saudi Arabian Oil Company, or Saudi Aramco, and became the world's largest and most valuable oil company. The move to nationalize the oil industry allowed Saudi Arabia to have greater control over its oil resources and revenues.

Technological Advancements: Over the decades, technological advancements in drilling and oil extraction techniques played a crucial role in maximizing the recovery of oil reserves. Horizontal drilling and enhanced oil recovery methods have been employed to increase the efficiency of oil production.

Impact on Saudi Society and Economy: The wealth generated by the oil industry had a transformative impact on Saudi society and the economy. It funded ambitious development projects, infrastructure improvements, and social programs. It also led to urbanization and modernization, with cities like Riyadh and Jeddah experiencing significant growth.

In summary, early explorations and drilling efforts in Saudi Arabia laid the groundwork for the kingdom's emergence as a major player in the global oil industry. The discovery of oil, the signing of concession agreements, and the subsequent nationalization of the industry reshaped Saudi Arabia's economy, politics, and global standing. The kingdom's oil wealth has been a driving force behind its modernization and development, making it a prominent player in the global energy landscape.

The discovery of vast oil reserves in Saudi Arabia marked a pivotal moment in the country's history, transforming it from a relatively unknown and impoverished desert kingdom into one of the world's wealthiest and most influential nations. This discovery, which occurred in the early 20th century, had profound economic, political, and social consequences, shaping the trajectory of Saudi Arabia and the global oil industry.

Early Explorations: The story of Saudi Arabia's oil discovery began with early explorations conducted by American geologists employed by the Standard Oil Company of California (now Chevron). These geologists, led by Max Steineke, began prospecting for oil in the Eastern Province of Saudi Arabia in the 1930s. Their exploratory efforts aimed to identify commercial quantities of oil beneath the desert sands.

Dammam No. 7: The breakthrough came in March 1938 with the drilling of the Dammam No. 7 well. This well, located near the town of Dhahran, struck oil at a depth of approximately 1,440 feet. The oil gushed from the well, confirming the presence of vast oil reserves beneath the Arabian Peninsula. Dammam No. 7 was a landmark discovery and is often considered the birth of Saudi Arabia's oil industry.

Concession Agreements: The successful discovery of oil led to negotiations between the Saudi government and foreign oil companies. These negotiations resulted in the signing of concession agreements that granted foreign companies exclusive rights to explore, extract, and market Saudi Arabia's oil reserves. The first of these agreements was signed with the Arabian American Oil Company (ARAMCO), a consortium of American oil companies.

Expansion of Exploration: Encouraged by the success of the initial discovery, exploration efforts expanded across the Eastern Province and beyond. More wells were drilled, confirming the presence of substantial oil reserves in various locations. This expansion marked the beginning of widespread oil exploration in Saudi Arabia.

Infrastructure Development: To support oil exploration and production, extensive infrastructure was developed. This included the construction of pipelines, refineries, storage facilities, and export terminals. Dhahran, where ARAMCO established its headquarters, became a hub for the emerging oil industry, with infrastructure growing to accommodate the increasing production.

Geopolitical Significance: Saudi Arabia's vast oil reserves quickly assumed geopolitical significance. As the world's largest proven oil reserves became increasingly vital to global energy security, Saudi Arabia's political importance grew. The kingdom's oil resources played a critical role in supplying the Allied forces during World War II.

Economic Transformation: The discovery of oil brought about a dramatic economic transformation in Saudi Arabia. Revenues from oil exports provided the kingdom with a reliable source of income, enabling ambitious development projects, infrastructure investments, and social programs. The newfound wealth elevated Saudi Arabia from poverty to affluence.

Nationalization of Oil: In 1988, the Saudi government acquired full ownership of ARAMCO, marking the nationalization of the oil industry. The company was renamed Saudi Arabian Oil Company, or Saudi Aramco, and it became the world's largest and most valuable oil company. This move allowed Saudi Arabia to have greater control over its oil resources and revenues.

Impact on Society and Culture: The oil boom had a profound impact on Saudi society and culture. It led to urbanization, modernization, and increased access to education and healthcare. It also brought Western influence to the kingdom, impacting social norms, lifestyle, and cultural practices.

In summary, the discovery of vast oil reserves in Saudi Arabia was a transformative event that reshaped the kingdom's destiny. It turned Saudi Arabia into a global energy powerhouse, profoundly influencing its economy, politics, and society. The nation's oil wealth continues to be a driving force behind its modernization and development, making it a prominent player in the global energy landscape.

The impact of the discovery of vast oil reserves on Saudi society and economy has been nothing short of transformative. It has fundamentally altered the socio-economic landscape of the kingdom, propelling it from relative obscurity and poverty to unprecedented wealth and modernization. In this narrative, we delve into the multifaceted effects of the oil boom on Saudi Arabia's society and economy.

Economic Transformation:

The economic transformation brought about by the oil boom cannot be overstated. Before the discovery of oil, Saudi Arabia was predominantly an agrarian society with a subsistence economy. The sudden influx of oil revenues revolutionized the nation's economic outlook. It turned Saudi Arabia into one of the wealthiest countries in the world, with a GDP per capita that soared to levels previously unimaginable.

Infrastructure Development:
The oil windfall facilitated an ambitious program of infrastructure development. New roads, highways, ports, airports, and telecommunications networks were constructed across the country. Cities and urban centers underwent extensive modernization and expansion. These infrastructure projects not only improved the quality of life but also laid the foundation for future economic growth.

Urbanization:
The economic prosperity driven by oil revenues triggered a wave of urbanization. People from rural areas flocked to the cities in search of employment and better living conditions. This rapid urbanization led to the growth of major cities like Riyadh, Jeddah, and Dhahran, which became bustling metropolises with modern amenities and services.

Education and Healthcare:
Oil revenues were channeled into enhancing education and healthcare systems. Saudi Arabia established universities, colleges, and research institutions, fostering a more educated workforce. This investment in education contributed to a higher literacy rate and a pool of skilled professionals. Additionally, improved healthcare infrastructure led to better healthcare services and increased life expectancy.

Employment Opportunities:
The oil industry created a plethora of employment opportunities. Not only were jobs available in the oil sector itself, but the wealth generated by oil revenues also fueled growth in various other sectors, such as construction, manufacturing, and services. This resulted in

a significant reduction in unemployment rates and a higher standard of living for many Saudis.

Social Modernization:
The oil boom catalyzed social modernization. The newfound wealth allowed Saudi Arabia to open up to the world in various ways. Access to global media, including television and the internet, exposed Saudis to international trends, ideas, and lifestyles. This exposure triggered debates about cultural identity and societal norms.

Cultural Changes:
While traditional customs and religious conservatism remained influential, there was a discernible shift in cultural norms. Western-style clothing, music, and entertainment gained acceptance. Saudi society became more diverse and cosmopolitan, with a growing interest in international cuisine, fashion, and consumer products.

Status of Women:
The status of women in Saudi Arabia began to evolve. While gender roles remained largely traditional, women gained more access to education and employment opportunities. Changes in societal norms allowed women to participate in various fields, including medicine, education, and business.

Challenges of Modernization:
The rapid pace of modernization also posed challenges. Traditionalists expressed concerns about the erosion of Saudi Arabia's cultural and religious identity. Balancing the preservation of Islamic values with modernization efforts became a recurring theme in societal discourse.

Economic Diversification:

Recognizing the vulnerability of an economy heavily dependent on oil, Saudi Arabia embarked on efforts to diversify its economic base. Vision 2030, launched in 2016, is a comprehensive blueprint for economic transformation. It aims to promote sectors such as tourism, entertainment, technology, and renewable energy, fostering greater economic diversity and resilience to global economic shocks.

Income Inequality:

Despite the nation's immense wealth, income inequality remains a challenge. While some Saudis have benefited significantly from the oil boom, there are still disparities in wealth and living standards, particularly among marginalized communities and certain regions.

Global Influence:

The oil boom elevated Saudi Arabia's global influence. As one of the world's leading oil producers, the kingdom plays a pivotal role in global energy markets. Its influence extends beyond economics, as Saudi Arabia has become a key player in regional and international diplomacy.

Social Welfare Programs:

The government has implemented social welfare programs to distribute the benefits of oil wealth more broadly. Subsidies for basic goods and services, such as education, healthcare, and housing, have been introduced to improve the living standards of all Saudis.

Challenges and Future Prospects:

The challenges of managing a rapidly changing society and diversifying the economy persist. Vision 2030 represents a concerted effort to address these challenges by fostering economic diversification, promoting cultural openness, and preparing Saudi Arabia for a post-oil future.

In summary, the impact of the discovery of vast oil reserves on Saudi society and economy has been multifaceted and profound. It has spurred economic transformation, urbanization, social modernization, and cultural change. While the oil boom has brought immense wealth and opportunities, it has also posed challenges and necessitated careful planning for the future. Saudi Arabia's journey from a desert kingdom to a modern nation continues to be shaped by the legacy of its oil riches.

Chapter 2: Petrodollars and Political Power: Oil Wealth and Influence (Mid-20th Century)

Oil exportation and the revenue generated from it have been the lifeblood of Saudi Arabia's economy, driving the nation's growth and development since the discovery of vast oil reserves. This narrative explores the intricate relationship between oil exportation and revenue, highlighting their significance and impact on the kingdom's economy and global influence.

Key Driver of Economic Growth:
Oil exportation has been the primary driver of Saudi Arabia's economic growth. The kingdom possesses some of the world's largest proven oil reserves, and it consistently ranks among the top oil producers. The revenue generated from oil exports has fueled extensive infrastructure development, social programs, and economic diversification efforts.

Global Energy Supplier:
Saudi Arabia plays a pivotal role in global energy markets as one of the leading oil exporters. The kingdom's ability to consistently supply oil to international markets has made it a reliable energy supplier. This role has helped stabilize global energy prices and ensured a steady flow of oil to meet global demand.

OPEC Membership:
Saudi Arabia is a founding member of the Organization of the Petroleum Exporting Countries (OPEC), an influential international organization of oil-producing nations. As a member, Saudi Arabia collaborates with other oil-producing countries to manage oil production levels and

stabilize global oil prices. The kingdom's role within OPEC enhances its influence in shaping global energy policies.

Revenue Generation:
Oil exportation accounts for a substantial portion of Saudi Arabia's government revenue. The kingdom heavily relies on oil-related income to finance public expenditures, including infrastructure projects, social welfare programs, education, and healthcare. The stability and predictability of oil revenue have allowed the government to plan and execute long-term development initiatives.

Economic Diversification:
While oil exportation has been the dominant source of revenue, Saudi Arabia recognizes the need for economic diversification to reduce its dependence on oil. The government has launched initiatives like Vision 2030 to promote non-oil sectors such as tourism, entertainment, technology, and renewable energy. These efforts aim to create a more balanced and resilient economy.

Impact of Oil Price Volatility:
The kingdom is susceptible to fluctuations in global oil prices. Periods of high oil prices can result in substantial windfalls, while price declines can strain the budget. Saudi Arabia has, at times, adjusted its oil production to stabilize prices, reflecting its commitment to maintaining oil market stability.

Strategic Diplomacy:
Saudi Arabia's status as a major oil exporter has conferred geopolitical significance on the kingdom. It has leveraged its oil resources and influence within OPEC to strengthen diplomatic ties with both regional and global powers. Saudi Arabia's foreign policy often aligns with its energy interests, making it a key player in international affairs.

Investment in Oil Infrastructure:
To support oil exportation, Saudi Arabia has made significant investments in oil infrastructure. This includes the construction of pipelines, storage facilities, refineries, and export terminals. Dhahran, home to the headquarters of Saudi Aramco, is a critical hub for the nation's oil operations.

Efforts to Increase Efficiency:
Saudi Arabia continuously invests in technological advancements and operational efficiencies to optimize oil production and exportation. Enhanced oil recovery techniques, advanced drilling technologies, and well management practices have been adopted to maximize the recovery of oil reserves.

Revenue Distribution:
The government has implemented social welfare programs and subsidies to distribute the benefits of oil revenue more equitably among the population. These programs encompass education, healthcare, housing, and other essential services, enhancing the quality of life for Saudi citizens.

Environmental Considerations:
As global awareness of environmental concerns grows, Saudi Arabia is exploring strategies to balance its reliance on oil revenue with sustainable practices. Initiatives to diversify the energy sector through investments in renewable energy sources, such as solar and wind power, are being pursued.

In summary, oil exportation and the revenue derived from it have played a central role in shaping Saudi Arabia's economy and global influence. As a leading oil exporter and a key player in OPEC, the kingdom's oil resources have propelled it to international prominence. While oil revenue has driven economic growth and development, Saudi Arabia is actively working to diversify its economy and adapt to changing global energy dynamics, ensuring a sustainable future beyond oil.

Saudi Arabia's emergence as a global energy player is a testament to the kingdom's vast oil reserves, strategic positioning, and its role in shaping the global energy landscape. Over the years, Saudi Arabia has become a dominant force in the international energy arena, influencing markets, diplomacy, and geopolitics. This narrative explores the factors that have contributed to Saudi Arabia's status as a global energy powerhouse.

Abundant Oil Reserves:
Saudi Arabia boasts some of the world's largest proven oil reserves. These vast reserves have positioned the kingdom as a reliable supplier of oil to global markets. The sheer magnitude of its reserves ensures a steady flow of oil, contributing to market stability.

OPEC Leadership:
As a founding member of the Organization of the Petroleum Exporting Countries (OPEC), Saudi Arabia plays a pivotal role in the organization's policies and decisions. OPEC's coordination of oil production levels has a direct impact on global oil prices, and Saudi Arabia's influence within OPEC allows it to shape these price dynamics.

Stabilizing Global Oil Prices:
Saudi Arabia has historically taken on the role of a "swing producer" in the oil market. This means that the kingdom can adjust its oil production levels to help stabilize global oil prices during times of price volatility. This stabilizing

role has been critical in preventing extreme price fluctuations.

Diplomatic Clout:
Saudi Arabia's significant oil reserves and its central role in OPEC have given it diplomatic leverage on the global stage. The kingdom uses its energy resources as a tool for diplomacy, forging alliances and influencing international relations. Its ability to impact global energy markets enhances its geopolitical importance.

Strategic Partnerships:
Saudi Arabia has cultivated strategic partnerships with major oil-consuming nations, such as the United States and China. These partnerships often extend beyond energy and encompass economic, political, and security interests. Saudi Arabia's role as an energy supplier has cemented these relationships.

Investment in Infrastructure:
To facilitate its position as a global energy player, Saudi Arabia has invested heavily in oil infrastructure. This includes the construction of pipelines, storage facilities, refineries, and export terminals. The kingdom's oil infrastructure ensures efficient production, transportation, and exportation of oil.

Technological Advancements:
Saudi Arabia has adopted advanced technologies and practices in its oil industry to maximize production efficiency. Innovations such as horizontal drilling and enhanced oil recovery techniques have been employed to increase the recovery of oil reserves.

Economic Diversification Efforts:
Recognizing the need to diversify its economy, Saudi Arabia has embarked on initiatives like Vision 2030. These

efforts aim to reduce the kingdom's dependence on oil revenue by promoting non-oil sectors such as tourism, entertainment, and technology. Diversification enhances economic resilience.

Environmental Considerations:

As environmental concerns and the push for renewable energy gain prominence, Saudi Arabia is exploring sustainable energy solutions. Investments in renewable energy sources like solar and wind power are part of the kingdom's strategy to adapt to changing global energy dynamics.

Global Energy Leadership:

Saudi Arabia's leadership in the global energy sector extends beyond oil. The kingdom has become a significant player in natural gas markets, with investments in liquefied natural gas (LNG) infrastructure. This diversification of energy assets underscores Saudi Arabia's commitment to remaining a key player in the evolving energy landscape.

In summary, Saudi Arabia's emergence as a global energy player is the result of a confluence of factors, including abundant oil reserves, OPEC membership, strategic partnerships, infrastructure investments, and diplomatic clout. The kingdom's influence in global energy markets and its ability to stabilize oil prices have solidified its status as a key player in the complex world of energy geopolitics. As the global energy landscape continues to evolve, Saudi Arabia remains a central figure in shaping its future.

Saudi Arabia's political clout and diplomatic relationships on the global stage are deeply intertwined with its strategic positioning, abundant oil reserves, and regional significance. As one of the world's leading oil producers and a key player in the Middle East, the kingdom wields substantial influence in international affairs. This narrative explores how Saudi Arabia has leveraged its political clout and cultivated diplomatic relationships to advance its interests and shape global geopolitics.

Energy Diplomacy:
Saudi Arabia's status as a major oil exporter has been a cornerstone of its diplomacy. The kingdom has used its energy resources as a diplomatic tool, forging alliances and partnerships with oil-consuming nations. These relationships are often multifaceted, encompassing economic, political, and security interests. Saudi Arabia's ability to influence global energy markets has made it a valuable partner for many nations.

OPEC Leadership:
As a founding member of the Organization of the Petroleum Exporting Countries (OPEC), Saudi Arabia plays a central role in the organization's policies and decisions. OPEC's coordination of oil production levels has a direct impact on global oil prices. Saudi Arabia's leadership within OPEC allows it to shape these price dynamics, and it has often acted as a stabilizing force during times of oil price volatility.

Regional Diplomacy:
Saudi Arabia's position in the Middle East grants it significant influence in regional politics. The kingdom has been actively involved in mediating conflicts and promoting stability in the region. Its diplomatic efforts extend to issues such as the Israeli-Palestinian conflict, the war in Yemen, and relations with neighboring Gulf states.

Counterterrorism Cooperation:

Saudi Arabia has been a crucial partner in international counterterrorism efforts. The kingdom's intelligence and security agencies have cooperated with their counterparts in various countries to combat terrorism and extremist ideologies. This cooperation has been particularly vital in the global fight against terrorism.

Strategic Partnerships:

Saudi Arabia has cultivated strategic partnerships with major global powers, including the United States and China. These partnerships encompass a range of interests, from energy cooperation and defense agreements to economic investments. Saudi Arabia's diplomatic relationships with these nations have significant implications for global politics and security.

Humanitarian Assistance:

The kingdom has played an active role in providing humanitarian assistance to countries in need. This includes contributions to international relief efforts during crises such as natural disasters and conflicts. Saudi Arabia's humanitarian initiatives have demonstrated its commitment to global stability and well-being.

Cultural and Religious Diplomacy:

As the birthplace of Islam and home to its two holiest cities, Mecca and Medina, Saudi Arabia wields significant influence in the Muslim world. The kingdom has used cultural and religious diplomacy to promote its vision of moderate Islam and counter extremist ideologies. Initiatives like the King Salman Center for International Peace have furthered these efforts.

Economic Investments:

Saudi Arabia has made substantial economic investments in various countries, contributing to job creation, infrastructure development, and economic growth. These investments serve both Saudi Arabia's economic interests and its diplomatic goals, strengthening its ties with partner nations.

Global Diplomacy:

The kingdom's diplomacy extends beyond the Middle East. Saudi Arabia has engaged in diplomatic outreach to nations around the world, seeking to expand its influence and bolster its standing on the global stage. Its participation in international organizations and forums allows it to address a wide range of global issues.

In summary, Saudi Arabia's political clout and diplomatic relationships are a reflection of its multifaceted approach to international affairs. The kingdom's role as a major oil exporter, regional mediator, and strategic partner has positioned it as a key player in global geopolitics. Its diplomatic endeavors encompass energy diplomacy, regional stability, counterterrorism cooperation, humanitarian assistance, and cultural outreach, all contributing to its influential position in the international arena. Saudi Arabia's diplomacy continues to evolve in response to changing global dynamics, ensuring that it remains a significant force in shaping global affairs.

Chapter 3: The OPEC Era: Saudi Arabia's Role in Global Energy Markets (1970s)

The formation and influence of the Organization of the Petroleum Exporting Countries (OPEC) represent a pivotal chapter in the history of global energy markets and international diplomacy. OPEC, a coalition of oil-producing nations, has played a central role in shaping the world's oil industry, influencing oil prices, and exerting political and economic influence on a global scale. This narrative delves into the formation of OPEC, its evolution, and the significant impact it has had on the energy sector and geopolitics.

The Origins of OPEC:

The roots of OPEC can be traced back to the mid-20th century when several oil-producing countries, including Venezuela, Iran, Iraq, and Kuwait, were grappling with the effects of a global oil industry dominated by major multinational corporations. These nations sought greater control over their oil resources and a fairer share of the industry's profits.

In September 1960, representatives from these oil-producing countries gathered in Baghdad, Iraq, for the First Arab Petroleum Congress. During this meeting, they recognized the need for collective action to achieve their objectives. This recognition laid the groundwork for the formation of OPEC.

The Birth of OPEC:

OPEC officially came into existence on September 14, 1960, when five founding members—Saudi Arabia, Iran, Iraq, Kuwait, and Venezuela—signed the Organization's

Charter in Baghdad. The primary objective of OPEC was to coordinate and unify the petroleum policies of its member countries to stabilize oil markets, ensure fair prices for oil producers, and secure a steady income from oil exports.

OPEC's Early Years:

In its early years, OPEC faced numerous challenges. The Organization's ability to influence global oil markets was limited, as it represented a relatively small portion of the world's oil production. Additionally, the global oil industry was dominated by the "Seven Sisters," a group of major multinational oil companies, which controlled a significant share of oil reserves and production.

OPEC's Rise to Influence:

OPEC's influence began to grow in the 1970s as member countries took control of their oil production and began to nationalize their oil industries. The pivotal moment in OPEC's history came in 1973 when the Organization, along with other Arab oil-producing nations, imposed an oil embargo on countries that supported Israel during the Yom Kippur War. This embargo led to a significant increase in oil prices and marked the beginning of OPEC's ascendancy in the global energy landscape.

The Oil Crises of the 1970s:

The 1970s witnessed two major oil crises that catapulted OPEC to global prominence. The first crisis occurred in 1973 during the Arab-Israeli War, resulting in an oil embargo and a quadrupling of oil prices. The second crisis unfolded in 1979 due to the Iranian Revolution and the Iran-Iraq War, causing further disruptions in the global oil supply. These crises led to a surge in oil prices and underscored OPEC's ability to influence global energy markets.

The Formation of OPEC's Pricing Mechanism:
During this period, OPEC introduced a pricing mechanism that linked oil prices to a basket of major currencies, making oil less susceptible to fluctuations in the value of a single currency, such as the U.S. dollar. This pricing mechanism allowed OPEC to maintain relatively stable oil prices, benefiting both oil producers and consumers.

Challenges and Internal Dynamics:
Despite its successes, OPEC faced internal challenges, including disagreements among member countries over production quotas and pricing strategies. These internal divisions occasionally led to overproduction and price fluctuations.

OPEC in the Modern Era:
OPEC's influence has continued into the modern era, with the Organization growing to include 13 member countries by 2021. While OPEC's market share has fluctuated, it remains a significant player in the global oil industry. OPEC, in cooperation with non-OPEC oil-producing nations, has implemented production cuts and agreements to stabilize oil prices and prevent oversupply.

OPEC's Geopolitical Role:
Beyond its economic influence, OPEC has played a geopolitical role in shaping international relations. The Organization's decisions, such as oil production cuts or embargoes, have the potential to impact the economies and foreign policies of major oil-importing nations. OPEC has leveraged its oil resources as a diplomatic tool and has engaged in diplomacy with both oil-consuming and oil-producing nations.

Challenges in the 21st Century:

In the 21st century, OPEC has faced new challenges, including the rise of shale oil production in the United States and the growing global demand for renewable energy sources. These factors have added complexity to OPEC's efforts to balance the global oil market.

OPEC's Response to Market Dynamics:

OPEC has adapted to changing market dynamics by engaging in cooperation agreements with non-OPEC oil producers, most notably the OPEC+ alliance with Russia and other oil-producing nations. These agreements aim to stabilize oil markets by adjusting production levels in response to changing demand.

Environmental Considerations:

OPEC has also recognized the need to address environmental concerns, including climate change and the transition to cleaner energy sources. Some member countries have initiated efforts to diversify their economies and reduce their dependence on oil revenues.

In summary:

The formation and influence of OPEC represent a significant chapter in the history of global energy markets and diplomacy. From its humble beginnings in Baghdad in 1960, OPEC has grown into a formidable organization that has shaped the global oil industry, influenced oil prices, and played a crucial role in international relations. As the world continues to grapple with energy challenges and transitions, OPEC's role in the energy landscape remains a subject of global importance and scrutiny.

Saudi Arabia's leadership within the Organization of the Petroleum Exporting Countries (OPEC) has been a defining feature of the global oil industry and international energy diplomacy. As one of the founding members of OPEC, Saudi Arabia has played a central role in shaping the Organization's policies, influencing oil production levels, and steering the course of global oil markets. This narrative explores Saudi Arabia's leadership in OPEC, its historical significance, and its impact on the global energy landscape.

Founding Member and OPEC's Birth:
Saudi Arabia was among the five founding members of OPEC when the Organization was officially established in Baghdad on September 14, 1960. At that time, the kingdom, along with Iran, Iraq, Kuwait, and Venezuela, recognized the need to unite in response to the dominance of major multinational oil corporations and to gain greater control over their oil resources.

Early Leadership and Vision:
From the outset, Saudi Arabia assumed a leadership role within OPEC. The kingdom's representatives were instrumental in the drafting of OPEC's Charter, which outlined the Organization's objectives, including the coordination of petroleum policies and the pursuit of fair oil prices. Saudi Arabia's leadership was driven by a vision of achieving stability in oil markets and securing a fair share of oil revenues for producing nations.

The 1973 Oil Crisis:
Saudi Arabia's leadership within OPEC came to the forefront during the 1973 oil crisis, which was triggered by the Yom Kippur War and the subsequent oil embargo imposed by OPEC members and other Arab oil-producing nations. This embargo led to a quadrupling of oil prices and demonstrated OPEC's collective power to influence global energy markets.

Swing Producer Role:
One of the key elements of Saudi Arabia's leadership in OPEC has been its role as a "swing producer." As a swing producer, Saudi Arabia has the capacity to adjust its oil production levels to stabilize global oil prices during times of price volatility. This ability has made Saudi Arabia a linchpin for oil market stability and has earned it the nickname "central bank of oil."

Stabilizing Oil Prices:
Saudi Arabia's leadership has been instrumental in stabilizing global oil prices. The kingdom has, on numerous occasions, increased or decreased its oil production to counteract sudden disruptions in supply or demand. This stabilizing influence has been crucial for both oil producers and consumers, providing predictability in an inherently volatile market.

Oil Pricing Mechanism:
Saudi Arabia also played a pivotal role in introducing a pricing mechanism within OPEC that linked oil prices to a basket of major currencies. This innovation made oil prices less vulnerable to fluctuations in the value of a single currency, such as the U.S. dollar. The pricing mechanism contributed to price stability and transparency.

OPEC Diplomacy and Mediation:
Saudi Arabia's leadership extends beyond production levels and pricing. The kingdom has frequently engaged in diplomatic efforts within OPEC to mediate disputes and broker agreements among member countries. These efforts have been crucial in maintaining unity and cooperation within the Organization.

OPEC and Non-OPEC Cooperation:

Saudi Arabia has also played a pivotal role in fostering cooperation between OPEC and non-OPEC oil-producing nations. The OPEC+ alliance, which includes Russia and several other countries, was formed to coordinate oil production levels and stabilize oil prices. Saudi Arabia's leadership in bridging gaps between OPEC and non-OPEC nations has been instrumental in achieving production agreements.

Challenges and Adaptations:
Saudi Arabia's leadership in OPEC has not been without challenges. The rise of shale oil production in the United States and the emergence of renewable energy sources have introduced complexities into global energy dynamics. In response, Saudi Arabia has adapted its strategies and engaged in production agreements to balance the global oil market.

Environmental Considerations:
Saudi Arabia has also recognized the importance of addressing environmental concerns and reducing its carbon footprint. Initiatives to diversify the kingdom's economy and invest in renewable energy sources reflect its commitment to a sustainable future beyond oil.

Geopolitical Significance:
Saudi Arabia's leadership in OPEC has conferred significant geopolitical significance on the kingdom. It has used its oil resources as a diplomatic tool, fostering ties with both oil-consuming and oil-producing nations. This diplomatic influence extends beyond energy and impacts international relations.

In summary, Saudi Arabia's leadership in OPEC has been a cornerstone of the global oil industry and international energy diplomacy. As a founding member and swing producer, the kingdom has shaped OPEC's policies, stabilized oil prices, and played a central role in mediating disputes. Saudi Arabia's leadership continues to be pivotal in the ever-evolving global energy landscape, where challenges and opportunities reshape the dynamics of the oil industry and international relations.

Oil crises and global energy shocks have been significant events that have shaped the world's economic and political landscape, leading to profound changes in energy policies, international relations, and global economic stability. This narrative explores the impact of major oil crises and energy shocks, highlighting their causes, consequences, and long-term effects on the global energy sector.

The 1970s Oil Crises:

The 1970s witnessed two major oil crises that had a profound impact on the global economy:

The 1973 Oil Crisis: This crisis was triggered by the Yom Kippur War, during which OPEC members and other Arab oil-producing nations imposed an oil embargo on countries supporting Israel. The embargo led to a sharp increase in oil prices, quadrupling the cost of a barrel of oil. This event highlighted the vulnerability of oil-importing nations and exposed their dependence on Middle Eastern oil.

The 1979 Oil Crisis: This crisis resulted from the Iranian Revolution and the Iran-Iraq War. Oil production disruptions and geopolitical tensions in the region contributed to another surge in oil prices. Additionally, the Iranian Revolution led to a significant reduction in oil supply from Iran, a major oil producer. These events intensified global concerns about energy security.

Consequences of the 1970s Oil Crises:
The oil crises of the 1970s had far-reaching consequences:
Economic Impact: The sharp increase in oil prices strained the economies of oil-importing nations, leading to stagflation—a combination of stagnant economic growth and high inflation. It forced many countries to reassess their energy policies and energy efficiency measures.
Shift in Geopolitical Dynamics: The crises highlighted the geopolitical significance of oil-producing nations, particularly those in the Middle East. Oil became a potent diplomatic tool, and the influence of OPEC, led by major oil-producing nations like Saudi Arabia, increased significantly.
Energy Policy Reforms: In response to the crises, many countries implemented energy policy reforms, including measures to reduce dependence on oil, promote energy conservation, and invest in alternative energy sources.
Emergence of Strategic Reserves: Several nations, including the United States, established strategic oil reserves to buffer against future oil supply disruptions. These reserves were intended to enhance energy security.
The 1980s and Beyond:
While the oil crises of the 1970s had a lasting impact, the subsequent decades witnessed fluctuations in oil prices and shifts in the global energy landscape:
1980s: Oil prices began to stabilize during the 1980s as the Iran-Iraq War ended and production levels normalized. However, the memory of the 1970s crises led to a continued focus on energy security and the pursuit of diversification strategies.
1990s: The Gulf War in 1990-1991, sparked by Iraq's invasion of Kuwait, created short-term disruptions in oil

supply and raised concerns about regional stability. The war highlighted the continued geopolitical significance of oil-rich regions.

21st Century: The 21st century brought new challenges, including the rise of shale oil production in the United States, which altered global oil supply dynamics. Environmental concerns and the push for renewable energy sources further reshaped the energy landscape.

The 2000s and Beyond:

The 21st century has seen a range of energy-related developments and challenges:

Renewable Energy: The growing awareness of climate change and the need for sustainable energy sources have led to increased investments in renewable energy, such as solar, wind, and hydropower.

Shale Oil and Gas: The U.S. shale revolution, driven by technologies like hydraulic fracturing, has transformed the country into a major oil and natural gas producer. This has had a significant impact on global oil markets and reduced the influence of traditional oil-producing nations.

Energy Transitions: Many countries have set ambitious goals for transitioning to cleaner energy sources, aiming to reduce greenhouse gas emissions and combat climate change. This transition has influenced energy policies and investments worldwide.

Geopolitical Tensions: Geopolitical tensions in energy-rich regions, such as the Middle East, continue to affect global energy markets. Conflicts and political instability in these areas can disrupt oil supply and impact oil prices.

The Ongoing Energy Landscape:

Today, the global energy landscape is characterized by a complex interplay of factors, including geopolitics, technology advancements, environmental concerns, and the pursuit of energy security. Major oil crises and energy shocks of the past have left a lasting legacy, shaping the policies and strategies of nations and organizations worldwide.

In summary, oil crises and global energy shocks have been pivotal events that have reshaped the world's energy outlook and influenced the course of international relations and economic policies. These events have underscored the need for energy diversification, energy conservation, and the development of alternative energy sources. As the world continues to grapple with energy challenges, the lessons learned from past crises remain relevant in navigating the evolving energy landscape.

Chapter 4: Royal Intrigues and Succession Struggles: The House of Saud's Internal Dynamics (1980s)

Power struggles within the Saudi Arabian royal family have been a recurring theme in the kingdom's history, as the complex dynamics of succession and influence have played out behind the scenes. These internal rivalries and conflicts often have far-reaching implications for the governance and stability of Saudi Arabia, a nation with significant global influence due to its vast oil reserves and strategic position in the Middle East.

Historical Context:
The House of Saud, the ruling family of Saudi Arabia, has a vast and intricate network of princes and branches. The kingdom's founder, Abdulaziz Ibn Saud, had numerous sons who played key roles in establishing the Saudi state. This extensive royal family has resulted in competition for power and influence among various branches and generations.

Traditional Succession:
Traditionally, the Saudi throne has passed from one brother to another, in keeping with the principle of seniority among Abdulaziz Ibn Saud's sons. This system aimed to maintain a degree of stability and consensus within the royal family. However, it also generated tensions, as the line of succession became increasingly lengthy and complex.

Transition to the Third Generation:
By the late 20th century, the Saudi royal family faced a significant transition. The second generation of princes,

who had been the main players in the early years of the kingdom, was giving way to the third generation. This generational shift heightened competition for positions of power and influence, as younger princes sought to secure their futures.

Power Centers and Alliances:
Within the royal family, several power centers and alliances have emerged over the years. These alliances are often built around influential princes who hold key positions in government, the military, or the business sector. Rivalries between these power centers can impact government policies and decision-making.

Succession Challenges:
Succession within the Saudi royal family has historically been a source of tension and rivalry. When a king or crown prince is selected, it can lead to competition and rival factions vying for control. The appointment of the crown prince, in particular, is a critical decision, as it determines the future direction of the kingdom.

Allegiances and Loyalties:
Princes within the royal family are often divided by their allegiances and loyalties. Some may align themselves with certain factions or powerful princes to increase their chances of ascending to positions of authority. These alliances can shift over time, further complicating the internal dynamics.

Impact on Governance:
Power struggles within the royal family can impact the governance of Saudi Arabia. Conflicting interests and disagreements among influential princes can lead to policy gridlock or the prioritization of certain agendas over

others. This, in turn, can affect the kingdom's domestic and foreign policies.

Influence on Foreign Relations:
The internal dynamics of the Saudi royal family also have implications for the kingdom's foreign relations. The appointment of key princes to diplomatic or ministerial positions can shape Saudi Arabia's stance on regional and global issues. Additionally, internal conflicts can make the leadership less predictable, which can influence international partners and allies.

Challenges to Stability:
While the Saudi royal family has managed to navigate power struggles and maintain its grip on the country for decades, internal divisions and rivalries always pose a potential challenge to the stability of the kingdom. Managing these tensions and ensuring a smooth transition of power remains a critical concern for Saudi leadership.

Modern Developments:
In recent years, Saudi Arabia has witnessed significant changes in its leadership and power dynamics. Crown Prince Mohammed bin Salman (MBS), from the third generation of the royal family, has consolidated power and implemented a series of ambitious reforms, including Vision 2030—a plan aimed at diversifying the Saudi economy. These reforms have generated both support and opposition within the royal family and among the broader population.

In summary, power struggles within the Saudi Arabian royal family have been a recurring feature of the kingdom's history. As Saudi Arabia faces challenges and transitions, the internal dynamics of the royal family will continue to play a pivotal role in shaping the nation's governance, policies, and relations with the wider world. Balancing these internal rivalries while maintaining stability and unity remains a central challenge for the kingdom's leadership.

Succession planning within the Saudi Arabian royal family is a highly complex and crucial aspect of the kingdom's governance. Given the large number of royals and the significance of Saudi Arabia on the global stage due to its oil wealth and strategic position in the Middle East, ensuring a smooth transition of power is of paramount importance. However, the process is fraught with challenges and complexities that have the potential to impact the stability and direction of the kingdom.

Abdulaziz Ibn Saud's Legacy:

The succession process in Saudi Arabia is rooted in the legacy of Abdulaziz Ibn Saud, the founder of the kingdom. His principle of seniority among his sons established a tradition of fraternal succession. The throne passes from one of Abdulaziz's sons to another in accordance with their age, ensuring a smooth transition within the family.

Generational Shift:

One of the key challenges facing the Saudi royal family is the generational shift from the second generation to the third. Many of the powerful princes from the second generation, who played key roles in the early years of the kingdom, have passed away. This shift has led to increased competition and rivalries among the third generation of princes, who are seeking to secure positions of power and influence.

Crown Prince Selection:

The selection of the crown prince is a critical decision in Saudi Arabia's succession process. The crown prince is typically the deputy prime minister and is positioned to become the future king. This appointment can be contentious, as it determines the future direction of the kingdom. Decisions regarding the crown prince can lead to competition and power struggles among influential princes.

Allegiances and Loyalties:

Princes within the royal family often form alliances and allegiances to advance their positions and influence within the kingdom. These alliances can shift over time and can be a source of tension and rivalry within the family. Decisions about succession may also be influenced by these alliances.

Challenges to Tradition:

While the tradition of seniority among Abdulaziz's sons has been a cornerstone of Saudi succession, there have been deviations from this tradition. Crown Prince Mohammed bin Salman (MBS), from the third generation, was appointed crown prince in 2017, bypassing older princes. This move disrupted the established order and generated both support and opposition within the royal family.

Consensus and Stability:

Maintaining consensus within the royal family is essential to ensure a smooth succession process and overall stability. Disagreements or fractures within the family can have far-reaching consequences for the kingdom. Striking a balance between tradition and the changing dynamics of leadership is a continuous challenge.

Impact on Governance and Policies:

Succession planning and the appointment of key princes to various government positions can influence Saudi

Arabia's domestic and foreign policies. Different princes may have varying agendas and priorities, leading to shifts in policy direction. Managing these differences while maintaining stability is a delicate task.

Modernization and Vision 2030:
Crown Prince Mohammed bin Salman's Vision 2030 plan, aimed at diversifying the Saudi economy and modernizing the kingdom, has introduced a new dimension to succession planning. The success of these reforms is closely tied to the stability and effectiveness of the leadership transition.

The Role of the King:
The reigning king plays a pivotal role in the succession process. King Salman's appointment of MBS as crown prince and his support for Vision 2030 reflect the influence of the monarch in shaping the kingdom's future. Ensuring a smooth transition of power from one king to the next is a core responsibility.

In summary, succession planning within the Saudi Arabian royal family is a complex and multifaceted process that has significant implications for the kingdom's governance, stability, and direction. Balancing tradition with the evolving dynamics of leadership, managing internal rivalries, and ensuring consensus among influential princes are central challenges. As Saudi Arabia continues to undergo social and economic transformations, the succession process will remain a critical factor in shaping the nation's future.

Chapter 5: Desert Storm and Regional Realignment: Saudi Arabia in the Gulf War (1990s)

Iraq's invasion of Kuwait in 1990 was a seismic event in the Middle East that had profound regional and global implications. The invasion, led by then-Iraqi President Saddam Hussein, marked a dramatic escalation in the already tense relations between Iraq and its neighbors. This narrative explores the background, events, and consequences of Iraq's invasion of Kuwait, shedding light on the regional tensions that were at the heart of the crisis.

Background and Historical Context:

Iraq-Iran War: One of the key factors leading to Iraq's invasion of Kuwait was the financial strain caused by the Iraq-Iran War (1980-1988). Iraq emerged from the war heavily indebted and sought to alleviate its economic woes by increasing oil production and revenues.

Oil Price Disputes: Iraq accused Kuwait of overproducing oil, which drove down global oil prices and, in turn, reduced Iraq's oil income. Iraq also claimed that Kuwait was slant-drilling into Iraq's oil fields, further exacerbating tensions.

The Invasion:

August 2, 1990: Iraqi forces, under Saddam Hussein's command, invaded Kuwait, citing historical claims to Kuwaiti territory and alleging economic and political provocations.

International Condemnation: The invasion was met with international condemnation, and the United Nations (UN) passed a series of resolutions, including UN Security Council Resolution 660, calling for Iraq's immediate withdrawal from Kuwait.

The Gulf War: The subsequent military buildup by a coalition of countries, led by the United States and authorized by the UN, marked the beginning of the Gulf War (1990-1991).

Regional Tensions:

Territorial Disputes: Iraq's invasion of Kuwait heightened concerns among its neighbors, particularly Saudi Arabia, which feared it could be Iraq's next target. Iraq's historical claims to certain territories in Saudi Arabia added to these concerns.

Iranian Perspective: Iran, which had been at war with Iraq for most of the 1980s, viewed the invasion with suspicion. Iran had a contentious relationship with both Iraq and Kuwait and sought to exploit the situation to its advantage.

Arab League and Regional Responses: The Arab League condemned the invasion, leading to strained relations between Iraq and its fellow Arab states. Egypt and Syria joined the coalition against Iraq, while others expressed varying degrees of support.

Economic and Energy Concerns: The invasion disrupted the flow of oil from the region, leading to a spike in oil prices and concerns about the global economy. It also highlighted the vulnerability of the world's oil supply to regional conflicts.

The Gulf War and Liberation of Kuwait:

Coalition Operations: The Gulf War began in January 1991, with a coalition of countries launching Operation Desert Storm to liberate Kuwait. The coalition's air campaign was followed by a ground offensive, leading to the liberation of Kuwait in February 1991.

Ceasefire and Consequences: A ceasefire was declared, and Iraq was subjected to a series of disarmament and sanctions measures. Kuwait faced the challenging task of post-invasion reconstruction.

Long-Term Consequences and Legacy:

Iraqi Isolation: Iraq was diplomatically and economically isolated following the Gulf War. This isolation would continue for years, leading to further regional instability.

Economic Impact: The Gulf War had significant economic consequences, not only for Iraq but also for the wider region. It highlighted the vulnerability of oil-dependent economies to geopolitical conflicts.

US Military Presence: The Gulf War marked the beginning of a long-term U.S. military presence in the Gulf region, aimed at ensuring the security of key allies and protecting access to oil resources.

Regional Security: The Gulf War reshaped regional security dynamics and led to increased cooperation among Gulf Cooperation Council (GCC) member states in defense and security matters.

Iraqi Political Shifts: The post-Gulf War era saw internal challenges in Iraq, including uprisings by Kurdish and Shiite populations in the north and south. These events contributed to a shifting political landscape in Iraq.

In summary, Iraq's invasion of Kuwait in 1990 was a pivotal moment in Middle Eastern history, characterized by regional tensions, international intervention, and far-reaching consequences. It highlighted the fragility of regional stability and the critical importance of the Gulf region in global geopolitics, particularly in relation to energy resources. The legacy of the Gulf War continues to influence the political and security landscape of the Middle East to this day.

Saudi Arabia played a significant role in the Gulf War coalition that liberated Kuwait from Iraqi occupation in 1990-1991. The invasion of Kuwait by Iraq, led by President Saddam Hussein, posed a direct threat to Saudi Arabia's security and regional stability. As a result, Saudi Arabia became a crucial partner in the international effort to expel Iraqi forces from Kuwait. Here, we delve into Saudi Arabia's role in the Gulf War coalition:

1. Hosting Coalition Forces:
Saudi Arabia served as a primary base of operations for the multinational coalition forces. This was strategically important for launching air and ground operations against Iraqi forces in Kuwait. The country's vast desert terrain provided ample space for deploying military units and infrastructure.

2. Military Support:
Saudi Arabia committed a substantial military force to the coalition effort. This included ground troops, tanks, armored vehicles, and aircraft. Saudi forces actively participated in the liberation of Kuwait alongside their coalition partners.

3. King Fahd's Diplomatic Leadership:
King Fahd bin Abdulaziz Al Saud, then the king of Saudi Arabia, played a key diplomatic role in building and maintaining the Gulf War coalition. He was instrumental in rallying regional and international support for the liberation of Kuwait.

4. Financial Contributions:

Saudi Arabia provided significant financial support to the coalition effort, contributing to the costs of the war. The kingdom's financial resources helped sustain the coalition's military operations.

5. Hosting Coalition Leaders:
Riyadh, the capital of Saudi Arabia, served as a hub for diplomatic negotiations and coordination among coalition leaders. King Fahd and other Saudi officials hosted meetings and discussions with leaders from various coalition nations.

6. Air Campaign:
Saudi Arabia's Prince Sultan Air Base was a critical hub for coalition air operations. The base hosted U.S. and coalition aircraft, which conducted extensive air strikes against Iraqi targets in Kuwait and Iraq.

7. Patriot Missile Defense:
Saudi Arabia received and deployed Patriot missile batteries, which played a vital role in defending against Iraqi Scud missile attacks on Saudi cities. These missile defense systems were provided by the United States and other coalition partners.

8. Regional Security Concerns:
Saudi Arabia viewed Iraq's invasion of Kuwait as a direct threat to its own security and stability. The kingdom's leadership was deeply concerned about the potential for further Iraqi aggression in the region.

9. Arab League Support:
Saudi Arabia's active participation in the Gulf War coalition enjoyed broad support from other Arab states within the Arab League. The league passed resolutions condemning Iraq's invasion and endorsed the coalition's efforts to liberate Kuwait.

10. Post-War Reconstruction Support:
After the liberation of Kuwait, Saudi Arabia contributed to post-war reconstruction efforts in the country, providing financial aid and assistance for rebuilding infrastructure.

In summary, Saudi Arabia played a pivotal role in the Gulf War coalition, contributing military forces, hosting coalition troops and bases, and providing diplomatic and financial support. The kingdom's leadership recognized the gravity of the situation and the need to counter the Iraqi invasion of Kuwait. Saudi Arabia's active involvement helped ensure the success of the coalition's mission to liberate Kuwait and restore regional stability.

The Gulf War in 1990-1991 had profound geopolitical shifts and long-lasting consequences for the Middle East and the wider international community. It reshaped regional dynamics, altered alliances, and left a legacy that continues to influence the geopolitics of the region today. Here, we explore the geopolitical shifts and aftermath of the conflict:

1. U.S. Dominance in the Gulf Region:
The Gulf War solidified the United States' status as the dominant military and political power in the Gulf region. The presence of U.S. forces during the conflict and the subsequent establishment of long-term military bases in the region underscored America's commitment to Gulf security.

2. Security Alliances and Coalitions:
The formation of a multinational coalition to liberate Kuwait highlighted the importance of international alliances in addressing regional conflicts. The experience of working together in the Gulf War paved the way for

continued cooperation among coalition partners in addressing future challenges.

3. Strengthening of Gulf Cooperation Council (GCC):
The Gulf War prompted Gulf Arab states, such as Saudi Arabia, Kuwait, and the United Arab Emirates, to enhance their security cooperation within the Gulf Cooperation Council (GCC). This regional organization became more influential in addressing security concerns in the Gulf.

4. Containment of Iraq:
The Gulf War contributed to the containment of Iraq, limiting its regional ambitions and military capabilities. This containment policy, enforced through UN sanctions and no-fly zones, remained in place until the 2003 Iraq War.

5. Kurdish and Shiite Uprisings:
The aftermath of the Gulf War witnessed uprisings by Kurdish and Shiite populations in Iraq's north and south. While these uprisings were ultimately crushed by the Iraqi regime, they further complicated Iraq's internal dynamics.

6. Impact on Iran:
The Gulf War had implications for Iran's regional role. While Iran cautiously supported the coalition's actions against Iraq, it remained wary of U.S. military presence in the region. The war indirectly led to a subtle rapprochement between Iran and some Gulf Arab states.

7. Economic Consequences:
The conflict and subsequent sanctions had economic consequences for Iraq, as well as the wider region. Iraq's economy was severely impacted, and the region experienced fluctuations in oil prices and production.

8. Palestinian Issue:

The Gulf War strained relations between some Gulf states and the Palestine Liberation Organization (PLO) due to the PLO's perceived support for Iraq. This had repercussions for the Palestinian issue and the broader Arab-Israeli conflict.

9. Legacy of U.S. Bases:

The establishment of U.S. military bases in the Gulf during and after the Gulf War has had a lasting impact on regional security and U.S. policy in the Middle East. These bases continue to play a role in U.S. military operations and diplomacy in the region.

10. Regional Instability:

While the Gulf War resolved the immediate crisis in Kuwait, it left a legacy of regional instability. Iraq's weakened state and internal tensions contributed to subsequent conflicts, including the 2003 Iraq War and ongoing instability in the region.

In summary, the Gulf War marked a significant turning point in the geopolitics of the Middle East. It solidified U.S. influence in the region, altered security dynamics, and had far-reaching consequences for Iraq and its neighbors. The legacy of the conflict continues to shape the politics and security of the Middle East today, with enduring implications for regional stability and global diplomacy.

Chapter 6: Islam, Extremism, and the House of Saud: Challenges and Responses (Late 20th Century)

The rise of extremism in the Middle East is a complex and multifaceted phenomenon that has had profound consequences for the region and the world. While extremism has deep historical roots, several key factors have contributed to its growth and spread in the modern era. Here, we explore the rise of extremism in the region and its various causes:

1. Historical and Religious Context:
Extremism in the Middle East has historical roots in various religious and ideological movements. The region is home to major world religions, including Islam, Christianity, and Judaism, and has witnessed religious and sectarian tensions for centuries.

2. Political Instability:
Political instability in the Middle East has created fertile ground for extremist groups to flourish. Authoritarian regimes, governance failures, and conflicts have fueled grievances that extremists exploit to gain support.

3. Socioeconomic Factors:
High levels of poverty, unemployment, and economic inequality have contributed to the appeal of extremist ideologies. Extremist groups often promise social justice and economic opportunities to recruit marginalized individuals.

4. Radicalization and Recruitment:
Extremist organizations use sophisticated recruitment strategies, including online propaganda and social media,

to attract followers from across the globe. The internet has become a key tool for radicalization.

5. Regional Conflicts:
Ongoing conflicts in the region, such as the Israeli-Palestinian conflict, the Iraq War, the Syrian Civil War, and the Yemeni Civil War, have provided fertile ground for extremist groups to recruit fighters and gain support.

6. Sectarianism:
Sectarian tensions, particularly between Sunni and Shia Muslims, have been exploited by extremist groups to further their agendas. The Syrian and Iraqi conflicts, in particular, have exacerbated sectarian divides.

7. Foreign Interventions:
The involvement of foreign powers in the Middle East has also played a role in the rise of extremism. The U.S.-led invasion of Iraq in 2003 and other military interventions have had unintended consequences, including the strengthening of extremist groups.

8. Ideological Influences:
Extremist ideologies, such as Salafism and Jihadism, have gained prominence in the region. These ideologies often reject pluralism and advocate for a strict interpretation of Islamic law.

9. Funding Sources:
Extremist groups have received funding from various sources, including wealthy individuals, charities, and even state actors. These funds are used to support recruitment, propaganda, and terrorist activities.

10. Globalization of Extremism:
Extremism in the Middle East has transcended national boundaries and become a global phenomenon. The

influence of groups like al-Qaeda and ISIS has extended well beyond the region.

11. State Sponsorship:
Some states have been accused of providing support to extremist groups as a means of pursuing their own geopolitical objectives. This has further complicated efforts to combat extremism.

12. Counterterrorism Efforts:
Efforts to counter extremism have included military operations, intelligence sharing, and counter-radicalization programs. However, these efforts have often faced significant challenges and limitations.

In summary, the rise of extremism in the Middle East is the result of a complex interplay of historical, political, socioeconomic, and ideological factors. Addressing extremism in the region requires a multifaceted approach that addresses both the root causes and the manifestations of radicalization. Additionally, international cooperation and regional stability are crucial for effectively countering the spread of extremism in the Middle East and its global implications.

Saudi Arabia has taken various steps to counter extremism and combat the spread of extremist ideologies within its borders and beyond. The kingdom recognizes the importance of addressing this issue for both its domestic stability and its international reputation. Here are some key efforts and initiatives Saudi Arabia has undertaken to counter extremism:

Educational Reforms:
Saudi Arabia has implemented significant reforms in its education system to remove or revise materials that promote extremist ideologies. The government has

worked to eliminate extremist content from textbooks and promote a more moderate and tolerant interpretation of Islam.

Counter-Radicalization Programs:
The kingdom has established rehabilitation and counseling programs for individuals who have been radicalized. These programs aim to reintegrate former extremists into society and provide them with an alternative to extremist ideologies.

Monitoring and Surveillance:
Saudi authorities have increased efforts to monitor and track individuals and groups associated with extremism. This includes monitoring online activities and social media platforms where extremist content may be shared.

Religious Reforms:
Saudi Arabia has made efforts to promote a more moderate and tolerant form of Islam, often referred to as "moderate Islam" or "open Islam." These reforms include encouraging religious leaders to promote tolerance and counter extremist interpretations of Islam.

International Collaboration:
The kingdom has worked closely with international partners in the fight against extremism and terrorism. Saudi Arabia has been an active member of international coalitions and has supported efforts to combat extremist groups globally.

Financial Regulations:
Saudi Arabia has implemented stricter financial regulations to prevent the flow of funds to extremist groups. The government has also worked to prevent the use of charitable organizations as fronts for financing extremism.

Counterterrorism Legislation:
The kingdom has enacted counterterrorism legislation to strengthen its legal framework for combating extremism. This includes measures to prosecute individuals and groups involved in promoting extremist ideologies or planning acts of terrorism.

Intellectual and Media Initiatives:
Saudi Arabia has launched intellectual and media initiatives to counter extremist narratives. This includes organizing conferences, seminars, and cultural events that promote dialogue and tolerance.

CVE (Countering Violent Extremism) Programs:
Saudi Arabia has implemented programs aimed at countering violent extremism (CVE) by addressing the root causes of radicalization. These programs focus on social, economic, and psychological factors that may contribute to extremism.

Preventing Hate Speech:
The kingdom has taken measures to prevent hate speech and incitement to violence, both in public spaces and online. These efforts include regulating religious sermons and monitoring online content for extremist rhetoric.

De-radicalization Centers:
Saudi Arabia has established de-radicalization centers where individuals who have been radicalized can undergo rehabilitation and counseling. These centers offer education, vocational training, and psychological support.

Promotion of Moderate Islam:
The kingdom has actively promoted the concept of "moderate Islam" as an alternative to extremist ideologies. This includes supporting institutions and

scholars that advocate for a more moderate interpretation of Islam.

While Saudi Arabia has made significant efforts to counter extremism, challenges remain. The kingdom continues to work on strengthening its measures and addressing underlying factors that contribute to radicalization. The fight against extremism is an ongoing process that requires sustained efforts both domestically and internationally.

The Gulf War had a significant impact on both Saudi Arabia's domestic policies and its approach to international affairs. These impacts were shaped by the kingdom's experiences during and after the conflict, as well as the broader regional and global context. Here are some key ways in which the Gulf War influenced Saudi Arabia's policies:

Domestic Policies:

Security and Defense: The Gulf War heightened Saudi Arabia's security concerns. As a result, the kingdom invested heavily in its military and defense infrastructure, seeking to enhance its capacity to deter potential threats. This included acquiring advanced military equipment and modernizing its armed forces.

Economic Diversification: The economic consequences of the Gulf War, particularly the fluctuation in oil prices, prompted Saudi Arabia to accelerate its efforts to diversify its economy. The kingdom launched economic diversification initiatives aimed at reducing its dependency on oil revenues and promoting non-oil sectors such as tourism, entertainment, and technology.

Social and Cultural Reforms: In the post-Gulf War era, Saudi Arabia embarked on a series of social and cultural reforms. These reforms aimed to promote a more open and moderate form of Islam, encourage cultural exchange, and expand opportunities for women in various sectors, including education and the workforce.

Counterterrorism Measures: The Gulf War exposed Saudi Arabia to the threat of extremism and terrorism. In response, the kingdom implemented counterterrorism measures, including intelligence sharing, monitoring of extremist activities, and the establishment of rehabilitation programs for former extremists.

Foreign Labor Policies: The influx of foreign troops and labor during the Gulf War prompted Saudi Arabia to reevaluate its foreign labor policies. The kingdom implemented stricter regulations on foreign workers, seeking to balance its need for foreign labor with national employment priorities.

International Policies:

Regional Alliances: The Gulf War led Saudi Arabia to strengthen its alliances with regional partners, particularly the Gulf Cooperation Council (GCC) states. The kingdom sought to bolster collective security within the GCC and enhance cooperation on regional issues.

U.S.-Saudi Relations: The Gulf War deepened Saudi Arabia's strategic partnership with the United States. The kingdom welcomed the U.S. military presence in the region as a means of deterring potential threats. This partnership continued to evolve in the post-Gulf War era, with shared interests in regional security and stability.

Support for International Initiatives: Saudi Arabia became a proponent of international initiatives aimed at promoting peace and stability in the Middle East. The kingdom supported efforts to resolve the Israeli-

Palestinian conflict and played a diplomatic role in regional conflicts and crises.

Humanitarian Assistance: In the aftermath of the Gulf War, Saudi Arabia provided humanitarian assistance to countries affected by the conflict, including Kuwait. The kingdom contributed to post-war reconstruction efforts and supported humanitarian organizations.

Counterterrorism Cooperation: Saudi Arabia actively cooperated with international partners in the fight against terrorism and extremism. The kingdom participated in global counterterrorism initiatives, shared intelligence, and worked to prevent the financing of extremist groups.

Diplomatic Engagement: The Gulf War experience reinforced Saudi Arabia's commitment to diplomacy and peaceful resolution of conflicts. The kingdom became an advocate for diplomatic solutions to regional disputes and crises.

In summary, the Gulf War had a profound impact on Saudi Arabia's domestic policies, leading to changes in defense, economics, social reforms, and security measures. It also shaped the kingdom's international policies, strengthening its alliances, deepening its partnership with the United States, and influencing its diplomatic engagement in the region and beyond. The lessons learned from the Gulf War continue to shape Saudi Arabia's approach to regional and global affairs.

Chapter 7: Modernization and Globalization: Saudi Arabia in a Changing World (Late 20th Century)

Saudi Arabia has embarked on a series of socioeconomic reforms and modernization initiatives aimed at diversifying its economy, promoting social development, and preparing for a post-oil future. These initiatives, often grouped under the banner of "Vision 2030," represent a fundamental transformation of the kingdom's economic and social landscape. Here are key aspects of these reforms and initiatives:

1. Vision 2030:

Vision Statement: Vision 2030 is a comprehensive plan unveiled by Saudi Arabia in 2016, with the goal of reducing the country's dependence on oil, stimulating economic growth, and improving the quality of life for its citizens.

Diversification: One of the primary objectives of Vision 2030 is to diversify the Saudi economy. This involves developing sectors such as tourism, entertainment, technology, and renewable energy to reduce the reliance on oil revenues.

2. Economic Reforms:

Privatization: Saudi Arabia aims to privatize state-owned assets and companies, including portions of the oil giant Saudi Aramco. This move seeks to stimulate private sector growth and attract foreign investment.

Fiscal Discipline: The government is working to improve fiscal discipline and reduce budget deficits. This involves measures like subsidy reforms and the introduction of new taxes, such as the Value Added Tax (VAT).

Investment Promotion: Saudi Arabia has made efforts to attract foreign investment through initiatives like the Saudi Arabian General Investment Authority (SAGIA) and the opening of the Saudi Stock Exchange (Tadawul) to foreign investors.

3. Social and Cultural Reforms:

Women's Empowerment: The kingdom has implemented a series of reforms aimed at empowering women. These include allowing women to drive, attend sports events, work in various sectors, and obtain passports and travel without male consent.

Entertainment and Tourism: Saudi Arabia is investing in its entertainment and tourism sectors to create new job opportunities and diversify the economy. The country has opened theaters, hosted international events, and developed tourist destinations.

Education and Training: The government is investing in education and vocational training to equip Saudi citizens with the skills needed for a modern workforce. Initiatives like the King Salman Scholarship Program aim to send Saudi students abroad for higher education.

4. Technology and Innovation:

Tech Hubs: Saudi Arabia is building technology and innovation hubs, such as the NEOM smart city project and the King Abdullah University of Science and Technology (KAUST). These hubs aim to attract talent and foster innovation.

Digital Transformation: The kingdom is promoting digital transformation in various sectors, including government services, healthcare, and education. This includes initiatives like the National Digital Transformation Strategy.

5. Environmental Sustainability:
Renewable Energy: Saudi Arabia is investing in renewable energy sources, particularly solar power. The country aims to diversify its energy mix and reduce its carbon footprint.
Green Initiatives: The Green Saudi and Green Middle East initiatives seek to enhance environmental protection, increase green spaces, and combat desertification in the region.
6. Cultural and Artistic Promotion:
Cultural Initiatives: Saudi Arabia is fostering cultural and artistic expression through events like the Riyadh Season, which features concerts, art exhibitions, and cultural festivals.
Cinema: The kingdom has reopened cinemas, allowing Saudis to enjoy films in public theaters for the first time in decades.
These socioeconomic reforms and modernization initiatives represent a significant shift in Saudi Arabia's approach to governance and development. While they face challenges and resistance, they are crucial steps in preparing the kingdom for a more diversified and sustainable future beyond its reliance on oil revenues.

Saudi Arabia plays a significant role in the global economy due to its status as a major oil producer, its strategic geographic location, and its efforts to diversify its economy. Here are key aspects of Saudi Arabia's role in the global economy:
Oil Production and Export: Saudi Arabia is one of the world's largest oil producers and exporters. The kingdom possesses vast reserves of crude oil, and its production capacity gives it considerable influence over global oil

markets. Saudi Arabia is a key member of the Organization of the Petroleum Exporting Countries (OPEC) and plays a central role in coordinating oil production levels and prices.

Energy Security: The stability of Saudi Arabia's oil production is crucial for global energy security. Any disruption in Saudi oil exports can have a significant impact on global oil prices and supply. The kingdom's role as a reliable oil supplier is essential for the stability of the global energy market.

Investment and Sovereign Wealth Funds: Saudi Arabia has established sovereign wealth funds, such as the Public Investment Fund (PIF), to invest in diverse sectors both domestically and internationally. These funds are used for strategic investments, which can impact global financial markets and industries.

Geopolitical Significance: Saudi Arabia's location in the Middle East, along with its status as a regional power, gives it geopolitical significance. The kingdom's diplomatic and security policies can have repercussions on regional stability and international relations.

Trade and Commerce: Saudi Arabia is a member of the World Trade Organization (WTO) and has actively engaged in trade agreements and partnerships. It is an important market for international companies and a source of goods and services for the global economy.

Economic Diversification: Recognizing the need to reduce its dependence on oil, Saudi Arabia has launched economic diversification initiatives under its Vision 2030 plan. These initiatives aim to promote sectors such as tourism, entertainment, technology, and renewable energy, contributing to global economic growth.

Infrastructure Investment: The kingdom's infrastructure development projects, including transportation networks, ports, and urban development, provide opportunities for international companies and have the potential to stimulate economic growth in the region.

Financial Services: Saudi Arabia has a well-developed financial sector, including a stock exchange (Tadawul), banks, and investment firms. These institutions play a role in the global financial system and facilitate investment in the kingdom.

Global Partnerships: Saudi Arabia collaborates with various countries and international organizations on economic and development initiatives. This includes partnerships in sectors such as technology, healthcare, and renewable energy.

Human Capital: The kingdom's efforts to invest in education and training programs, including scholarships for Saudi students to study abroad, contribute to the global pool of skilled professionals.

Islamic Finance: Saudi Arabia is a hub for Islamic finance, with a well-established Islamic banking sector. It contributes to the development of Sharia-compliant financial products and services globally.

Global Philanthropy: Saudi Arabia engages in philanthropic activities, including humanitarian aid and development projects, which have a global impact, particularly in the Muslim world.

In summary, Saudi Arabia's role in the global economy is multifaceted and extends beyond its position as a major oil producer. The kingdom's economic diversification efforts, strategic investments, and participation in international organizations contribute to its influence on the global stage. Moreover, Saudi Arabia's stability and economic policies have implications for the stability and prosperity of the broader international community.

Cultural and social changes in a globalized context are at the forefront of discussions about the evolving nature of societies worldwide. As the world becomes increasingly interconnected through technology, trade, and communication, cultures and societies are experiencing profound shifts that impact individuals, communities, and nations. These changes are multifaceted and complex, often blurring the lines between traditional and contemporary norms, values, and practices.

At the heart of these transformations is the phenomenon of globalization, which refers to the interconnectedness and interdependence of countries and cultures across the globe. Globalization has facilitated the exchange of ideas, information, goods, services, and people on an unprecedented scale. Here, we delve into the cultural and social changes that have emerged within this globalized context.

Cultural Hybridity:

One of the most noticeable effects of globalization on culture is the rise of cultural hybridity. Cultures are no longer confined to geographical boundaries, and people from diverse backgrounds interact more frequently. This intermingling has led to the blending of cultural elements, resulting in hybrid identities and expressions. For example, the fusion of Western and Eastern fashion trends or the incorporation of international cuisine into local diets showcases this cultural blending.

Language Evolution:

Language is a crucial aspect of culture, and globalization has influenced how languages evolve. English, as a global lingua franca, has become a common medium of communication across borders. This widespread use of English has had both positive and negative effects. While it facilitates international business and cultural exchange, it can also lead to the dominance of one language over others, potentially endangering linguistic diversity.

Cultural Exchange and Diversity:

Globalization has opened the doors to greater cultural exchange and diversity. People have more opportunities to engage with different cultures through travel, media, and the internet. This exposure fosters cultural understanding and appreciation. Additionally, multiculturalism is increasingly celebrated as societies become more diverse due to immigration and the movement of people.

Media and Pop Culture:

Globalized media, including television, film, music, and the internet, has a significant impact on shaping cultural norms and values. Hollywood movies, K-pop music, and online streaming platforms have gained international followings, influencing fashion, lifestyle choices, and even political opinions. These cultural exports transcend borders and help create shared global cultural references.

Consumer Culture:

The globalization of consumer culture is evident in the spread of multinational corporations, fast-food chains, and global brands. People around the world often share similar consumer preferences and access to products. This standardization of consumer culture can sometimes lead to concerns about cultural homogenization and the loss of local traditions.

Religious Pluralism:
Globalization has contributed to increased religious pluralism in many societies. As people migrate and communities become more diverse, religious traditions from around the world coexist in the same geographic areas. This diversity can promote religious tolerance and dialogue but can also lead to tensions and conflicts.

Digital Connectivity:
The digital age has brought about unprecedented connectivity and communication. Social media platforms, in particular, have allowed individuals to connect with others globally, share their cultures, and engage in cross-cultural conversations. This digital interconnectedness has both positive and negative consequences, including the rapid spread of information, but also the spread of misinformation and polarization.

Challenges to Cultural Identity:
While globalization fosters cultural exchange, it can also challenge cultural identities. As societies embrace global trends and values, there can be a sense of cultural erosion or loss of traditional practices. Some argue that globalization threatens the authenticity of cultural expressions.

Cultural Diplomacy:
Nations increasingly use cultural diplomacy as a tool to enhance their global influence. Cultural exchanges, art exhibitions, and international festivals are mechanisms for countries to showcase their culture and promote soft power. These initiatives foster international collaboration and mutual understanding.

Global Challenges and Solutions:
Globalization has also intensified the interconnectedness of global challenges, such as climate change, pandemics, and economic crises. Addressing these issues requires international cooperation and the sharing of knowledge and resources across borders. Cultural and social changes play a role in shaping societies' responses to these global challenges.

In summary, cultural and social changes in a globalized context are dynamic and multifaceted. While globalization has facilitated greater cultural exchange and diversity, it has also raised questions and challenges related to cultural identity, linguistic diversity, and the preservation of traditions. As societies continue to navigate these changes, they must strike a balance between embracing global influences and preserving their unique cultural heritage and values. Moreover, recognizing the role of culture in addressing global challenges underscores the importance of cross-cultural collaboration and understanding in an increasingly interconnected world.

Chapter 8: The 21st Century Awakening: Saudi Arabia's Quest for Economic Diversification (Early 2000s)

The 21st century has witnessed a multitude of economic challenges on a global scale, affecting nations, businesses, and individuals. These challenges have been shaped by various factors, including technological advancements, financial crises, demographic shifts, and environmental concerns. Here, we explore some of the prominent economic challenges that have emerged in the 21st century.

1. Financial Crises:
Financial instability has been a recurring issue in the 21st century. The global financial crisis of 2007-2008, triggered by the collapse of Lehman Brothers, led to a worldwide recession. The crisis exposed vulnerabilities in the global financial system and highlighted the interconnectedness of economies.

2. Income Inequality:
Income inequality has become a pressing concern in many countries. The gap between the wealthy and the rest of the population has widened, leading to social and political tensions. The concentration of wealth in the hands of a few has raised questions about fairness and social cohesion.

3. Technological Disruption:
Rapid technological advancements, including automation, artificial intelligence, and the gig economy, have disrupted traditional industries and job markets. While these technologies offer opportunities for efficiency and

innovation, they also pose challenges, such as job displacement and the need for workforce retraining.

4. Trade Tensions:

Trade tensions between major economies, particularly the United States and China, have had a significant impact on global trade. Tariffs and trade disputes have disrupted supply chains, increased costs for businesses, and contributed to uncertainty in international trade.

5. Demographic Changes:

Demographic shifts, including aging populations in many developed countries and youth bulges in some developing nations, have economic implications. Aging populations strain social welfare systems, while youth populations require job opportunities and education.

6. Climate Change and Environmental Sustainability:

Climate change and environmental degradation have economic consequences, from the increasing frequency of natural disasters to the need for sustainable business practices. Mitigating climate change and transitioning to a green economy require substantial investments and policy changes.

7. Public Debt:

Many countries have experienced rising levels of public debt, partly due to economic stimulus measures during financial crises. High levels of debt can limit governments' ability to respond to future economic challenges and may lead to fiscal instability.

8. Global Health Crises:

The COVID-19 pandemic, which began in late 2019, had profound economic implications. Lockdowns, travel restrictions, and disruptions to supply chains caused economic recessions in many countries. Governments implemented massive stimulus packages to support businesses and individuals affected by the pandemic.

9. Access to Education and Healthcare:
Access to quality education and healthcare remains a challenge in many parts of the world. Inadequate access to these essential services can hinder human capital development and economic growth.

10. Geopolitical Uncertainty:
Geopolitical tensions and conflicts, such as those in the Middle East and Ukraine, create uncertainty for global markets and investments. Political instability can deter foreign investment and disrupt economic activities.

11. Digital Divide:
The digital divide, the gap in access to and use of digital technologies, remains a challenge, particularly in developing regions. Unequal access to the internet and digital tools can limit economic opportunities and social inclusion.

12. Pandemic Preparedness:
The COVID-19 pandemic underscored the need for better pandemic preparedness and global health infrastructure. The economic costs of future pandemics could be substantial if adequate measures are not in place.

Addressing these economic challenges requires international cooperation, innovative policies, and adaptability. Governments, businesses, and individuals must navigate the evolving economic landscape while striving for inclusive and sustainable growth. Policymakers must consider strategies that promote economic resilience, reduce inequality, and address the unique challenges posed by the 21st century.

Saudi Arabia's Vision 2030 is a bold and ambitious plan aimed at transforming the kingdom's economy and society for a post-oil era. Launched in 2016, this comprehensive vision seeks to diversify the Saudi economy, reduce its dependency on oil revenues, and promote social development. It represents a significant departure from traditional economic models and encompasses various sectors and initiatives designed to usher in a new era of growth and prosperity.

Diversification Beyond Oil:
One of the central pillars of Vision 2030 is economic diversification. Saudi Arabia recognizes the vulnerabilities of relying solely on oil revenues and aims to broaden its economic base. This involves developing sectors such as tourism, entertainment, technology, renewable energy, and mining. By nurturing these non-oil industries, the kingdom seeks to create jobs, stimulate economic growth, and increase revenue sources.

Privatization and Investment:
To bolster economic transformation, Vision 2030 includes plans to privatize state-owned assets and companies. This privatization drive aims to attract foreign investment, boost the private sector, and improve the efficiency of government-owned enterprises. Key state assets, such as Saudi Aramco and various utilities, are part of this ambitious privatization agenda.

Fiscal Reforms:
The fiscal reforms outlined in Vision 2030 seek to improve the government's financial sustainability. Initiatives include reducing subsidies, introducing taxes like the Value Added Tax (VAT), and implementing measures to enhance fiscal discipline. These reforms aim to address

budget deficits and create a more sustainable fiscal framework.

Human Capital Development:
Investing in the development of human capital is a core component of Vision 2030. The Saudi government has launched numerous initiatives to enhance education and vocational training, equipping the Saudi workforce with the skills needed for a modern and diversified economy. The King Salman Scholarship Program, for example, sends Saudi students abroad for higher education.

Women's Empowerment:
Vision 2030 recognizes the importance of women's participation in the workforce and society. It has led to a series of reforms to empower women, including granting them the right to drive, expanding career opportunities, and encouraging their participation in various sectors. These changes aim to tap into the full potential of Saudi Arabia's female population.

Entertainment and Tourism:
To diversify the economy further, Saudi Arabia has invested in its entertainment and tourism sectors. The kingdom has opened cinemas, hosted international events, and developed tourist destinations. These efforts aim to create new job opportunities and make Saudi Arabia a vibrant cultural and entertainment hub.

Technology and Innovation:
Innovation and technology play a critical role in Vision 2030. Initiatives like the NEOM smart city project and the King Abdullah University of Science and Technology (KAUST) are aimed at fostering innovation and attracting talent. Saudi Arabia seeks to become a global player in

areas such as artificial intelligence, renewable energy, and space exploration.

Environmental Sustainability:

As part of its commitment to sustainable development, Vision 2030 includes efforts to address environmental challenges. Saudi Arabia is investing in renewable energy sources, particularly solar power, to diversify its energy mix and reduce carbon emissions. The Green Saudi and Green Middle East initiatives aim to enhance environmental protection and combat desertification in the region.

Global Partnerships:

Saudi Arabia actively collaborates with various countries and international organizations on economic and development initiatives. These partnerships contribute to global economic growth and foster mutual understanding and cooperation.

In summary, Vision 2030 represents a comprehensive and ambitious roadmap for Saudi Arabia's economic transformation. While challenges and obstacles remain, the plan's multifaceted approach, ranging from diversification and privatization to education and technology, demonstrates the kingdom's commitment to building a more sustainable and prosperous future. As the world watches Saudi Arabia's progress, Vision 2030 serves as a model for countries seeking to navigate the complexities of a changing global economy.

Saudi Arabia's efforts to diversify its economy are central to the Vision 2030 plan. Diversification aims to reduce the kingdom's reliance on oil revenues, promote economic growth in non-oil sectors, and create a more sustainable economic future. To achieve these objectives, Saudi

Arabia has undertaken various diversification strategies and initiatives:

1. Tourism and Entertainment:

Tourism Development: Saudi Arabia is investing in tourism infrastructure and marketing to attract international and domestic tourists. The kingdom has opened up tourist destinations, including historical sites, and hosted cultural and sporting events to boost the tourism sector.

Entertainment Industry: The development of the entertainment industry is a key aspect of diversification. Saudi Arabia has launched cinemas, music festivals, and entertainment complexes to provide leisure options and create jobs.

2. Technology and Innovation:

Smart City Projects: The NEOM project is a flagship initiative aimed at creating a futuristic, technology-driven smart city in the northwest of Saudi Arabia. NEOM aims to attract talent, foster innovation, and promote economic diversification.

Research and Development: The government is investing in research and development centers, including the King Abdullah University of Science and Technology (KAUST), to support innovation and technology-driven sectors.

3. Renewable Energy:

Solar Energy: Saudi Arabia has set ambitious targets for renewable energy production, with a particular focus on solar power. The country aims to develop its renewable energy capacity to reduce its reliance on fossil fuels.

The Green Saudi and Green Middle East Initiatives: These initiatives focus on environmental protection and combating desertification, promoting sustainable agricultural practices, and preserving biodiversity.

4. Mining and Minerals:

Mining Sector Development: Saudi Arabia is working to develop its mining and minerals sector, including the extraction of phosphates and rare earth minerals. This diversification strategy aims to tap into the kingdom's rich mineral resources.

Value Addition: Initiatives aim to move beyond raw material exports and promote the processing and manufacturing of minerals within the country.

5. Financial Services:

Financial Sector Expansion: Saudi Arabia is working to expand its financial services sector, including banking and insurance, to diversify its revenue sources. The kingdom is opening up its financial markets to foreign investors to attract international capital.

6. Manufacturing and Industry:

Local Manufacturing: The Saudi government encourages local manufacturing and industrialization through incentives and support for industries like petrochemicals, automotive manufacturing, and aerospace.

Special Economic Zones: Special economic zones (SEZs) have been established to attract foreign investors and promote industrial growth.

7. Small and Medium-sized Enterprises (SMEs):

SME Development: Initiatives to support SMEs aim to create job opportunities and stimulate economic growth. Funding, training, and mentorship programs are available to help SMEs thrive.

8. Agriculture and Food Security:

Agricultural Investment: Saudi Arabia is investing in agriculture to enhance food security. The government is promoting sustainable agricultural practices, such as aquaculture and hydroponics, to increase local food production.

9. Healthcare and Pharmaceuticals:

Healthcare Investments: The kingdom is investing in healthcare infrastructure, medical research, and pharmaceutical manufacturing to develop a competitive healthcare sector.

Chapter 9: Leadership Transition: The Post-9/11 Era and Beyond (2000s)

The September 11, 2001 terrorist attacks in the United States had a profound impact on Saudi Arabia and its leadership. The attacks, carried out by al-Qaeda operatives, exposed the kingdom's vulnerabilities, strained its relationship with the United States, and prompted significant changes in Saudi leadership's approach to counterterrorism and domestic policies. Here, we examine Saudi Arabia's leadership in the wake of 9/11:

1. Leadership Response:

Immediate Condemnation: In the immediate aftermath of the 9/11 attacks, Saudi leaders, including Crown Prince Abdullah (later King Abdullah), issued strong condemnations of the terrorist acts. They expressed condolences to the American people and reaffirmed their commitment to counterterrorism efforts.

Support for the U.S.: Saudi Arabia provided crucial support to the United States in its response to 9/11. This included intelligence cooperation, sharing financial information to track terrorist financing, and allowing the use of Saudi military bases in the campaign against al-Qaeda and the Taliban in Afghanistan.

2. Counterterrorism Measures:

Crackdown on Extremists: In the years following 9/11, Saudi Arabia intensified its efforts to combat extremism within its borders. The government launched a series of campaigns to root out radical elements and arrest individuals linked to terrorist organizations.

Rehabilitation Programs: Saudi Arabia established rehabilitation programs for former extremists, aimed at reintegrating them into society. These programs offered counseling, religious re-education, and vocational training to individuals with extremist ideologies.

Enhanced Security: The Saudi government invested heavily in enhancing its security apparatus and border controls to prevent the infiltration of terrorists and the smuggling of weapons.

3. Domestic Policy Changes:

Educational Reforms: Saudi leadership recognized the need for educational reforms to counter extremist ideologies. Efforts were made to revise school curricula and promote a more moderate interpretation of Islam.

Promotion of Moderate Islam: The government actively promoted a more moderate form of Islam and sought to counter the extremist ideologies propagated by groups like al-Qaeda. This included supporting moderate religious leaders and scholars.

4. Social and Cultural Initiatives:

Cultural and Social Reforms: Saudi Arabia initiated a series of cultural and social reforms aimed at countering extremism and promoting a more open and tolerant society. These reforms included allowing entertainment and cultural events and expanding opportunities for women in various sectors.

5. U.S.-Saudi Relations:

Strained Relations: While Saudi Arabia cooperated with the United States in counterterrorism efforts, relations between the two countries became strained due to suspicions that some Saudi individuals had connections to the 9/11 attackers. These suspicions led to increased scrutiny of Saudi nationals traveling to the U.S.

Continued Cooperation: Despite challenges, the U.S. and Saudi Arabia continued to collaborate on counterterrorism efforts and regional security issues. Both countries recognized the importance of maintaining stability in the Gulf region.

6. Leadership Transitions:

King Abdullah's Reign: King Abdullah, who ascended to the throne in 2005, played a pivotal role in the post-9/11 era. He continued to pursue counterterrorism measures and initiated domestic reforms aimed at modernizing Saudi society.

King Salman and Crown Prince Mohammed bin Salman: Subsequent leadership changes, with King Salman taking the throne in 2015 and his son, Crown Prince Mohammed bin Salman (MbS), emerging as a prominent figure, brought about significant reforms and a more assertive foreign policy.

In summary, the aftermath of 9/11 led to significant changes in Saudi Arabia's approach to counterterrorism, domestic policies, and international relations. Saudi leadership recognized the need to address extremism within its borders and actively cooperated with the United States and the international community in countering terrorism. The legacy of these changes continues to shape Saudi Arabia's approach to domestic and foreign policy, as well as its ongoing efforts to modernize and reform the kingdom.

The transition to a new generation of leaders in Saudi Arabia has been a prominent and transformative development in recent years. Under the leadership of

Crown Prince Mohammed bin Salman (MbS), Saudi Arabia has undergone significant political, social, and economic reforms. Here, we examine the transition to this new generation of leaders and its impact:

1. Rise of Crown Prince Mohammed bin Salman (MbS):

Elevation to Crown Prince: In June 2017, King Salman named his son, Mohammed bin Salman, as Crown Prince, effectively making him the heir to the throne. This marked a departure from the tradition of seniority in succession.

Vision 2030: MbS introduced Vision 2030, a comprehensive reform plan aimed at diversifying the Saudi economy, reducing dependence on oil, and modernizing various aspects of society. This ambitious vision reflects the young prince's desire to reshape Saudi Arabia for the 21st century.

2. Economic Reforms:

Diversification Efforts: Vision 2030 places a strong emphasis on diversifying the Saudi economy. Initiatives include the partial privatization of Saudi Aramco, the development of NEOM (a futuristic city), and investments in various non-oil sectors.

Foreign Investments: MbS has actively sought foreign investments and partnerships to drive economic growth. This includes the NEOM project's collaboration with international companies and the development of the Red Sea Project to boost tourism.

3. Social Reforms:

Women's Rights: Under MbS's leadership, Saudi Arabia has witnessed significant advancements in women's rights. Women have gained the right to drive, travel without a male guardian's permission, and participate in various sectors, including sports and entertainment.

Entertainment and Culture: Saudi Arabia has opened up to international entertainment and cultural events, hosting concerts, film festivals, and sporting events. These reforms aim to diversify leisure options and promote a more open and vibrant society.

4. Political Changes:

Anti-Corruption Crackdown: MbS initiated a high-profile anti-corruption campaign in 2017, detaining numerous princes, businessmen, and officials. This move aimed to tackle corruption within the government and improve transparency.

Centralization of Power: The Crown Prince has consolidated power within the royal family, leading to changes in the country's decision-making structure. This centralization has allowed for more streamlined decision-making.

5. Regional and Foreign Policy:

Foreign Policy Shifts: Saudi Arabia has adopted a more assertive foreign policy under MbS, including its involvement in the Yemeni civil war and the blockade of Qatar. These policies have had regional ramifications and have drawn both support and criticism.

Vision for the Region: MbS has expressed a vision for a more moderate and economically integrated Middle East through initiatives like the Middle East Green Initiative, designed to combat desertification and promote sustainable development.

6. Challenges and Controversies:

Criticism and Human Rights Concerns: MbS's leadership has faced international criticism over issues such as human rights violations, including the murder of journalist Jamal Khashoggi, and the conflict in Yemen.

Economic Challenges: The ambitious economic reforms outlined in Vision 2030 face challenges, including economic diversification, job creation, and global economic fluctuations.

7. Ongoing Transformation:

Continued Reforms: The transition to a new generation of leaders is an ongoing process, and Saudi Arabia is expected to continue implementing reforms and modernization initiatives. These reforms may face resistance from conservative elements within the society.

Global Engagement: Saudi Arabia under MbS has sought to engage more with the international community, fostering partnerships and collaborations across various sectors, including technology, investment, and culture.

In summary, the transition to a new generation of leaders in Saudi Arabia, led by Crown Prince Mohammed bin Salman, has brought about significant changes in the kingdom's political, social, and economic landscape. These changes reflect a vision for a more modern and diversified Saudi Arabia, but they also face challenges and controversies both domestically and internationally. The impact of these reforms on the kingdom and the broader region will continue to be a subject of global interest and scrutiny.

The post-9/11 era ushered in a period of significant challenges and heightened expectations, not only for the United States but also for the international community as a whole. The devastating terrorist attacks on September 11, 2001, fundamentally altered the global landscape and posed multifaceted challenges that demanded collective responses and proactive measures. Next, we will explore the challenges faced by nations worldwide and the corresponding expectations in the post-9/11 era.

The foremost challenge that emerged in the wake of 9/11 was the urgent need to counter the global threat of terrorism. The attacks demonstrated the ability of transnational terrorist groups like al-Qaeda to carry out large-scale, coordinated acts of violence on a global stage. This necessitated a paradigm shift in how nations approached security and intelligence sharing.

Additionally, the attacks raised concerns about the vulnerabilities of critical infrastructure, such as transportation systems, financial institutions, and energy facilities, to terrorist attacks. Governments worldwide were compelled to reassess their security measures and invest in protecting these vital assets.

The expectation in the post-9/11 era was that nations would collaborate more closely on intelligence sharing and counterterrorism efforts. The international community anticipated enhanced cooperation and the creation of a united front against global terrorism. The establishment of the U.S. Department of Homeland Security and the development of organizations like INTERPOL underscored the commitment to a collective response.

Another significant challenge was the need to strike a balance between national security and individual civil liberties. The heightened security measures that followed 9/11, including increased surveillance, airport screenings, and counterterrorism legislation, raised concerns about potential infringements on privacy and civil rights. Nations were expected to navigate this delicate balance by ensuring security without unduly compromising personal freedoms.

Moreover, the post-9/11 era witnessed a shift in foreign policy priorities for many countries, particularly those in the West. The United States, in particular, embarked on a global War on Terror, which included military interventions in Afghanistan and Iraq. These actions had far-reaching consequences, including destabilizing entire regions, contributing to the rise of insurgent groups, and prompting debates about the legality and efficacy of such interventions.

The international community expected nations to exercise prudence in their foreign policy decisions and to work collaboratively to address the root causes of terrorism, such as political instability, socioeconomic disparities, and the spread of radical ideologies. There was an anticipation of greater emphasis on diplomacy, conflict resolution, and nation-building.

The economic fallout from the 9/11 attacks also posed challenges. Stock markets plummeted, and economic uncertainty prevailed. The aviation and tourism industries were severely impacted, resulting in job losses and financial strain. The expectation was that nations would implement measures to stabilize their economies, restore investor confidence, and ensure the resilience of critical sectors.

Furthermore, the attacks amplified concerns about the proliferation of weapons of mass destruction (WMDs) and the potential use of these weapons by terrorist organizations. Nations were challenged to strengthen non-proliferation efforts, secure WMD stockpiles, and prevent the acquisition of such weapons by rogue states or extremist groups.

In the realm of international law, the post-9/11 era prompted debates about the legality of actions taken in the name of counterterrorism. Questions arose regarding the adherence to international humanitarian law, human rights conventions, and the treatment of detainees. The expectation was that nations would uphold the principles of legality, proportionality, and accountability in their counterterrorism efforts.

Moreover, the post-9/11 era highlighted the importance of addressing the root causes of extremism and radicalization. Nations faced the challenge of developing comprehensive strategies for countering violent extremism (CVE) and promoting community resilience. The expectation was that governments would invest in programs that tackled the underlying factors that drive individuals toward radical ideologies, such as social marginalization and lack of economic opportunities.

Another pressing challenge was the rise of cyberterrorism and cyberattacks in the post-9/11 era. As digital technologies became increasingly integrated into critical infrastructure and communication systems, the vulnerability to cyber threats grew. Nations were expected to bolster their cybersecurity measures and collaborate internationally to mitigate the risks posed by cyberterrorism.

Additionally, the post-9/11 era saw a surge in Islamophobia and anti-Muslim sentiment in many parts of the world. Hate crimes and discrimination against Muslim communities became a concerning issue. Nations were challenged to promote tolerance, inclusivity, and interfaith dialogue while combating extremism.

In terms of expectations, the international community anticipated a commitment to promoting cultural exchange, fostering understanding among different faiths and cultures, and countering extremist narratives. The goal was to build societies that embraced diversity and rejected intolerance.

Furthermore, the post-9/11 era brought renewed attention to humanitarian crises resulting from conflict and terrorism. The displacement of populations, the destruction of homes and infrastructure, and the suffering of civilians in conflict zones necessitated a robust humanitarian response. Nations were expected to contribute to humanitarian efforts, provide aid to affected populations, and support peace and reconciliation initiatives.

In summary, the post-9/11 era presented nations with a complex web of challenges, from countering terrorism and protecting civil liberties to addressing economic instability and promoting tolerance. The expectations were high, with an emphasis on international cooperation, diplomacy, and a commitment to upholding human rights and the rule of law. The ongoing pursuit of these goals remains central to the global response to the challenges posed by the post-9/11 landscape.

Chapter 10: Vision 2030 and Beyond: Saudi Arabia's Ambitious Transformation (21st Century)

In April 2016, Saudi Arabia unveiled an ambitious and transformative plan known as "Vision 2030." Spearheaded by Crown Prince Mohammed bin Salman (MbS), this comprehensive vision aimed to reshape the kingdom's economy, society, and overall outlook for the future. At its core, Vision 2030 sought to diversify the Saudi economy, reduce its dependency on oil, and foster a more vibrant and open society. This essay delves into the unveiling and objectives of Vision 2030.

The Unveiling of Vision 2030:
The official launch of Vision 2030 occurred in April 2016 with a series of announcements, interviews, and statements. At the heart of this vision was a recognition of the challenges that Saudi Arabia faced in the 21st century. The kingdom's economy had long relied on oil exports, leaving it vulnerable to fluctuations in global oil prices. Moreover, demographic trends indicated a growing youth population with increasing aspirations and demands for better opportunities.

Crown Prince Mohammed bin Salman, who was instrumental in crafting and promoting Vision 2030, outlined the need for a new economic and social direction. He emphasized the importance of unlocking the potential of Saudi Arabia's youth, promoting innovation, and reducing the nation's dependence on oil revenue.

Objectives of Vision 2030:
Diversification of the Economy:

A central objective of Vision 2030 was to diversify the Saudi economy by reducing its reliance on oil. This diversification was envisioned through the development of various economic sectors, including tourism, entertainment, technology, and renewable energy. The goal was to create new revenue streams and job opportunities outside the oil sector.

Privatization and Investment:

Vision 2030 aimed to stimulate economic growth by privatizing certain state-owned assets and encouraging foreign investment. The privatization of Saudi Aramco, the state-owned oil company, was one of the most prominent aspects of this initiative. By allowing private ownership of a portion of the company, the government sought to attract foreign investment and generate revenue for further development.

Job Creation and Empowerment of Saudi Youth:

With a significant youth population, job creation was a pressing concern. Vision 2030 aimed to create opportunities for Saudi youth through various means, including investments in education and training programs, the promotion of entrepreneurship, and the development of a vibrant private sector.

Promotion of Tourism and Entertainment:

The plan sought to transform Saudi Arabia into a tourist destination by promoting its rich cultural heritage, historical sites, and natural landscapes. Investments in entertainment and cultural events were intended to make the kingdom a more appealing destination for both domestic and international tourists.

Enhancement of Healthcare and Education:

Vision 2030 included objectives to improve the quality of healthcare and education in Saudi Arabia. This included the development of world-class healthcare facilities, the enhancement of educational curricula, and the promotion of lifelong learning.

Sustainable Development and Renewable Energy:
Recognizing the importance of sustainability, Vision 2030 set forth objectives related to environmental conservation and the development of renewable energy sources. Initiatives like the NEOM project, a futuristic city powered by renewable energy, exemplified these goals.

Women's Empowerment:
A key social objective was the empowerment of Saudi women. The plan aimed to expand women's participation in the workforce, remove barriers to their economic and social engagement, and promote their leadership roles in various sectors.

Cultural and Social Initiatives:
Vision 2030 included cultural and social reforms to promote a more open and vibrant society. Initiatives like the reintroduction of cinema, the organization of cultural events, and the expansion of entertainment options aimed to enrich the cultural landscape of Saudi Arabia.

International Partnerships and Collaboration:
The vision emphasized Saudi Arabia's commitment to international collaboration and partnerships. It aimed to position the kingdom as a global player, foster economic ties with other nations, and promote cultural exchange and dialogue.

Fiscal Responsibility:
To ensure the sustainability of the reforms, Vision 2030 included measures to enhance fiscal responsibility and

efficiency in government spending. This involved fiscal reforms, including the introduction of value-added tax (VAT) and efforts to combat corruption.

In summary, Vision 2030 marked a pivotal moment in Saudi Arabia's history as it embarked on a journey of economic diversification, social reform, and cultural revitalization. The vision aimed to address the challenges of the 21st century while harnessing the nation's untapped potential. While it set ambitious goals, the success of Vision 2030 depended on effective implementation, adaptation to changing circumstances, and the engagement of both domestic and international stakeholders. As Saudi Arabia progresses toward its 2030 objectives, it continues to be a subject of global interest and scrutiny.

The implementation of Vision 2030 in Saudi Arabia has been a dynamic and evolving process, marked by both progress and challenges. Since its unveiling in 2016, Vision 2030 has sought to transform various aspects of Saudi society and the economy, with a focus on diversifying the economy, promoting social reforms, and fostering a more open and vibrant society. Next, we will examine the progress made and the challenges faced in the journey of implementing Vision 2030.

Economic Diversification and Investment:
One of the key objectives of Vision 2030 was to diversify the Saudi economy away from its heavy dependence on oil. Significant progress has been made in this regard. The government has actively sought foreign investments and partnerships, attracting global companies to invest in the kingdom's burgeoning non-oil sectors. Initiatives such as

the privatization of Saudi Aramco, the state-owned oil company, and the establishment of the Public Investment Fund (PIF) to support domestic and international investments have been instrumental in diversifying revenue streams.

Challenges:

Oil Price Volatility: The Saudi economy remains closely tied to oil prices, and fluctuations in global oil markets can impact economic stability. While diversification efforts are ongoing, the economy is still vulnerable to oil price shocks.

Job Creation and Empowerment:

Vision 2030 set ambitious targets for job creation, particularly among the Saudi youth. Several programs and initiatives have been launched to promote employment opportunities and empower Saudi youth. Notably, the establishment of the Quality of Life Program aims to create jobs in various sectors, including entertainment, sports, and tourism.

Challenges:

Job Market Realignment: Transitioning from a predominantly oil-based economy to a diversified one requires realigning the job market and equipping the workforce with new skills. This process can be complex and time-consuming.

Promotion of Tourism and Entertainment:

Saudi Arabia has made significant strides in promoting tourism and entertainment. The kingdom opened up to international tourists, introducing e-visas and launching the "Visit Saudi" campaign to attract visitors to its rich cultural and historical sites. Additionally, the entertainment sector has seen rapid growth, with the organization of concerts, sporting events, and cultural festivals.

Challenges:

Cultural and Social Norms: Balancing the promotion of entertainment and tourism with conservative cultural and social norms remains a challenge. Striking the right balance while respecting the values of the society can be delicate.

Enhancement of Healthcare and Education:

Vision 2030 included objectives to improve the quality of healthcare and education in Saudi Arabia. Investments in healthcare infrastructure and education programs have led to notable improvements in these sectors. The "Transformation of Healthcare" program, for instance, has aimed to enhance healthcare services and accessibility.

Challenges:

Quality Assurance: Ensuring that healthcare and education reforms result in measurable improvements in quality and access remains a challenge. Maintaining consistent standards across the country can be demanding.

Sustainable Development and Renewable Energy:

The vision emphasized sustainability and the development of renewable energy sources. Saudi Arabia launched the NEOM project, a futuristic city powered by renewable energy, as part of its commitment to environmental conservation. The kingdom has also invested in solar and wind energy projects.

Challenges:

Transitioning to Renewable Energy: While progress has been made, transitioning from fossil fuels to renewable energy sources is a complex and costly endeavor.

Challenges include infrastructure development, energy storage, and grid integration.

Women's Empowerment:

Empowering women and increasing their participation in the workforce has been a central goal of Vision 2030. Saudi women have gained the right to drive, travel independently, and access various professional fields. The government has also introduced initiatives to support female entrepreneurs.

Challenges:

Cultural and Social Norms: Changing deeply ingrained cultural and social norms around the role of women in society can take time and necessitates a careful approach.

Cultural and Social Initiatives:

Saudi Arabia has witnessed a cultural renaissance with the reintroduction of cinemas, cultural events, and entertainment options. The goal is to create a more open and vibrant society that embraces culture and creativity.

Challenges:

Navigating Social Sensitivities: As Saudi Arabia introduces cultural and social reforms, it must navigate the sensitivities and values of its diverse population.

International Partnerships and Collaboration:

The vision emphasizes international collaboration and partnerships across various sectors, including technology, investment, and culture. Saudi Arabia seeks to position itself as a global player and engage with the international community.

Challenges:

Geopolitical Dynamics: The kingdom's foreign policy and international partnerships are influenced by complex geopolitical dynamics in the Middle East. Navigating these relationships can be challenging.

Fiscal Responsibility:

To ensure the sustainability of the reforms, Vision 2030 includes measures to enhance fiscal responsibility and efficiency in government spending. The introduction of value-added tax (VAT) and efforts to combat corruption reflect a commitment to responsible fiscal management.

Challenges:

Economic Downturn: Economic challenges, such as the impact of the COVID-19 pandemic and oil price fluctuations, have tested the resilience of fiscal reforms.

In summary, the implementation of Vision 2030 in Saudi Arabia has seen notable progress in diversifying the economy, empowering Saudi youth, promoting tourism, and advancing social and cultural initiatives. However, it has also encountered challenges related to cultural norms, economic dependencies, and the need for sustained reforms. As Saudi Arabia continues to work toward achieving the objectives of Vision 2030, the kingdom's progress and challenges remain of great interest to the international community, as they have implications not only for the country but also for the broader region.

Saudi Arabia's future beyond the Vision 2030 initiative holds promise and potential, yet it also presents a set of complex challenges and uncertainties. The ambitious roadmap laid out by the kingdom seeks to transform its economy, society, and international standing, setting the stage for a new era in Saudi history. Next, we will explore the prospects, opportunities, and challenges that Saudi Arabia may encounter as it looks ahead to a post-Vision 2030 future.

Economic Transformation and Diversification:
One of the most significant prospects for Saudi Arabia's future is the continued economic transformation and diversification. Vision 2030 has set the foundation for reducing the country's reliance on oil revenues and expanding non-oil sectors such as technology, entertainment, and tourism. In a post-Vision 2030 era, the kingdom can build upon these achievements and further cultivate a diverse and resilient economy.

Opportunities:

Innovation and Technology: Saudi Arabia can harness the potential of innovation and technology to drive economic growth. By investing in research and development, fostering a culture of entrepreneurship, and attracting global tech companies, the kingdom can position itself as a regional technology hub.

Challenges:

Economic Sustainability: Maintaining economic sustainability and resilience will be an ongoing challenge. Ensuring the long-term success of economic diversification efforts requires adaptability and effective management of resources.

Regional Leadership and Geopolitical Influence:
Saudi Arabia has long played a significant role in the Middle East and the wider Islamic world. Beyond Vision 2030, the kingdom has the opportunity to expand its regional leadership and diplomatic influence. By engaging in conflict resolution, fostering peace agreements, and promoting regional stability, Saudi Arabia can strengthen its position as a key player in the region.

Opportunities:

Diplomatic Initiatives: The kingdom can continue to engage in diplomatic initiatives, such as mediating conflicts, to shape regional dynamics and promote cooperation.

Challenges:

Regional Conflicts: Ongoing regional conflicts, such as the Yemeni civil war and tensions with Iran, pose challenges to Saudi Arabia's efforts to maintain stability and security in the region.

Socio-Cultural Reforms and Women's Empowerment:

Vision 2030 initiated a wave of socio-cultural reforms aimed at modernizing Saudi society and empowering women. In the future, Saudi Arabia has the potential to build upon these reforms and further enhance social inclusivity, tolerance, and gender equality. Advancements in these areas can lead to a more vibrant and progressive society.

Opportunities:

Cultural Exchange: Expanding cultural exchange programs, hosting international events, and promoting dialogue can foster a more open and diverse society.

Challenges:

Social Traditions: Balancing social reforms with cultural traditions and conservative values may pose challenges. Navigating these complexities will require careful planning and communication.

Environmental Sustainability and Renewable Energy:

Environmental sustainability and renewable energy will play an increasingly vital role in Saudi Arabia's future. The kingdom has the opportunity to become a global leader in clean energy production and environmental conservation. Investments in renewable energy sources, such as solar and wind power, can reduce carbon emissions and address climate change.

Opportunities:

Global Leadership: Saudi Arabia can lead by example in adopting sustainable practices and collaborating with other nations to combat climate change.

Challenges:

Transitioning to Clean Energy: The transition from fossil fuels to clean energy sources can be a complex process that requires significant infrastructure development and investment.

Youth Empowerment and Education:

Saudi Arabia's youthful population presents both an opportunity and a challenge. The kingdom can further empower its youth through education, skill development, and job creation. Initiatives aimed at fostering innovation and entrepreneurship among young Saudis can drive economic growth and social progress.

Opportunities:

Youth Innovation: Encouraging youth to innovate and create can lead to the development of a dynamic and competitive knowledge-based economy.

Challenges:

Youth Unemployment: Ensuring that the youth population is gainfully employed and contributing to the economy is essential to avoid potential social challenges.

International Alliances and Trade Relations:

Saudi Arabia's future lies in its ability to foster international alliances and strengthen trade relations. By engaging in mutually beneficial partnerships, the kingdom can enhance its global standing and diversify its sources of economic growth.

Opportunities:
Trade Diversification: Expanding trade beyond oil exports and building partnerships with a diverse range of nations can reduce economic vulnerability.
Challenges:
Geopolitical Instability: Ongoing geopolitical tensions in the Middle East may affect Saudi Arabia's ability to forge stable international alliances.
Political Stability and Governance:
Political stability and effective governance are critical factors in shaping Saudi Arabia's future. Ensuring transparent and accountable governance, as well as addressing social and political demands, can contribute to long-term stability.
Opportunities:
Good Governance: Emphasizing good governance practices and transparency can enhance public trust and confidence in government institutions.
Challenges:
Political Transition: Preparing for a smooth transition of leadership and maintaining political stability during periods of change will be essential.
Cultural Exchange and Soft Power:
Saudi Arabia can leverage its rich cultural heritage and historical significance to expand its soft power on the global stage. Promoting cultural exchange, supporting the arts, and showcasing the kingdom's traditions can enhance its influence and reputation.
Opportunities:
Cultural Diplomacy: Utilizing cultural diplomacy as a means to connect with other nations and foster understanding can enhance Saudi Arabia's global image.

Challenges:

Perception and Stereotypes: Addressing stereotypes and misconceptions about the kingdom will be necessary to effectively wield cultural soft power.

In summary, Saudi Arabia's future beyond Vision 2030 is a multifaceted landscape characterized by opportunities for economic diversification, regional leadership, social progress, and global engagement. However, the kingdom also faces challenges related to economic sustainability, regional conflicts, social reforms, and environmental transitions. The path forward will require visionary leadership, adaptability, and the ability to navigate a rapidly changing world. As Saudi Arabia charts its course into the future, it does so with the potential to shape not only its own destiny but also the dynamics of the broader Middle East and the international stage.

BOOK 3
MODERNIZATION AND TRADITION
HOUSE OF SAUD'S VISION 2030 (2000S-PRESENT)

BY A.J. KINGSTON

Chapter 1: The Visionary Roadmap: Unveiling Vision 2030 (Early 2000s)

The genesis of Vision 2030, Saudi Arabia's ambitious blueprint for economic and social transformation, can be traced to a confluence of factors that compelled the kingdom to chart a new course for its future. This visionary initiative, officially unveiled in April 2016, emerged as a response to the pressing challenges facing Saudi Arabia and the need for a sustainable and diversified economy. Next, we will delve into the genesis of Vision 2030, exploring the historical context, economic imperatives, and visionary leadership that led to its inception.

Historical Context:
The historical context of Vision 2030 is rooted in Saudi Arabia's evolution as a modern nation-state. Since its founding in 1932 by Abdulaziz Ibn Saud, the kingdom had largely relied on its vast oil reserves as the primary source of revenue. While oil brought immense wealth and development, it also engendered economic vulnerabilities, as the Saudi economy remained heavily dependent on the fluctuating price of oil in global markets.

Over the decades, Saudi Arabia had undertaken various development plans to diversify its economy, but the scale and urgency of the challenge grew in the early 21st century. The global economic landscape was shifting, and the kingdom recognized the need to reduce its reliance on oil to ensure long-term prosperity and stability.

Economic Imperatives:
The economic imperatives that underpinned Vision 2030 were multifaceted and compelling. Key factors included:

Oil Price Volatility: The early 2010s saw significant fluctuations in oil prices, with prices plummeting in 2014. This exposed the vulnerability of Saudi Arabia's oil-dependent economy to external market forces and underscored the need for diversification.

Youth Unemployment: A burgeoning youth population, with high rates of unemployment, presented both a demographic dividend and a potential challenge. The government recognized the importance of providing job opportunities and economic prospects for its young citizens.

Budget Deficits: Plummeting oil prices led to budget deficits, necessitating fiscal reforms to maintain economic stability. Reducing government reliance on oil revenues became imperative to address these deficits.

Economic Efficiency: The desire to enhance economic efficiency and productivity, reduce waste, and streamline government operations played a crucial role in shaping Vision 2030. The kingdom sought to optimize the utilization of its resources.

Visionary Leadership:

The genesis of Vision 2030 was profoundly influenced by the visionary leadership of Crown Prince Mohammad bin Salman (MbS). As the architect of the initiative, MbS recognized the urgency of addressing Saudi Arabia's economic challenges and seized the opportunity to redefine the kingdom's future. Several key aspects of visionary leadership contributed to the inception of Vision 2030:

Strategic Thinking: MbS demonstrated a strategic approach to addressing the nation's challenges. He envisioned a Saudi Arabia that could thrive in a post-oil era and laid out a comprehensive roadmap to achieve this vision.

Bold Reforms: The Crown Prince initiated a series of bold reforms, including the decision to allow women to drive, the launch of the entertainment sector, and the privatization of state-owned enterprises. These reforms signaled a commitment to change and modernization.

Global Engagement: MbS recognized the importance of Saudi Arabia's engagement with the global community. He promoted international partnerships, attracted foreign investments, and aimed to transform the kingdom into a global hub for business and tourism.

Youth Empowerment: Empowering the youth played a central role in Vision 2030. MbS aimed to tap into the potential of Saudi Arabia's youthful population by providing them with opportunities for education, entrepreneurship, and innovation.

Key Pillars of Vision 2030:

The genesis of Vision 2030 also involved the identification of key pillars that would serve as the foundation for the kingdom's transformation:

Economic Diversification: The core objective was to reduce the kingdom's reliance on oil by diversifying the economy. This entailed investments in sectors such as tourism, entertainment, technology, and renewable energy.

Vibrant Society: Vision 2030 aimed to create a more open and vibrant society by fostering cultural and recreational activities. Initiatives like "Saudi Seasons" sought to promote tourism and cultural events.

Efficient Government: Improving government efficiency and accountability was a fundamental pillar. The National Transformation Program (NTP) aimed to streamline government operations and enhance public services.

Quality of Life: Enhancing the quality of life for Saudi citizens was central to the vision. This included improvements in healthcare, education, and housing, as well as promoting a healthy lifestyle.

Public Engagement and Feedback:

The genesis of Vision 2030 involved extensive public engagement and feedback. The government sought the input of Saudi citizens, experts, and stakeholders through various channels, including town hall meetings and online platforms. This inclusive approach aimed to ensure that the vision reflected the aspirations and needs of the Saudi population.

International Collaboration:
The kingdom recognized the importance of international collaboration in realizing its vision. Saudi Arabia sought partnerships with global organizations, corporations, and governments to attract investments, transfer knowledge, and leverage international expertise in various sectors.

The genesis of Vision 2030 marked a pivotal moment in Saudi Arabia's history. It was a response to economic imperatives, historical context, and visionary leadership that recognized the need for transformative change. As Saudi Arabia continues its journey toward 2030, the vision remains a dynamic and evolving roadmap that will shape the kingdom's future, fostering economic diversification, societal openness, and global engagement. The success of Vision 2030 hinges on the kingdom's ability to navigate challenges, harness opportunities, and maintain its commitment to a prosperous and sustainable future.

Vision 2030, Saudi Arabia's comprehensive blueprint for economic and social transformation, is built upon a set of key objectives and components designed to guide the nation's path toward a more diversified, prosperous, and sustainable future. These objectives and components serve as the building blocks for achieving the overarching vision of the initiative. Next, we will explore the essential elements of Vision 2030, emphasizing its key objectives and components.

Key Objectives:

Economic Diversification:
A primary objective of Vision 2030 is to reduce Saudi Arabia's dependency on oil revenues by diversifying its economy. This includes expanding non-oil sectors, such as tourism, entertainment, technology, and renewable energy. The aim is to create a more resilient and dynamic economy that is less susceptible to fluctuations in oil prices.

Enhanced Quality of Life:
Improving the quality of life for Saudi citizens is a central focus. This encompasses a wide range of initiatives aimed at providing better healthcare, education, and housing options. It also includes promoting a healthy lifestyle and enhancing recreational and cultural opportunities.

Vibrant Society:
Vision 2030 seeks to cultivate a more open and vibrant society by encouraging cultural and recreational activities. Initiatives like "Saudi Seasons" promote tourism and cultural events, fostering a sense of community and engagement among citizens.

Efficient Government:
Streamlining government operations and increasing efficiency is a critical objective. The National Transformation Program (NTP) is a key component designed to achieve this goal by optimizing government services and processes, ultimately improving the delivery of public services.

Global Engagement:
Saudi Arabia aims to strengthen its global standing by engaging with the international community. This involves promoting international partnerships, attracting foreign investments, and positioning the kingdom as a global hub for business and tourism.

Youth Empowerment:
Empowering the youth is a fundamental objective. Vision 2030 recognizes the potential of Saudi Arabia's youthful

population and aims to provide them with opportunities for education, entrepreneurship, and innovation.

Key Components:

Economic Transformation:
The economic transformation component focuses on diversifying the economy away from oil dependence. It involves significant investments in sectors such as tourism, entertainment, technology, and renewable energy. The privatization of state-owned enterprises is also part of this component.

Quality of Life Enhancement:
Enhancing the quality of life encompasses multiple facets, including improvements in healthcare, education, and housing. The "Quality of Life Program" aims to create a healthier and more livable environment for Saudi citizens.

Vibrant Society and Culture:
Promoting a vibrant society and culture involves fostering cultural and recreational activities. The "Quality of Life Program" includes initiatives to enhance the cultural scene and promote tourism and entertainment.

Government Efficiency and Effectiveness:
Achieving efficient government operations is a key component. The National Transformation Program (NTP) is responsible for optimizing government services, enhancing public sector efficiency, and streamlining processes.

Global Partnerships and Investment:
Building global partnerships and attracting foreign investments is crucial for economic diversification. Initiatives such as the Future Investment Initiative (FII) aim to position Saudi Arabia as an attractive destination for international investors.

Youth and Human Capital Development:
Developing human capital, particularly among the youth, is vital for the nation's future. Programs and initiatives are

designed to provide education and training opportunities, support entrepreneurship, and foster innovation.

Environmental Sustainability:

Environmental sustainability is increasingly important. Vision 2030 includes initiatives to address environmental challenges and promote responsible resource management, including investments in renewable energy sources.

Digital Transformation:

Embracing digital transformation is essential for modernization. The "Digital Transformation Program" focuses on harnessing digital technologies to enhance government services, foster innovation, and drive economic growth.

National Identity and Cultural Heritage:

Preserving and promoting national identity and cultural heritage are key components of Vision 2030. Initiatives are aimed at showcasing Saudi Arabia's historical and cultural significance to the world.

Vision 2030's key objectives and components collectively represent a comprehensive and forward-thinking strategy for Saudi Arabia's transformation. By addressing economic diversification, quality of life, government efficiency, global engagement, youth empowerment, and more, the initiative aims to shape a vibrant and prosperous future for the kingdom. As Saudi Arabia continues its journey toward 2030, these key elements will serve as the pillars upon which the nation's success and sustainability are built.

In the early years following the unveiling of Vision 2030, Saudi Arabia's ambitious blueprint for economic and social transformation received a range of reactions both domestically and internationally. While it garnered optimism and support for its visionary goals, it also faced significant challenges and skepticism. This essay explores the early reception of Vision 2030 and the challenges it encountered in its initial phases.

Domestic Reception:

Optimism and Hope: Among many Saudis, Vision 2030 was met with optimism and hope for a brighter future. The plan's promises of economic diversification, improved quality of life, and greater opportunities for the youth resonated with citizens who aspired for a more prosperous and open society.

Youth Empowerment: The emphasis on youth empowerment and the development of human capital was particularly well-received. Young Saudis saw the potential for education, entrepreneurship, and innovation as avenues to shape their own destinies.

Cultural and Social Reforms: The introduction of cultural and social reforms, such as allowing women to drive and promoting entertainment and tourism, marked a significant departure from the past. Many Saudis welcomed these changes as steps toward a more inclusive and vibrant society.

Economic Optimism: The economic transformation component, which aimed to reduce the country's reliance on oil, also generated optimism. The potential for new job opportunities, investments in non-oil sectors, and the diversification of the economy appealed to those seeking economic stability.

Challenges and Skepticism:

Implementation Hurdles: One of the early challenges facing Vision 2030 was the complexity of implementation. Transforming an oil-dependent economy into a diversified one required significant reforms, and some doubted the government's ability to execute these changes effectively.

Dependency on Oil Revenues: Critics pointed out that while Vision 2030 aimed to reduce oil dependency, it still relied on oil revenues to fund many of its initiatives. This raised concerns about the sustainability of the plan in the face of volatile oil prices.

Societal Resistance: Not all segments of Saudi society welcomed the cultural and social reforms. Some conservative factions expressed resistance to changes they viewed as incompatible with traditional values and norms.

Economic Realities: Vision 2030 was unveiled at a time when the kingdom faced economic challenges due to low oil prices. Skeptics questioned whether the government could fund the ambitious initiatives while grappling with budget deficits.

Global Uncertainties: Internationally, the vision faced skepticism regarding its feasibility and impact. Some doubted Saudi Arabia's ability to diversify its economy successfully and questioned whether the plan would truly lead to greater social and political openness.

Government Response:

To address these early challenges and skepticism, the Saudi government took several strategic measures:

Fiscal Reforms: The government implemented fiscal reforms to reduce budget deficits and enhance financial sustainability, including measures like the introduction of a value-added tax (VAT).

Investor-Friendly Policies: Saudi Arabia actively sought foreign investments and implemented investor-friendly policies to attract international capital into non-oil sectors.

Social Initiatives: The government continued to roll out social and cultural initiatives to promote the vision's objectives, such as expanding entertainment options and hosting international events.

International Engagement: Saudi Arabia engaged with the international community to promote Vision 2030, showcasing its commitment to modernization and reforms.

In its early years, Vision 2030 faced a mixed reception, with optimism among many Saudis and skepticism from various quarters. The government's response to implementation challenges, fiscal constraints, and societal resistance demonstrated a commitment to realizing the vision's goals. As Saudi Arabia moved forward with the ambitious transformation plan, it sought to address concerns, build partnerships, and adapt to evolving circumstances, laying the foundation for the journey toward a diversified, prosperous, and sustainable future as outlined in Vision 2030.

Chapter 2: Economic Transformation: Diversifying Beyond Oil (2000s-2010s)

The imperative for economic diversification lies at the heart of Vision 2030, Saudi Arabia's ambitious blueprint for transformation. This imperative reflects the recognition that the nation's heavy reliance on oil as its primary source of revenue and economic sustenance poses significant risks and limitations in a rapidly changing global landscape. To understand the imperative for economic diversification, we must delve into the multifaceted reasons that make this transformation not just desirable but necessary.

Vulnerability to Oil Price Volatility:

One of the most compelling reasons for economic diversification is the inherent vulnerability that comes with being heavily reliant on oil revenues. Historically, Saudi Arabia's economic fortunes have risen and fallen with the price of oil in international markets. When oil prices are high, the kingdom experiences economic prosperity, but when prices plummet, as they did in 2014, it can lead to budget deficits, austerity measures, and economic uncertainty.

This vulnerability stems from the fact that oil prices are subject to a multitude of factors beyond Saudi Arabia's control, including geopolitical tensions, production decisions by other major oil-producing nations, and shifts in global demand. Economic diversification is seen as a way to mitigate this vulnerability by reducing the kingdom's dependence on oil.

Youth Unemployment and Demographic Challenges:

Another imperative for economic diversification is the need to address the challenges posed by a rapidly growing and youthful population. Saudi Arabia has one of the world's highest youth unemployment rates, with a significant portion of its population under the age of 30. While this demographic can be a source of strength, it also presents a challenge in terms of providing meaningful employment opportunities and a sustainable future for the nation's youth.

Economic diversification offers the potential to create new industries, sectors, and jobs outside of the traditional oil-based economy. By fostering entrepreneurship, innovation, and education, Saudi Arabia aims to tap into the energy and potential of its young population.

Budget Deficits and Fiscal Sustainability:

Budget deficits resulting from fluctuations in oil prices have been a recurring issue for Saudi Arabia. These deficits have often necessitated fiscal adjustments, cuts in government spending, and the depletion of financial reserves. Addressing these deficits is crucial for the nation's fiscal sustainability.

Economic diversification seeks to provide alternative sources of revenue that can help balance the budget and reduce reliance on oil revenues. Initiatives such as privatization, investments in non-oil sectors, and the introduction of new taxes like the value-added tax (VAT) are all part of the broader strategy to address budget deficits.

Economic Efficiency and Productivity:

Improving economic efficiency and productivity is another key driver of economic diversification. Over the years, the Saudi economy has faced challenges related to inefficiencies in government operations, misallocation of resources, and the need for greater private sector participation.

Economic diversification involves structural reforms that aim to enhance economic efficiency by streamlining government processes, encouraging competition, and optimizing resource allocation. These reforms are intended to make the economy more dynamic and responsive to market forces.

Reducing Reliance on Oil Revenues:

The imperative for reducing reliance on oil revenues is perhaps the most fundamental reason for economic diversification. Oil has long been the lifeblood of the Saudi economy, accounting for the majority of government revenues. While oil has provided immense wealth, it has also engendered a sense of complacency and dependency.

By diversifying the economy, Saudi Arabia aims to create a more balanced revenue mix. This not only reduces the vulnerability to oil price fluctuations but also ensures that the nation can sustain economic growth and development in the long term, even as global energy dynamics evolve.

Environmental Sustainability:

As the world increasingly focuses on environmental sustainability and climate change mitigation, diversifying the economy is seen as a step toward aligning with these global imperatives. The oil industry, while lucrative, is also associated with environmental challenges and concerns, including greenhouse gas emissions.

Economic diversification includes investments in renewable energy sources and sustainable practices, contributing to a more environmentally responsible economic framework.

The imperative for economic diversification in Saudi Arabia is driven by a combination of factors that encompass economic vulnerability, demographic challenges, fiscal sustainability, efficiency improvements, reduced reliance on oil revenues, and environmental considerations. These imperatives collectively underscore the need for a diversified economy that can weather global economic shifts, provide opportunities for the nation's youth, and secure a sustainable future. Vision 2030 represents a comprehensive response to these imperatives, charting a course for a transformed and resilient Saudi Arabia.

The development of non-oil sectors and investments is a pivotal component of Vision 2030, Saudi Arabia's ambitious blueprint for economic transformation. This strategic emphasis reflects the kingdom's recognition of the need to diversify its economy away from heavy dependence on oil revenues. Non-oil sectors encompass a wide range of industries and areas that have the potential to drive economic growth, create jobs, and enhance the nation's overall prosperity. In this discussion, we explore the significance and trajectory of non-oil sectors and investments within the context of Vision 2030.

Diversification for Economic Resilience:
The primary rationale behind the focus on non-oil sectors is to reduce Saudi Arabia's vulnerability to the volatile fluctuations in global oil prices. Historically, the kingdom's economic fortunes have been closely tied to the oil market, making it susceptible to revenue fluctuations. By investing in non-oil sectors, Saudi Arabia aims to create a more balanced and resilient economy that can withstand oil price volatility.

Key Non-Oil Sectors:

Tourism and Entertainment:
One of the most prominent non-oil sectors targeted for development is tourism and entertainment. Saudi Arabia seeks to position itself as a tourist destination by promoting its cultural heritage, historical sites, and natural beauty. Initiatives such as the "Saudi Seasons" and the development of tourism infrastructure are designed to attract domestic and international visitors.

Technology and Innovation:
The technology and innovation sector is a focal point for economic diversification. Investments in technology startups, research and development centers, and digital infrastructure are aimed at fostering innovation and

entrepreneurship. The goal is to create a thriving tech ecosystem that contributes to economic growth.

Renewable Energy:
As the world moves toward cleaner and more sustainable energy sources, Saudi Arabia is investing in renewable energy. Solar and wind projects, along with the development of a sustainable energy industry, are integral to the diversification strategy. The kingdom aims to become a global leader in renewable energy production.

Manufacturing and Industry:
Expanding the manufacturing and industrial base is crucial for reducing import dependence and creating jobs. Saudi Arabia is investing in industrial zones, such as NEOM and the Red Sea Project, to attract manufacturing and industrial enterprises.

Mining and Mineral Resources:
The mining sector holds significant potential, with vast mineral resources, including phosphate, gold, and rare earth elements. Investment in mining infrastructure and exploration is part of the plan to unlock the economic value of these resources.

Healthcare and Life Sciences:
Enhancing healthcare and life sciences is another non-oil sector priority. Investments in medical facilities, research institutions, and pharmaceutical manufacturing aim to improve healthcare services and promote medical tourism.

Foreign Investments and Partnerships:
To accelerate the development of non-oil sectors, Saudi Arabia actively seeks foreign investments and international partnerships. The kingdom has implemented a series of reforms to create a more attractive investment environment, including the establishment of the Saudi Arabian General Investment Authority (SAGIA) and the opening up of various sectors to foreign ownership.

Local Entrepreneurship and Innovation:
While foreign investments are crucial, Vision 2030 also emphasizes the importance of nurturing local entrepreneurship and innovation. Initiatives like the "Misk Innovation" program and the establishment of innovation hubs aim to empower Saudi youth to contribute to economic diversification through their innovative ideas and startups.

Challenges and Opportunities:
Developing non-oil sectors and investments is not without challenges. It requires significant capital, infrastructure development, regulatory reforms, and the cultivation of a skilled workforce. However, the potential benefits are substantial, including job creation, reduced fiscal dependence on oil, and economic resilience.

The development of non-oil sectors and investments is a linchpin of Vision 2030's strategy for transforming Saudi Arabia's economy. By diversifying its economic base, the kingdom aims to reduce its vulnerability to oil price volatility, unlock new sources of growth, and create a more sustainable and prosperous future. This strategic shift towards non-oil sectors and investments is not only essential for Saudi Arabia's economic resilience but also aligns with broader global trends and sustainability imperatives.

Chapter 3: Societal Reforms: Women's Rights, Entertainment, and Social Change (2010s)

Expanding women's rights and opportunities is a pivotal aspect of Vision 2030, Saudi Arabia's comprehensive plan for economic and social transformation. The kingdom has long been characterized by conservative social norms and strict gender segregation, but in recent years, there has been a concerted effort to empower women, promote gender equality, and provide more avenues for their participation in various sectors of society. This shift reflects a recognition of the significant untapped potential that women represent and the importance of their full inclusion in the nation's development. In this discussion, we explore the significance and trajectory of expanding women's rights and opportunities within the context of Vision 2030.

Historical Context:
Saudi Arabia's conservative social and cultural norms have historically limited women's participation in public life and the workforce. For decades, women faced restrictions on their mobility, access to education, and employment opportunities. However, recent years have witnessed a series of reforms aimed at expanding women's rights and opportunities.

Empowering Women in the Workforce:
One of the central goals of Vision 2030 is to significantly increase women's participation in the labor market. Historically, Saudi Arabia had one of the world's lowest rates of female workforce participation. To address this, the kingdom has implemented a range of measures, including:

Lifting the Driving Ban: The decision to allow women to drive in 2018 marked a significant milestone. It not only granted women greater mobility but also expanded their access to education and employment.

Access to Education: Saudi women have made substantial strides in education, with increasing numbers pursuing higher education and advanced degrees. The government has invested in educational opportunities for women, enabling them to compete in various fields.

Workplace Reforms: Reforms have been introduced to make workplaces more accommodating for women. This includes efforts to provide safe and suitable working environments and facilitate work-from-home options.

Promoting Entrepreneurship: Initiatives like the "Qimam Fellowship" program support young Saudi women in pursuing entrepreneurship and leadership roles in various sectors.

Leadership Roles and Decision-Making:

Vision 2030 seeks to increase women's representation in leadership positions and decision-making roles. This is evident in initiatives like the appointment of women to key government positions, including ministerial roles and leadership positions in various sectors. Additionally, quotas have been introduced to ensure greater representation of women on boards of directors and in other decision-making bodies.

Cultural and Social Reforms:

The expansion of women's rights and opportunities extends beyond the workplace. Cultural and social reforms aim to create a more inclusive and diverse society. Some key developments include:

Entertainment and Leisure: The promotion of entertainment and leisure activities has provided more recreational opportunities for women, contributing to a more vibrant cultural scene.

Access to Public Spaces: Efforts have been made to ensure that women have equal access to public spaces, including parks, restaurants, and cultural events.

Guardianship Reforms: Changes to the male guardianship system have granted women greater autonomy in making life decisions, such as travel and healthcare choices.

Challenges and Progress:

While significant progress has been made in expanding women's rights and opportunities, challenges remain. Some conservative segments of society continue to resist these reforms, and gender equality advocates sometimes face opposition. Nevertheless, the momentum for change is palpable, and Saudi women are increasingly playing active roles in diverse fields, from business and academia to sports and the arts.

Expanding women's rights and opportunities is a transformative aspect of Vision 2030 that is reshaping Saudi Arabia's social and economic landscape. As women are empowered to contribute to the nation's progress, their increased participation in the workforce and society at large promises to drive innovation, enhance economic growth, and foster a more inclusive and equitable society. While challenges persist, the commitment to gender equality and the recognition of the invaluable role of women in Saudi Arabia's development are driving a historic transformation that holds great promise for the nation's future.

Cultural and entertainment reforms are integral components of Vision 2030, Saudi Arabia's ambitious blueprint for economic and societal transformation. These reforms reflect a significant departure from the kingdom's historically conservative cultural norms and strict interpretations of Islamic law, signaling a commitment to embracing a more open and diverse cultural landscape. The objective is to enrich the lives of Saudi citizens, promote creativity and artistic expression, and position the kingdom as a vibrant cultural hub in the region. In this discussion, we delve into the significance and trajectory of cultural and entertainment reforms within the context of Vision 2030.

Historical Context:
Saudi Arabia's cultural landscape has long been characterized by its adherence to conservative interpretations of Islam, which influenced various aspects of daily life. This included restrictions on music, dance, cinema, and public entertainment, as they were perceived as incompatible with religious values.

Cultural Reforms:
Cultural reforms aim to promote Saudi Arabia's rich heritage, artistic expression, and cultural diversity. Some key developments in this domain include:

Cultural Events and Festivals: Saudi Arabia has witnessed a proliferation of cultural events and festivals. The "Saudi Seasons" initiative, for example, brings together art exhibitions, music performances, and other cultural activities, providing a platform for artists and creatives to showcase their work.

Cultural Heritage Preservation: Efforts to preserve and celebrate the nation's cultural heritage have been a priority. This includes the restoration and maintenance of historical sites and museums that showcase Saudi Arabia's history and traditions.

Support for the Arts: Initiatives to support local artists and creatives have been launched. Grants and funding opportunities enable artists to pursue their creative endeavors, contributing to a thriving cultural scene.

Entertainment Reforms:

Entertainment reforms aim to provide diverse and engaging leisure activities for citizens and residents. Some notable changes in this regard include:

Cinema Reintroduction: After a 35-year ban, cinemas were reintroduced in Saudi Arabia in 2018. This marked a significant shift in the entertainment landscape, with theaters screening a variety of international and regional films.

Concerts and Live Performances: International and local artists have performed in Saudi Arabia, attracting audiences and creating a vibrant music scene.

Theme Parks and Attractions: The kingdom has invested in theme parks and entertainment attractions. Projects like Qiddiya aim to provide a wide range of recreational activities, from amusement parks to sports facilities.

Sports and Sporting Events: Saudi Arabia has hosted various international sporting events, such as Formula E races and golf tournaments, fostering a culture of sports and entertainment.

Challenges and Progress:

While cultural and entertainment reforms have garnered widespread support and enthusiasm, they have also faced resistance from conservative segments of society. Some argue that these reforms challenge traditional values and norms. Balancing these reforms with the preservation of cultural heritage and Islamic identity remains a challenge.

Nevertheless, the progress made in transforming the cultural and entertainment landscape is undeniable. The reforms have invigorated the cultural scene, stimulated economic activity in related industries, and provided opportunities for Saudi citizens to engage in a wider array of leisure and entertainment activities.

Cultural and entertainment reforms are key pillars of Vision 2030 that are reshaping Saudi Arabia's cultural and social fabric. These reforms not only offer citizens and residents more avenues for entertainment and creative expression but also contribute to economic diversification by developing cultural and entertainment industries. While challenges persist, the commitment to fostering a vibrant and dynamic cultural environment aligns with the kingdom's vision of a more inclusive and forward-looking society. Saudi Arabia's journey toward becoming a cultural and entertainment hub in the region is a reflection of its determination to embrace change and progress in the 21st century.

Chapter 4: Megaprojects and Modern Infrastructure: Redefining Urban Landscapes (2010s-Present)

Ambitious megaprojects are a central feature of Vision 2030, Saudi Arabia's comprehensive plan for economic diversification and development. These large-scale initiatives aim to transform various sectors of the economy and society, contributing to the kingdom's long-term growth and prosperity. Megaprojects in Saudi Arabia represent a substantial commitment to innovation, infrastructure development, and economic diversification. In this discussion, we explore the significance and goals of some of these ambitious megaprojects within the context of Vision 2030.

NEOM:

Goal: NEOM, a futuristic city planned for the northwest of Saudi Arabia, is envisioned as a hub for innovation, technology, and sustainable living. The goal is to create a globally competitive city that attracts talent and investment, fostering economic growth.

The Red Sea Project:

Goal: Located along the Red Sea coast, this project aims to establish a luxury tourism destination known for its natural beauty and cultural heritage. It seeks to boost the tourism sector, create jobs, and enhance the kingdom's reputation as a tourist destination.

Qiddiya:

Goal: Qiddiya is a vast entertainment and leisure project designed to provide diverse recreational activities, including theme parks, sports facilities, and cultural attractions. Its goal is to develop the entertainment sector, promote leisure activities, and enhance the quality of life for Saudi citizens.

Diriyah Gate:
Goal: Diriyah Gate is a historical and cultural preservation project located in Riyadh. Its goal is to celebrate Saudi Arabia's heritage, attract tourists, and create a vibrant cultural district that contributes to the nation's cultural identity.

Red Sea Tourism Project:
Goal: This project focuses on developing a series of luxury resorts and recreational facilities along the Red Sea coast. The goal is to position Saudi Arabia as a premier destination for international tourists, thus diversifying the economy.

Saudi Arabian Green Initiative and the Middle East Green Initiative:
Goal: These initiatives are part of the kingdom's commitment to environmental sustainability. The goal is to address climate change, reduce carbon emissions, and promote renewable energy projects, aligning with global sustainability goals.

The Amaala Project:
Goal: Amaala is envisioned as an ultra-luxury destination centered around wellness, art, and culture. The goal is to attract high-end tourism, investment, and talent to the kingdom.

Tourism in Asir:
Goal: The development of Asir aims to highlight its natural beauty, including mountains and historical sites. The goal is to promote domestic tourism and preserve the region's heritage.

Fadhili Gas Plant:
Goal: The Fadhili Gas Plant is a critical component of the kingdom's energy strategy. It aims to process natural gas and reduce reliance on oil for electricity generation.

The Jeddah Tower (formerly Kingdom Tower):

Goal: This megatall skyscraper, set to be one of the tallest buildings in the world, symbolizes Saudi Arabia's commitment to modernization and urban development. Its goal is to enhance Jeddah's status as a global city.

These ambitious megaprojects are tangible manifestations of Saudi Arabia's commitment to realizing the goals of Vision 2030. They span various sectors, from tourism and entertainment to technology and sustainability, and reflect the kingdom's determination to diversify its economy, create jobs, and improve the quality of life for its citizens. While these projects are not without challenges and complexities, they represent a bold vision for Saudi Arabia's future and its aspirations to play a leading role in the global economy and innovation landscape.

The modernization of infrastructure and urban development is a fundamental component of Vision 2030, Saudi Arabia's comprehensive plan for economic and societal transformation. This initiative aims to revitalize cities, upgrade critical infrastructure, and create sustainable urban environments that can accommodate the kingdom's growing population and diverse economic activities. It represents a commitment to fostering economic growth, enhancing the quality of life, and positioning Saudi cities as vibrant hubs for business and culture. In this discussion, we explore the significance and objectives of the modernization of infrastructure and urban development within the context of Vision 2030.

Historical Context:

Saudi Arabia has undergone significant urbanization and population growth in recent decades, leading to increased pressure on infrastructure and services. The modernization effort acknowledges the need to adapt to these changes while aligning with global urban development trends.

Goals and Objectives:

Infrastructure Upgrades:
The modernization effort includes substantial investments in transportation, utilities, and communication infrastructure. These upgrades aim to improve connectivity within and between cities, enhance logistics and supply chains, and support economic diversification.

Smart Cities:
Saudi Arabia envisions the development of smart cities that leverage technology to enhance efficiency, sustainability, and the quality of life. These cities will feature advanced infrastructure, integrated data systems, and innovative solutions for urban challenges.

Sustainable Urban Development:
Promoting sustainability is a key objective. This involves the development of eco-friendly buildings, green spaces, and public transportation systems to reduce carbon emissions and enhance overall environmental quality.

Economic Hubs:
Saudi cities are being transformed into economic hubs, with a focus on attracting foreign investment, fostering entrepreneurship, and creating job opportunities. Key cities like Riyadh, Jeddah, and Dammam are being positioned as global business destinations.

Cultural and Recreational Facilities:
The modernization effort includes the development of cultural and recreational amenities, including museums, theaters, sports complexes, and public parks. These facilities contribute to a vibrant urban lifestyle and enhance the cultural scene.

Housing and Affordable Housing:
There is an emphasis on providing affordable housing solutions for citizens. Initiatives like "Sakani" aim to address housing needs, reduce costs, and ensure adequate and comfortable housing for all.

Key Projects and Initiatives:

King Salman Park (Riyadh): This mega-project involves the creation of a massive urban park in Riyadh, covering an area of 13.4 square kilometers. It will include recreational areas, green spaces, and cultural attractions.

Riyadh Metro: The Riyadh Metro is one of the most extensive metro projects globally, with multiple lines designed to ease traffic congestion and enhance public transportation in the capital city.

Jeddah Corniche Revitalization: The Jeddah Corniche is undergoing a comprehensive redevelopment to transform it into a picturesque waterfront destination with parks, beaches, and entertainment facilities.

Red Sea Coastal Development: The development of the Red Sea coastline includes luxury resorts, residential communities, and entertainment options to boost tourism and economic growth in the region.

King Abdullah Financial District (Riyadh): This district is envisioned as a financial and business hub with world-class infrastructure, cutting-edge technology, and sustainable design principles.

Challenges and Progress:

Modernizing infrastructure and urban development is a complex and resource-intensive endeavor. Challenges include ensuring the sustainability of projects, mitigating environmental impacts, and maintaining cultural authenticity in a rapidly changing urban landscape. Nevertheless, significant progress has been made, with key projects already in various stages of development and implementation.

The modernization of infrastructure and urban development is a critical pillar of Vision 2030 that aims to reshape the urban landscape of Saudi Arabia. By creating sustainable, smart, and vibrant cities, the kingdom seeks to attract investment, stimulate economic diversification, and improve the quality of life for its citizens. As Saudi cities continue to evolve into dynamic centers of business, culture, and innovation, the modernization effort will play a pivotal role in realizing the broader goals of Vision 2030 and positioning Saudi Arabia as a global player in the 21st century.

Chapter 5: Investment and International Relations: Saudi Arabia's Global Outreach (2010s-Present)

Saudi Arabia's investment initiatives abroad are a significant component of the kingdom's economic diversification strategy, Vision 2030. These initiatives involve deploying Saudi Arabia's considerable financial resources to invest in various sectors and markets globally, aiming to generate returns, facilitate technological transfer, and enhance the kingdom's influence in the global economy. The investment strategy reflects a desire to reduce dependence on oil revenues, promote economic growth, and establish Saudi Arabia as a prominent player in international finance and investment. In this discussion, we explore the significance and objectives of Saudi Arabia's investment initiatives abroad within the context of Vision 2030.

Historical Context:
Saudi Arabia's economy has been heavily reliant on oil revenues for decades. Recognizing the vulnerability of this dependence, the kingdom has sought to diversify its investments globally. Historically, Saudi Arabia has been a prominent investor in the United States and Europe, particularly in sectors such as real estate and finance.

Goals and Objectives:
Economic Diversification:
A primary goal is to diversify Saudi Arabia's sources of income by generating returns on investments in various sectors and markets. This helps reduce the kingdom's reliance on oil revenues, making the economy more resilient to fluctuations in global energy markets.

Technology Transfer:

Investments in advanced industries and technology companies abroad enable Saudi Arabia to access cutting-edge technologies and expertise, which can be applied domestically to boost innovation and competitiveness.

Influence and Diplomacy:
Investment initiatives abroad can enhance Saudi Arabia's diplomatic and economic ties with partner countries. These investments can foster mutual economic interests and strengthen geopolitical relationships.

Sovereign Wealth Fund Growth:
Saudi Arabia's sovereign wealth fund, the Public Investment Fund (PIF), plays a crucial role in these investments. Expanding the fund's assets and diversifying its portfolio is a key objective.

Key Investments:

Technology and Innovation:
Saudi Arabia has made significant investments in technology companies, including major investments in firms like Uber, Tesla, and SoftBank's Vision Fund. These investments align with the kingdom's efforts to develop a knowledge-based economy.

Real Estate and Infrastructure:
The PIF has invested in real estate projects and infrastructure developments globally, with a focus on enhancing returns and contributing to economic growth.

Tourism and Entertainment:
Investments in the tourism and entertainment sectors abroad aim to strengthen the kingdom's position as a global tourist destination. Projects include partnerships with companies like Six Flags for theme parks and investments in entertainment giants like AMC.

Energy and Industry:

Saudi Arabia has invested in energy and industrial projects abroad, including partnerships with foreign companies in renewable energy ventures.

Agriculture and Food Security:
The kingdom has sought to ensure food security through investments in agriculture and agribusiness projects in various countries.

Challenges and Progress:
Investment initiatives abroad are not without challenges. They involve risks related to market volatility, economic conditions in host countries, and geopolitical factors. Additionally, ensuring that investments align with Saudi Arabia's economic and strategic objectives requires careful planning and management.

Despite these challenges, Saudi Arabia has made significant progress in diversifying its investments and expanding its international portfolio. The kingdom's investments abroad have garnered attention and contributed to its evolving role in the global economy.

Saudi Arabia's investment initiatives abroad are a vital element of Vision 2030, reflecting the kingdom's commitment to economic diversification and global engagement. By strategically deploying its financial resources, Saudi Arabia aims to create new sources of income, access advanced technologies, and strengthen its presence on the international stage. As these investments continue to evolve, they play a pivotal role in shaping Saudi Arabia's economic future and its position in the global economy.

Diplomatic and trade relationships with global partners are integral components of Saudi Arabia's foreign policy and economic diversification efforts under Vision 2030. The kingdom has actively sought to strengthen ties with nations around the world, fostering diplomatic cooperation, expanding trade networks, and attracting foreign investment. These efforts are aimed at enhancing Saudi Arabia's economic resilience, increasing its global influence, and promoting its role as a regional and international player. In this discussion, we explore the significance and objectives of Saudi Arabia's diplomatic and trade relationships with global partners within the context of Vision 2030.

Historical Context:

Saudi Arabia has historically maintained strong diplomatic ties with key allies, including the United States and Western European countries, owing to its position as a major oil producer and its strategic importance in the Middle East. Over the years, the kingdom has diversified its diplomatic and economic relationships to include a broader range of partners.

Goals and Objectives:

Economic Diversification:

A primary objective is to reduce Saudi Arabia's dependence on oil revenues by expanding its non-oil sectors through international trade and investment. This diversification helps shield the economy from fluctuations in global energy markets.

Attracting Foreign Investment:

Saudi Arabia seeks to attract foreign direct investment (FDI) by creating a favorable investment climate and offering opportunities in various sectors. This not only boosts economic growth but also promotes knowledge transfer and technology exchange.

Global Influence:

Strengthening diplomatic and trade relationships enhances Saudi Arabia's global influence and allows it to play a more significant role in international affairs, including conflict resolution and regional stability.

Market Access:
Access to global markets is crucial for Saudi Arabia's non-oil sectors. Trade agreements and partnerships with countries and regional blocs facilitate market access for Saudi goods and services.
Key Relationships and Initiatives:
United States:
The U.S.-Saudi relationship has historically been significant due to energy interests, security cooperation, and economic ties. Saudi Arabia continues to engage with the U.S. to attract investment and advance joint projects.
China:
Saudi Arabia has sought to deepen economic ties with China, including signing agreements related to the Belt and Road Initiative (BRI). The two countries cooperate on various projects, including infrastructure and energy.
Asia-Pacific:
The kingdom has fostered relationships with countries in the Asia-Pacific region, such as Japan, South Korea, and India. These partnerships include investments, energy cooperation, and trade agreements.
Arab Gulf States:
Saudi Arabia maintains close ties with its Gulf Cooperation Council (GCC) partners, aiming to strengthen regional stability and economic integration.
Africa:
The kingdom has expanded its presence in Africa through trade and investment, with a focus on sectors like agriculture, infrastructure, and telecommunications.
Europe:
Saudi Arabia engages with European countries on trade, technology, and defense cooperation. Agreements with the European Union promote economic collaboration.
Challenges and Progress:

Challenges to Saudi Arabia's diplomatic and trade relationships include geopolitical tensions in the region, shifts in global economic dynamics, and diversifying its economy while maintaining energy interests. However, the kingdom has made significant progress in expanding its network of partners, attracting foreign investment, and advancing its position in international organizations and forums.

Diplomatic and trade relationships with global partners are central to Saudi Arabia's pursuit of economic diversification and global influence under Vision 2030. These relationships enable the kingdom to access markets, attract investment, and promote technology transfer, ultimately contributing to its economic resilience and strategic role in regional and international affairs. As Saudi Arabia continues to strengthen its ties with diverse global partners, it seeks to position itself as a dynamic and influential player on the global stage in the 21st century.

Chapter 6: Challenges and Criticisms: Vision 2030's Hurdles and Controversies (2010s-Present)

Economic and social challenges are pivotal aspects of Saudi Arabia's Vision 2030, the kingdom's ambitious blueprint for transformation and diversification. While the vision outlines a comprehensive strategy for achieving economic sustainability and societal advancement, it is not without its set of challenges and complexities. In this discussion, we delve into some of the primary economic and social challenges faced by Saudi Arabia in its pursuit of Vision 2030.

1. Economic Dependency on Oil:

Challenge: Saudi Arabia has historically relied heavily on oil exports for government revenues and economic sustenance. The global volatility of oil prices poses a significant challenge to the kingdom's economic stability and growth prospects.

Progress: Vision 2030 seeks to reduce this dependency by diversifying the economy into non-oil sectors such as tourism, technology, and entertainment. Strategic investments aim to create alternative revenue streams.

2. Youth Unemployment:

Challenge: Saudi Arabia has a sizable youth population with a high unemployment rate, which is a pressing concern. The challenge lies in creating sufficient job opportunities for the growing youth demographic.

Progress: Initiatives under Vision 2030 target job creation through economic diversification, entrepreneurship support, and the development of a skilled workforce. Educational reforms are also geared towards aligning skills with market demands.

3. Gender Inequality:

Challenge: Historically, Saudi Arabia has faced gender inequality issues, particularly in relation to women's participation in the workforce and society.

Progress: Vision 2030 has introduced a series of social and economic reforms aimed at improving gender equality. These include granting women the right to drive, expanding employment opportunities for women, and fostering a more inclusive society.

4. Social Transformation and Cultural Acceptance:

Challenge: Rapid social transformation, including entertainment and cultural reforms, may face resistance from conservative segments of society.

Progress: The government has taken steps to balance modernization with cultural acceptance, promoting entertainment and tourism while respecting Saudi Arabia's cultural heritage.

5. Fiscal Sustainability:

Challenge: As Saudi Arabia pursues diversification, managing fiscal sustainability and ensuring the efficient allocation of resources remains a challenge.

Progress: The kingdom is implementing fiscal reforms to improve efficiency and transparency in public spending, including the introduction of value-added tax (VAT) and subsidy reforms.

6. Attracting Foreign Investment:

Challenge: Attracting foreign direct investment (FDI) in a competitive global landscape is essential for Vision 2030's success. Building investor confidence is a challenge.

Progress: The establishment of the Public Investment Fund (PIF) as a major driver of FDI, alongside business-friendly reforms and infrastructure development, is expected to boost investment.

7. Regional and Geopolitical Tensions:

Challenge: The Middle East is a region marked by geopolitical tensions and conflicts. Ensuring regional stability while implementing Vision 2030 is challenging.

Progress: Saudi Arabia continues to engage in regional diplomacy while focusing on its internal reforms. It seeks to maintain a balance between its national interests and regional stability.

8. Environmental Sustainability:

Challenge: Ensuring sustainability in a region prone to environmental challenges such as water scarcity and extreme heat is a critical challenge.

Progress: Vision 2030 includes initiatives for environmental conservation and the development of renewable energy sources to address these challenges.

9. Healthcare and Education Reforms:

Challenge: Enhancing the quality of healthcare and education services to meet the growing demands of a young population is a challenge.

Progress: The government has allocated significant resources to improve healthcare infrastructure and educational standards, focusing on skill development and research institutions.

Public and international criticisms of Saudi Arabia have been a prominent aspect of the kingdom's global image and diplomatic relations. These criticisms have often revolved around various issues, including human rights, regional conflicts, and political dynamics. It's essential to understand the nature of these criticisms and how Saudi Arabia has responded to them.

1. Human Rights Concerns:

Criticism: Saudi Arabia has faced widespread international criticism for its human rights record, including restrictions on freedom of expression, freedom of the press, and treatment of political dissidents. The kingdom's treatment of women's rights activists and its record on religious freedom have also been criticized.

Response: Saudi Arabia has initiated some social and legal reforms to address these concerns. For example, the kingdom has lifted the ban on women driving, granted women more rights in various areas, and announced plans to improve human rights conditions. However, critics argue that more significant reforms are needed.

2. Yemen Conflict:

Criticism: Saudi Arabia's involvement in the Yemen conflict, particularly its military intervention against Houthi rebels, has faced international condemnation. Critics have raised concerns about civilian casualties and the humanitarian crisis in Yemen.

Response: Saudi Arabia has stated that its intervention in Yemen is aimed at restoring the internationally recognized government and countering Houthi aggression. The kingdom has also provided humanitarian aid to Yemen and supported efforts to find a diplomatic solution to the conflict.

3. Jamal Khashoggi's Murder:

Criticism: The murder of journalist Jamal Khashoggi inside the Saudi consulate in Istanbul in 2018 drew widespread international condemnation. The incident raised concerns about press freedom, human rights, and the kingdom's treatment of dissidents.

Response: Saudi Arabia acknowledged the murder and arrested several individuals in connection with it. The government maintained that the murder was not sanctioned by top officials and has taken steps to reform its intelligence agencies.

4. International Relations:

Criticism: Saudi Arabia's foreign policy choices, including its stance on regional conflicts like Syria and Lebanon, have generated criticism and tensions with some countries in the Middle East.

Response: Saudi Arabia has sought to balance its foreign policy by engaging in diplomatic initiatives and regional partnerships. It has also emphasized its commitment to regional stability and counterterrorism efforts.

5. Dissident Crackdowns:

Criticism: The kingdom has faced criticism for its crackdowns on dissidents, including activists, bloggers, and political opponents.

Response: Saudi Arabia has defended its actions by stating that it aims to preserve national security and combat extremism. The government has also argued that some detained individuals were involved in illegal activities.

6. Khashoggi's Impact on Saudi's Image:

Criticism: The Khashoggi incident significantly damaged Saudi Arabia's international image, leading to calls for sanctions and boycotts.

Response: Saudi Arabia has taken steps to rebuild its reputation by implementing social and economic reforms, presenting itself as a destination for foreign investment, and emphasizing its role in regional stability.

It's important to note that Saudi Arabia's responses to criticisms vary depending on the nature and context of the issue. The kingdom continues to engage in diplomatic efforts to improve its international standing while pursuing its domestic reform agenda under Vision 2030. The extent to which Saudi Arabia addresses these criticisms and works to improve its global image remains a subject of ongoing international scrutiny and debate.

Chapter 7: Cultural Heritage and Identity: Balancing Tradition with Modernization (2010s-Present)

Preserving cultural heritage is a significant consideration for Saudi Arabia as it undergoes rapid social and economic transformations under Vision 2030. The kingdom is home to a rich and diverse cultural heritage that spans centuries, including historic sites, traditional arts, and archaeological treasures. Preserving this heritage while embracing modernization is a complex challenge. Here, we explore Saudi Arabia's efforts to safeguard its cultural heritage in the midst of transformative change.

1. Historic Sites and Architecture:
Saudi Arabia boasts numerous historic sites and architectural treasures, such as Diriyah, the old city of Riyadh, and the Nabatean tombs of Al-Ula. Preserving these sites is a top priority. The government has launched initiatives to restore and maintain historic structures, promoting them as tourist attractions and cultural landmarks. This includes the establishment of the Diriyah Gate Development Authority to oversee the preservation and development of Diriyah.

2. Museums and Cultural Centers:
The kingdom has invested in the construction of world-class museums and cultural centers. The National Museum in Riyadh, the King Abdulaziz Historical Center, and the upcoming Al-Ula Museum are examples of these efforts. These institutions serve to educate both Saudis and visitors about the country's history and culture.

3. Archaeological Discoveries:
Saudi Arabia continues to make significant archaeological discoveries that shed light on its pre-Islamic history. These discoveries are carefully excavated and studied to contribute

to the understanding of the Arabian Peninsula's past. Sites like Al-Ula and Madain Saleh have gained UNESCO World Heritage status, highlighting their cultural significance.

4. Traditional Arts and Crafts:

Efforts are underway to support and promote traditional Saudi arts and crafts, such as calligraphy, pottery, and weaving. These art forms are considered integral to the kingdom's cultural identity. Initiatives include workshops, festivals, and the establishment of artisan cooperatives.

5. Cultural Festivals and Events:

Saudi Arabia hosts various cultural festivals and events that celebrate its heritage. The Janadriyah Festival, for example, showcases traditional music, dance, and crafts from different regions of the country. These events provide opportunities for Saudis to connect with their cultural roots.

6. Cultural Education:

Cultural education is emphasized in schools and universities. Saudi students learn about the history, heritage, and traditions of their country as part of their curriculum. This helps instill a sense of pride and identity.

7. Balance with Modernization:

Preserving cultural heritage is a delicate balance with modernization. The government aims to modernize the country while respecting its traditions. For example, architectural designs for new buildings often incorporate elements of traditional Saudi design.

8. Tourism and Cultural Tourism:

Tourism plays a vital role in preserving cultural heritage. Saudi Arabia has been actively promoting tourism, attracting visitors to its cultural sites and heritage villages. This not only generates revenue but also raises awareness about the importance of preserving these sites.

9. Community Engagement:

Engaging local communities in the preservation of cultural heritage is crucial. Many heritage sites are located in rural areas, and involving local residents in conservation efforts fosters a sense of ownership and responsibility.

While preserving cultural heritage is a priority, it is not without its challenges. Rapid development, urbanization, and the impacts of climate change can threaten historical sites and artifacts. However, Saudi Arabia's commitment to cultural preservation, as reflected in Vision 2030, demonstrates a proactive approach to maintaining the country's rich and diverse cultural heritage for future generations. Balancing modernization and heritage preservation is an ongoing process, and the kingdom's efforts will continue to evolve as it progresses toward its goals. The impact of modernization on Saudi identity is a complex and multifaceted issue. Saudi Arabia's ambitious Vision 2030 plan aims to transform the country's economy and society, ushering in a new era of modernization. While modernization brings many benefits, it also raises questions and challenges concerning cultural, social, and national identity. Here, we explore how modernization is influencing Saudi identity.

1. Economic Transformation:

Modernization efforts are primarily focused on diversifying the economy away from oil dependency. This includes investing in industries such as technology, tourism, and entertainment. The economic transformation is creating new opportunities and job markets for Saudis, reshaping their roles and aspirations.

Impact on Identity: The shift from an oil-dependent economy to a more diverse and globally integrated one can lead to changes in the way Saudis perceive their economic identity. People may increasingly identify with a more entrepreneurial and technologically savvy identity.

2. Social and Cultural Changes:
Modernization initiatives have brought about significant social and cultural changes. Reforms in areas such as women's rights, entertainment, and cultural expression are reshaping societal norms and values.
Impact on Identity: These reforms are influencing how Saudis perceive their cultural identity. For example, greater social freedoms and the emergence of a vibrant entertainment industry can contribute to a sense of a more open and cosmopolitan identity. However, they can also spark debates about preserving traditional values and cultural authenticity.

3. Education and Innovation:
Modernization involves investing in education, research, and innovation. Saudi Arabia is fostering a knowledge-based economy and promoting scientific advancements.
Impact on Identity: This shift emphasizes intellectual growth and innovation, potentially leading to a stronger sense of a modern, knowledge-oriented identity among Saudis. It can also encourage a sense of global citizenship as Saudis engage with the international academic community.

4. Traditional Values vs. Modernity:
As Saudi Arabia modernizes, there is an ongoing debate about the balance between traditional values and modernity. Some may see modernization as a threat to cherished customs and traditions.
Impact on Identity: This debate can create tensions within Saudi society and contribute to a sense of identity crisis for some. Individuals may grapple with the challenge of maintaining their cultural and religious heritage while embracing the benefits of modernization.

5. Nationalism and Patriotism:
Modernization efforts are often framed as part of the broader goal of strengthening the nation. Initiatives such as

the "Quality of Life Program" aim to enhance the well-being of citizens and residents.

Impact on Identity: Modernization efforts can foster a sense of national pride and unity among Saudis, reinforcing their identity as citizens of a forward-looking, prosperous nation.

6. Youth Engagement:

Saudi Arabia's young population is at the forefront of modernization. Youth are actively participating in economic, cultural, and social changes, shaping the direction of the country.

Impact on Identity: The younger generation may identify more strongly with a modern and dynamic Saudi identity, embracing the opportunities and values associated with modernization.

7. Global Connections:

Modernization efforts are making Saudi Arabia increasingly interconnected with the global community. This exposure to diverse cultures, ideas, and perspectives can influence identity.

Impact on Identity: Saudis may develop a more globally oriented identity, appreciating the diversity and interconnectedness of the world while maintaining their Saudi heritage.

In summary, modernization is undoubtedly reshaping Saudi identity. While it brings economic prosperity and social progress, it also presents challenges in terms of maintaining cultural authenticity and traditional values. The evolving Saudi identity is likely to be a dynamic blend of tradition and modernity, reflecting the complexities and opportunities of the 21st century. How Saudi Arabia navigates these changes and strikes a balance between modernization and cultural preservation will play a crucial role in shaping the identity of its citizens in the years to come.

Chapter 8: Leadership and Succession: The Crown Prince's Role in Shaping the Vision (2010s-Present)

Crown Prince Mohammed bin Salman (commonly referred to as MbS) plays a central and influential role in Saudi Arabia's domestic and international affairs. His ascendancy to power has brought about significant changes and reforms, as well as sparked debates and controversies. Here, we examine the role of Crown Prince Mohammed bin Salman in shaping the kingdom's trajectory.

1. Vision 2030 Architect:

Crown Prince Mohammed bin Salman is the architect of Saudi Arabia's Vision 2030 plan, a comprehensive blueprint for the kingdom's transformation. Under his leadership, Vision 2030 aims to diversify the economy, reduce oil dependency, and promote social and cultural reforms.

2. Economic Reforms:

MbS has spearheaded economic reforms, including privatization, attracting foreign investments, and developing non-oil sectors. Initiatives like the Public Investment Fund (PIF) have been instrumental in driving economic diversification.

3. Social Reforms:

The crown prince has introduced a series of social reforms, including granting women the right to drive, promoting entertainment and tourism, and enhancing women's participation in the workforce. These changes are part of his vision for a more open and inclusive Saudi society.

4. Modernization and Innovation:

He has championed initiatives to foster innovation, support the technology sector, and promote digital transformation.

These efforts are part of Saudi Arabia's drive to become a regional tech hub.

5. Foreign Policy:
Crown Prince Mohammed bin Salman has played a key role in shaping Saudi Arabia's foreign policy. He has been involved in regional issues such as the Yemen conflict, the blockade of Qatar, and efforts to counter Iran's influence.

6. Regional Ambitions:
MbS has been associated with ambitious regional projects like NEOM, a futuristic city planned for the northwest of Saudi Arabia. These endeavors reflect his vision for modernizing the kingdom and diversifying its revenue sources.

7. Controversies and Criticisms:
His leadership has also been marked by controversies, including the Saudi-led intervention in Yemen, the blockade of Qatar, and the murder of journalist Jamal Khashoggi. These events have drawn international criticism and scrutiny.

8. Centralization of Power:
The crown prince's consolidation of power has been seen by some as a centralizing force in Saudi politics. His influence extends to various sectors, from the military to economic policy, which has both supporters and detractors.

9. Vision for Youth Engagement:
MbS has emphasized the importance of Saudi Arabia's youthful population. He seeks to engage and empower young Saudis through initiatives that promote entrepreneurship, education, and entertainment.

10. Ongoing Challenges:
While Crown Prince Mohammed bin Salman has made significant strides in pushing for reforms and modernization, he faces ongoing challenges, including balancing tradition with change, managing the economy's transition, and

addressing concerns about human rights and political freedoms.

In summary, Crown Prince Mohammed bin Salman is a transformative figure in Saudi Arabia. His leadership has brought about significant changes and reforms, both domestically and regionally. However, it has also generated controversies and international scrutiny. The extent to which his vision for Saudi Arabia will be realized and how the country navigates the complex challenges it faces will shape its future trajectory.

The leadership transition in Saudi Arabia and the implementation of Vision 2030 are closely intertwined and represent a pivotal period in the kingdom's history. Here, we delve into the relationship between the leadership transition and the ambitious Vision 2030 plan.

1. Ascension of Crown Prince Mohammed bin Salman (MbS):

The leadership transition was marked by the rise of Crown Prince Mohammed bin Salman, who was appointed as the heir apparent in 2017. His ascension to power brought about significant changes and reforms, setting the stage for Vision 2030.

2. Architect of Vision 2030:

Crown Prince Mohammed bin Salman is the chief architect of Vision 2030, which is his ambitious blueprint for the future of Saudi Arabia. His leadership and vision are instrumental in driving the plan's goals and initiatives.

3. Vision 2030's Objectives:

Vision 2030 aims to transform Saudi Arabia's economy and society by diversifying away from oil, promoting non-oil sectors, enhancing the business environment, and improving the quality of life for Saudi citizens. These objectives align with the broader goals of the leadership transition.

4. Economic Reforms:
The leadership transition and Vision 2030 are intertwined through economic reforms. The crown prince has pushed for economic diversification, privatization, and attracting foreign investment—key components of Vision 2030.

5. Modernization and Social Reforms:
Both the leadership transition and Vision 2030 emphasize modernization and social reforms. Initiatives like granting women the right to drive, promoting entertainment and tourism, and enhancing women's participation in the workforce are central to both agendas.

6. Regional and Global Engagement:
The leadership transition has influenced Saudi Arabia's regional and global engagement, and Vision 2030 aligns with the goal of projecting a more dynamic and open image of the kingdom.

7. Challenges and Controversies:
The implementation of Vision 2030 has not been without challenges and controversies. Economic diversification and social reforms have faced resistance and have generated debates within Saudi society.

8. Long-Term Vision:
Both the leadership transition and Vision 2030 reflect a long-term vision for Saudi Arabia. The transition ensures continuity in leadership, while Vision 2030 provides a roadmap for the kingdom's development over the next decade.

9. Youth Empowerment:
The leadership transition and Vision 2030 place a strong emphasis on engaging and empowering Saudi Arabia's youthful population. Initiatives that promote entrepreneurship, education, and entertainment are aimed at harnessing the potential of the youth.

10. The Road Ahead:

The leadership transition and Vision 2030 represent a commitment to modernizing Saudi Arabia while preserving its cultural and historical heritage. The kingdom faces ongoing challenges in balancing tradition with change, managing the economic transition, and addressing concerns about human rights and political freedoms.

In summary, the leadership transition in Saudi Arabia and the implementation of Vision 2030 are closely linked and represent a pivotal moment in the kingdom's history. Crown Prince Mohammed bin Salman's leadership is instrumental in driving the vision for a transformed and diversified Saudi Arabia. The success of Vision 2030 will depend on how effectively the leadership manages the challenges and opportunities that arise during this period of significant change and reform.

Chapter 9: Green Initiatives and Sustainability: Saudi Arabia's Environmental Commitments (2010s-Present)

Environmental challenges and awareness in Saudi Arabia have gained prominence in recent years as the kingdom grapples with the consequences of rapid development and industrialization. Here, we examine the environmental challenges facing Saudi Arabia and the efforts to raise awareness and address these issues.

1. Water Scarcity:
Saudi Arabia faces severe water scarcity due to its arid climate and high water consumption. The kingdom relies heavily on groundwater, which is depleting at an alarming rate. Efforts to raise awareness include promoting water conservation and more sustainable agricultural practices.

2. Desertification:
Desertification, the process of fertile land turning into desert, is a significant environmental challenge. This is exacerbated by overgrazing, urban expansion, and improper land use. Awareness campaigns focus on land preservation and afforestation projects.

3. Air Pollution:
Rapid industrialization and urbanization have led to air pollution in major cities like Riyadh and Jeddah. Awareness campaigns highlight the health risks associated with air pollution and encourage the use of cleaner technologies and public transportation.

4. Climate Change:
Saudi Arabia is vulnerable to the impacts of climate change, including rising temperatures and extreme weather events. The kingdom has taken steps to address climate change by

participating in international agreements like the Paris Agreement.

5. Biodiversity Loss:
The kingdom's unique ecosystems, such as coral reefs in the Red Sea and rare wildlife, are threatened by habitat destruction and overfishing. Conservation efforts and awareness campaigns aim to protect these natural treasures.

6. Marine Pollution:
Coastal areas in Saudi Arabia face marine pollution from industrial discharges and shipping activities. Awareness campaigns stress the importance of responsible waste disposal and marine conservation.

7. Renewable Energy:
Saudi Arabia is investing in renewable energy sources like solar and wind power to reduce its reliance on fossil fuels. Awareness campaigns emphasize the benefits of clean energy for the environment and the economy.

8. Environmental Education:
Environmental education is being integrated into the curriculum at schools and universities. This helps raise awareness among the younger generation about the importance of environmental protection.

9. Conservation Reserves:
The establishment of conservation reserves and protected areas is a step toward preserving Saudi Arabia's unique ecosystems and biodiversity. Awareness efforts highlight the significance of these reserves.

10. Sustainable Practices:
Businesses and industries are increasingly adopting sustainable practices, such as reducing waste and conserving resources. Awareness campaigns promote eco-friendly initiatives.

In summary, Saudi Arabia is actively addressing its environmental challenges and raising awareness about the importance of environmental conservation. The kingdom recognizes the need to balance its rapid development with sustainable practices to protect its natural resources and preserve its unique ecosystems. As awareness grows and initiatives are implemented, Saudi Arabia is taking steps toward a more environmentally sustainable future.

Saudi Arabia has launched several sustainability initiatives in recent years as part of its commitment to address environmental challenges and transition to a more sustainable and diversified economy. Here, we explore some of the key sustainability initiatives undertaken by the kingdom:

1. Vision 2030:
Vision 2030, spearheaded by Crown Prince Mohammed bin Salman, is the cornerstone of Saudi Arabia's sustainability efforts. It outlines a comprehensive plan to diversify the economy away from oil dependency, promote sustainable practices, and improve the quality of life for citizens.

2. NEOM:
NEOM is a futuristic, sustainable city planned for the northwest of Saudi Arabia. Designed to be powered by renewable energy, NEOM aims to be a global hub for innovation, technology, and sustainable living.

3. The Red Sea Project:
This ambitious initiative aims to develop tourism along the Red Sea coast in a sustainable manner. It includes plans for luxury resorts, natural conservation, and efforts to protect the marine ecosystem.

4. Amaala:
Amaala is another luxury tourism project on the Red Sea, with a strong focus on sustainable practices, conservation, and eco-friendly development.

5. The Line:

Part of the NEOM project, "The Line" is a revolutionary city development concept that emphasizes sustainability. It envisions a city built around nature, with zero cars and 100% renewable energy.

6. Renewable Energy:
Saudi Arabia is investing heavily in renewable energy sources, particularly solar and wind power. The country aims to generate a significant portion of its energy from renewables in the coming years.

7. Green Saudi and Green Middle East Initiatives:
These initiatives aim to increase green cover in Saudi Arabia and neighboring countries by planting billions of trees. The goal is to combat desertification, reduce carbon emissions, and enhance biodiversity.

8. Sustainable Agriculture:
The kingdom is implementing sustainable agricultural practices to reduce water consumption and promote food security.

9. Water Conservation:
Efforts are underway to promote water conservation through improved irrigation techniques and the reduction of water-intensive crops.

10. Circular Carbon Economy:
Saudi Arabia is exploring ways to reduce carbon emissions and increase energy efficiency through a circular carbon economy approach.

11. Environmental Education:
The government is integrating environmental education into the curriculum at schools and universities to raise awareness about sustainability.

12. Sustainable Transportation:
Initiatives like the Riyadh Metro and the expansion of public transportation networks aim to reduce traffic congestion and air pollution in major cities.

13. Waste Management:

Saudi Arabia is working on improving waste management practices and recycling programs to reduce landfill waste.

These sustainability initiatives reflect Saudi Arabia's commitment to addressing environmental challenges, reducing its carbon footprint, and transitioning to a more sustainable and diversified economy. While challenges remain, the kingdom is making significant strides toward a greener and more sustainable future.

Chapter 10: The Road Ahead: Prospects and Possibilities for Vision 2030 (Present and Beyond)

Vision 2030 is a comprehensive and ambitious plan for Saudi Arabia's future development, with a focus on economic diversification, social reforms, and sustainability. As the year 2030 approaches, the plan has set several milestones and targets to measure its progress and impact. Here are some of the future milestones envisioned under Vision 2030:

1. Economic Diversification:

Reduced Oil Dependency: By 2030, Saudi Arabia aims to significantly reduce its dependence on oil revenue by developing non-oil sectors. The plan targets specific percentages of non-oil revenue contributions to the GDP.

Growth of Non-Oil Sectors: Vision 2030 aims to see substantial growth in non-oil sectors, such as tourism, entertainment, technology, and manufacturing. Milestones include the development of tourism infrastructure and attracting foreign investments.

Privatization: The plan envisions the privatization of key sectors, including education, healthcare, and state-owned companies. Milestones involve the successful privatization of specific entities.

2. Social Reforms:

Women's Empowerment: Vision 2030 includes milestones related to increasing women's participation in the workforce and enhancing their rights. This involves the creation of more opportunities for women in various sectors.

Youth Engagement: The plan emphasizes engaging and empowering Saudi Arabia's youthful population through education, job creation, and entrepreneurship. Milestones include youth employment rates and educational improvements.

Entertainment and Cultural Initiatives: The plan encourages the growth of the entertainment and cultural sectors. Future milestones include the expansion of entertainment options and cultural events.

3. Sustainability and Environment:

Renewable Energy: Saudi Arabia has set ambitious targets for renewable energy production, including specific capacity goals for solar and wind energy by 2030.

Reduction in Carbon Emissions: The plan envisions a significant reduction in carbon emissions through the adoption of clean and sustainable practices.

Natural Conservation: Vision 2030 includes milestones related to the conservation of natural resources, including the establishment of protected areas and initiatives to combat desertification.

4. Governance and Transparency:

Improved Governance: The plan aims to enhance governance and transparency within government institutions. Future milestones may involve improvements in government services and anti-corruption measures.

E-Government: Vision 2030 promotes the adoption of e-government services to streamline administrative processes and enhance efficiency.

5. Regional and Global Engagement:

Diplomatic and Trade Relationships: Saudi Arabia seeks to strengthen its diplomatic ties and trade relationships with global partners. Future milestones may involve the signing of trade agreements and increased diplomatic initiatives.

Cultural Diplomacy: The plan encourages cultural diplomacy and Saudi Arabia's role as a cultural hub in the region.

Milestones could include the hosting of international cultural events and exhibitions.

6. Quality of Life:

Improved Quality of Life: Vision 2030 seeks to improve the overall quality of life for Saudi citizens through better healthcare, education, and infrastructure. Milestones include health and education indicators.

Housing: The plan includes initiatives to address housing affordability and availability. Future milestones may involve the completion of housing projects.

As 2030 approaches, Saudi Arabia will continue to track progress toward these milestones and adjust its strategies as needed to achieve its long-term goals. The successful realization of these milestones will be crucial in determining the overall impact of Vision 2030 on the kingdom's future.

Saudi Arabia's Vision 2030 and its associated initiatives have significant regional and global implications that extend beyond the kingdom's borders. Here are some of the key regional and global implications of Vision 2030:

1. Regional Economic Impact:

Economic Integration: Saudi Arabia's economic diversification efforts are likely to lead to increased economic integration with neighboring countries. This could stimulate regional trade and investment.

Regional Competitiveness: As Saudi Arabia develops key sectors like tourism and technology, it may become a regional hub, attracting businesses and talent from nearby countries.

2. Energy Markets:

Impact on Oil Markets: Saudi Arabia's plans to reduce oil dependency may have implications for global oil markets. Reduced oil production or exports from the kingdom could influence global oil prices.

Renewable Energy Leadership: The kingdom's investments in renewable energy could set an example for other oil-producing countries in the region, potentially accelerating the shift toward clean energy in the Middle East.

3. Geopolitical Dynamics:

Diplomatic Initiatives: Saudi Arabia's increased engagement with other countries, both in the region and globally, as part of Vision 2030 could reshape regional diplomatic dynamics.

Regional Conflicts: Economic diversification and stability in Saudi Arabia could contribute to regional stability and conflict resolution efforts, particularly in the Middle East.

4. Cultural and Social Influence:

Cultural Exchange: Saudi Arabia's efforts to promote culture and entertainment could facilitate cultural exchange and dialogue with other nations, leading to greater understanding and cooperation.

Moderation and Tolerance: The kingdom's emphasis on moderation and tolerance in its society could set an example for countering extremism and promoting religious and social tolerance regionally and globally.

5. Investment and Trade:

Foreign Investment: Saudi Arabia's efforts to attract foreign investment may result in increased investment from international businesses, which could have a positive economic impact both domestically and abroad.

Trade Relations: Enhanced trade relations between Saudi Arabia and other countries could open up new markets and business opportunities for global firms.

6. Environmental Sustainability:

Renewable Energy Adoption: Saudi Arabia's investments in renewable energy and environmental initiatives could encourage other countries to follow suit, contributing to global efforts to combat climate change.

Environmental Diplomacy: The kingdom's focus on sustainability and conservation may lead to collaborations with other nations on environmental issues and conservation efforts.

7. Human Capital Development:

Education Exchange: Saudi Arabia's investments in education and human capital development could lead to increased educational exchange programs and collaboration with international universities.

Workforce Mobility: A more skilled and diverse Saudi workforce could potentially contribute to the global labor market and facilitate labor mobility.

In summary, Saudi Arabia's Vision 2030 has wide-ranging implications for the Middle East and the world. The kingdom's economic diversification, cultural initiatives, and sustainability efforts have the potential to reshape regional dynamics, influence global markets, and contribute to broader international goals, including environmental sustainability and social development. The successful implementation of Vision 2030 will likely be closely watched and could serve as a model for other countries seeking to address similar challenges and opportunities.

**BOOK 4
DISSIDENCE AND THE HOUSE OF SAUD
A HISTORY OF OPPOSITION (20TH-21ST CENTURY)**

BY A.J. KINGSTON

Chapter 1: Seeds of Discontent: Early Opposition Movements (20th Century)

Early dissent and dissatisfaction in Saudi Arabia can be traced back to various factors, including political, social, and economic grievances. Here, we explore the key aspects of early dissent and dissatisfaction in the kingdom:

1. Tribal and Regional Tensions:

Historical Tribal Divisions: Saudi Arabia has a long history of tribal divisions, and these divisions sometimes led to local tensions and disputes with the central authority.

Regional Rivalries: Different regions of the kingdom had their own grievances, often related to issues like resource allocation, representation, and access to government resources.

2. Religious Discontent:

Religious Interpretations: Disagreements over religious interpretations and practices have historically fueled dissent, particularly among religious scholars and clerics who had differing views on religious matters.

Wahhabi Influence: The kingdom's religious establishment, closely tied to the strict Wahhabi interpretation of Islam, sometimes clashed with individuals and groups advocating for more liberal interpretations.

3. Economic Disparities:

Resource Distribution: Dissatisfaction often arose from perceived disparities in the distribution of the country's wealth and resources, with some regions feeling marginalized or excluded from economic development.

Job Opportunities: Unequal access to job opportunities and economic benefits led to frustration, particularly among young Saudis seeking employment.

4. Political Exclusion:

Lack of Political Representation: Dissent was fueled by the lack of political representation and the concentration of power in the hands of the royal family.

Limited Political Freedoms: The absence of political freedoms and civil liberties led to calls for greater political participation and freedom of expression.

5. Religious and Social Reforms:

Push for Social Reforms: Calls for social reforms, including greater gender equality, were met with resistance from conservative elements in society.

Restrictions on Freedom: Restrictions on personal freedoms, such as dress codes and social behavior, contributed to dissent among those seeking more liberal and open societies.

6. Intellectual Dissent:

Intellectuals and Writers: Intellectuals, writers, and academics often expressed dissenting views through literature, writing, and academic work that challenged traditional norms and values.

7. Regional and International Factors:

Influence of Pan-Arabism: During the mid-20th century, pan-Arabism and revolutionary movements in the region influenced political dissent in Saudi Arabia.

Cold War Dynamics: The kingdom's alignment with Western powers during the Cold War led to criticism and dissent from those advocating for a more independent foreign policy.

8. Suppression of Dissent:

Government Crackdowns: The Saudi government, at times, responded to dissent with arrests, censorship, and crackdowns on opposition movements.

Exile of Dissidents: Some dissidents and intellectuals chose to go into exile to avoid persecution and continue advocating for their causes from abroad.

It's important to note that early dissent and dissatisfaction in Saudi Arabia were often met with government suppression, making it challenging for dissenting voices to gain traction. Over time, these issues evolved and contributed to more complex challenges and opposition movements in the kingdom, which continue to shape Saudi society and politics today.

Opposition movements in Saudi Arabia have seen several pioneers who have played significant roles in advocating for various causes, including political reform, human rights, and social change. Here are some notable pioneers of opposition movements in the kingdom:

1. Sheikh Jafar Al-Shayeb:
Sheikh Jafar Al-Shayeb was a prominent Islamic scholar and reformist who advocated for political and social change in Saudi Arabia. He was known for his critique of the government's policies and his calls for greater political representation.

2. Dr. Saad Al-Faqih:
Dr. Saad Al-Faqih is a Saudi dissident and academic who founded the Movement for Islamic Reform in Arabia (MIRA). He has been an outspoken critic of the Saudi government and has called for political reform and greater civil liberties.

3. Manal al-Sharif:
Manal al-Sharif is an activist known for her campaign against the ban on women driving in Saudi Arabia. Her activism helped bring international attention to the issue of women's rights in the kingdom.

4. Raif Badawi:
Raif Badawi is a Saudi writer and activist who founded the Free Saudi Liberals website, where he discussed liberal and secular ideas. He was arrested in 2012 and sentenced to imprisonment and flogging for his writings.

5. Mohammed bin Nayef Al-Qarni:
Mohammed bin Nayef Al-Qarni is a prominent Islamic scholar and author known for his criticism of the Saudi government's policies and his calls for political reform.

6. Abdullah Al-Hamid:
Abdullah Al-Hamid was a Saudi human rights activist and founding member of the Saudi Civil and Political Rights Association (ACPRA). He was known for his advocacy for political reform and human rights.

7. Samar Badawi:
Samar Badawi is a Saudi women's rights activist who has campaigned for women's rights and the release of political prisoners. She was awarded the U.S. International Women of Courage Award in 2012.

8. Waleed Abulkhair:
Waleed Abulkhair is a Saudi human rights lawyer and activist who has represented clients in high-profile human rights cases. He was imprisoned for his activism and has received international recognition for his work.

Chapter 2: Islamist Challenges: Radicalism and the House of Saud (Late 20th Century)

The emergence of Islamist movements in Saudi Arabia has been a complex and multifaceted phenomenon, shaped by various historical, political, and social factors. Here is an overview of the key developments and drivers that contributed to the rise of Islamist movements in the kingdom:

1. Historical Background:

Wahhabi Influence: The religious and political influence of the Wahhabi movement, a conservative and puritanical interpretation of Islam, has deep historical roots in Saudi Arabia. The alliance between the House of Saud and the Wahhabi clerical establishment laid the foundation for the kingdom's religious and political identity.

2. Political Factors:

1979 Siege of the Grand Mosque: The 1979 takeover of the Grand Mosque in Mecca by Islamist militants had a profound impact on Saudi Arabia. The incident highlighted security vulnerabilities and led to a more conservative religious approach by the government.

Soviet-Afghan War: Saudi Arabia's support for the Afghan mujahideen during the Soviet-Afghan War in the 1980s contributed to the radicalization of some Saudis who fought in Afghanistan and later returned home with jihadist ideologies.

3. Influence of Islamist Ideologies:

Salafism: Salafism, a conservative Islamic ideology that seeks to emulate the practices of the early generations of Muslims, has gained influence in Saudi Arabia. Some Salafi groups have been involved in religious activism and missionary work.

Muslim Brotherhood: While not officially recognized in Saudi Arabia, the Muslim Brotherhood has influenced Islamist movements in the country, advocating for political reform and social justice.

4. Socioeconomic Factors:

Economic Disparities: Economic disparities and inequalities have fueled grievances, making some segments of the population receptive to Islamist narratives that promise social justice and redistribution of wealth.

5. Internet and Social Media:

Access to Information: The proliferation of the internet and social media platforms has provided a means for the dissemination of Islamist ideologies, enabling both radical and reformist voices to reach a broader audience.

6. Political Activism:

Calls for Reform: Some Islamist activists have called for political reform, greater political participation, and the establishment of constitutional rights within an Islamic framework.

Human Rights Advocacy: Islamist activists have also been involved in advocating for human rights and civil liberties, sometimes aligning with non-religious activists in these efforts.

7. Government Response:

Suppression of Dissent: The Saudi government has at times cracked down on Islamist activists and groups it perceives as a threat to its authority. This has included arrests, detentions, and censorship.

Counterterrorism Measures: In response to the rise of jihadist extremism, the government has implemented counterterrorism measures and sought to counter radicalization within the country.

8. Regional and International Influences:

Regional Unrest: Political instability and conflict in the Middle East, including the Arab Spring uprisings, have influenced the dynamics of Islamist movements in Saudi Arabia.

International Alliances: Saudi Arabia's alliances with Western powers, particularly the United States, have sometimes fueled anti-government sentiment and contributed to Islamist opposition narratives.

It's important to note that not all Islamist movements in Saudi Arabia advocate violence or radical ideologies. Some seek peaceful reform and social change within the framework of Islamic principles. The complex interplay of these various factors has shaped the landscape of Islamist movements in the kingdom, making it a dynamic and evolving phenomenon.

Al Qaeda and extremist threats have posed significant challenges to Saudi Arabia's stability and security. The kingdom has faced a series of attacks and attempts by extremist groups, including Al Qaeda, to undermine the government and promote their extremist ideologies. Here is an overview of Al Qaeda's activities and the broader extremist threats in Saudi Arabia:

1. Al Qaeda in the Arabian Peninsula (AQAP):

Formation: Al Qaeda in the Arabian Peninsula (AQAP) emerged as an affiliate of Al Qaeda in the early 2000s, primarily operating in Yemen and Saudi Arabia. It sought to establish a base for global jihad in the Arabian Peninsula.

Targets: AQAP targeted the Saudi government, security forces, and Western interests, viewing the Saudi monarchy as corrupt and aligned with Western powers.

Attacks: The group carried out numerous attacks in Saudi Arabia, including bombings, assassinations, and kidnappings. One of the most significant attacks was the 2003 Riyadh compound bombings, which killed dozens of people, including Westerners.

2. Government Response:

Counterterrorism Efforts: The Saudi government implemented robust counterterrorism measures to combat AQAP and other extremist groups. This included arrests, crackdowns on extremist networks, and intelligence cooperation with Western allies.

Rehabilitation Programs: Saudi Arabia also introduced rehabilitation programs for former extremists, aimed at reintegrating them into society through religious counseling and education.

3. Ideological and Religious Dimension:

Counterextremism Education: Saudi Arabia recognized the importance of addressing extremist ideologies and took steps to reform its educational curriculum to promote tolerance and counter radical interpretations of Islam.

Religious Scholars: Prominent religious scholars and clerics in the kingdom issued fatwas (religious rulings) condemning terrorism and extremist ideologies.

4. Social and Economic Factors:

Youth Vulnerability: High youth unemployment and feelings of marginalization among certain segments of the population made some young Saudis vulnerable to extremist recruitment.

Economic Reforms: The government's efforts to diversify the economy through Vision 2030 aimed to address some of the socioeconomic factors contributing to extremism.

5. Regional and International Context:

Regional Instability: Regional conflicts, such as the Syrian civil war and the rise of ISIS, created conditions that allowed extremist ideologies to flourish and facilitated the movement of fighters and funding across borders.

International Cooperation: Saudi Arabia cooperated with international partners, including the United States, in countering extremist threats. The U.S. provided support and intelligence sharing in the fight against AQAP.

6. Progress and Challenges:

Successes: Saudi Arabia has made significant strides in reducing the influence and operational capacity of AQAP within its borders. Counterterrorism efforts have disrupted many extremist networks.

Ongoing Challenges: Despite progress, the threat of extremism remains, and the government continues to grapple with countering radicalization and addressing root causes.

Saudi Arabia's experience with Al Qaeda and extremist threats underscores the complex interplay of political, ideological, socioeconomic, and regional factors that contribute to extremism. While significant efforts have been made to combat extremism and violence, ongoing vigilance and comprehensive strategies are essential to mitigate the risk of future threats.

Chapter 3: Regional Tensions: Saudi Arabia and Its Neighbors (20th Century)

Saudi Arabia's relations with neighboring states have been characterized by a mix of cooperation, competition, and occasional tensions. The kingdom shares borders with several countries, and its foreign policy is influenced by regional dynamics, security concerns, economic interests, and diplomatic initiatives. Here's an overview of Saudi Arabia's relations with its neighboring states:

1. Yemen:
Historical Ties: Saudi Arabia shares a long and complex history with Yemen. The two countries have historical, cultural, and economic ties. However, they have also experienced border disputes and intermittent conflicts.
Yemeni Civil War: The ongoing Yemeni civil war, which began in 2014, has strained relations between Saudi Arabia and Yemen. Saudi Arabia, along with a coalition of Arab states, has been involved in supporting the Yemeni government against Houthi rebels. The conflict has had significant humanitarian implications.

2. Iraq:
Post-Saddam Hussein Era: Following the fall of Saddam Hussein in Iraq, Saudi Arabia sought to engage with the new Iraqi government and rebuild diplomatic ties. Both countries have a shared interest in regional stability.
Religious Pilgrimages: The religious significance of Saudi Arabia as the host of Mecca and Medina makes it an important destination for Iraqi Shia pilgrims. This has cultural and religious significance for both countries.

3. Jordan:

Strengthened Ties: Saudi Arabia has maintained positive relations with Jordan, providing economic assistance and political support. Both countries have a shared interest in regional stability and counterterrorism efforts.

Economic Cooperation: Saudi Arabia has invested in various development projects in Jordan, contributing to economic growth and infrastructure development.

4. Kuwait:

Gulf Cooperation Council (GCC): Kuwait is a fellow member of the Gulf Cooperation Council (GCC) along with Saudi Arabia. The GCC promotes economic and political cooperation among its member states.

Border Disputes: Although Kuwait and Saudi Arabia have had disputes over their shared border, these issues have largely been resolved through diplomatic channels.

5. Qatar:

GCC Crisis: Saudi Arabia, along with the United Arab Emirates, Bahrain, and Egypt, imposed a blockade on Qatar in 2017, accusing it of supporting terrorism and having ties to Iran. This crisis strained relations within the GCC and disrupted regional cooperation.

Ongoing Tensions: While some diplomatic efforts have been made to resolve the crisis, tensions persist, and a full reconciliation has not been achieved.

6. United Arab Emirates (UAE):

Strong Ties: Saudi Arabia and the UAE have developed strong political, economic, and military ties. They cooperate closely on regional security issues and share common goals in counterterrorism efforts.

Economic Partners: The two countries are key partners in various economic initiatives, including investment projects and economic diversification efforts.

7. Oman:

Neutral Stance: Oman maintains a neutral and independent foreign policy. It has historically played a role in facilitating diplomatic dialogue and conflict resolution in the region.

Strategic Geography: Oman's strategic location at the entrance to the Strait of Hormuz makes it a key player in regional security and trade.

8. Bahrain:

Security Cooperation: Bahrain and Saudi Arabia share strong security and military cooperation. Saudi Arabia played a role in supporting Bahrain during the Arab Spring protests in 2011.

Economic Ties: Economic cooperation and investment projects have strengthened ties between the two countries.

Saudi Arabia's relations with neighboring states are shaped by a combination of geopolitical, security, economic, and cultural factors. The kingdom seeks to balance its regional interests and maintain stability in a complex and often volatile regional environment. Diplomatic efforts and regional organizations like the GCC play a role in managing and addressing regional challenges.

Saudi Arabia's involvement in regional conflicts and alliances has been influenced by its geopolitical position, security concerns, and efforts to protect its interests in the Middle East. The kingdom has played a prominent role in several regional conflicts and has sought to build alliances with like-minded countries. Here is an overview of Saudi Arabia's involvement in regional conflicts and alliances:

1. Yemen Conflict:

Saudi-Led Coalition: Saudi Arabia has been a key player in the ongoing conflict in Yemen, leading a coalition of Arab states in support of the Yemeni government against Houthi rebels. The conflict has been marked by a humanitarian crisis and ongoing hostilities.

Security Concerns: Saudi Arabia views the Houthi rebels, who are aligned with Iran, as a security threat due to their proximity to the Saudi border. The conflict has also been seen as part of the broader Saudi-Iran regional rivalry.

2. Syria Conflict:

Support for Syrian Opposition: Saudi Arabia has provided support to various Syrian opposition groups during the Syrian civil war. Its goal has been to weaken the Assad regime, which is backed by Iran, and to promote a political transition.

Humanitarian Assistance: The kingdom has also contributed to humanitarian efforts in Syria, providing aid to refugees and displaced persons.

3. Lebanese Politics:

Support for March 14 Alliance: Saudi Arabia has historically supported the March 14 Alliance in Lebanese politics, which is aligned with Sunni interests and opposed to Hezbollah, a Shia militant group with close ties to Iran.

Political Influence: The kingdom has used its influence to shape Lebanese politics and has at times been involved in political disputes in the country.

4. Gulf Cooperation Council (GCC):

Regional Alliance: Saudi Arabia is a member of the Gulf Cooperation Council (GCC), which includes Bahrain, Kuwait, Oman, Qatar, and the United Arab Emirates. The GCC is a regional alliance that promotes economic and political cooperation among its member states.

Security Cooperation: The GCC states have cooperated on security matters, including military alliances and joint defense agreements.

5. Anti-Terrorism Coalition:

Islamic Military Counter Terrorism Coalition (IMCTC): Saudi Arabia formed the IMCTC, a coalition of Islamic countries, to combat terrorism and extremism. The coalition seeks to enhance cooperation in the fight against terrorist groups.

6. Iranian Rivalry:

Saudi-Iran Rivalry: Saudi Arabia and Iran have a longstanding regional rivalry. They often find themselves on opposite sides of regional conflicts, such as in Yemen and Syria, due to their differing geopolitical interests and sectarian differences.

Proxy Conflicts: Regional conflicts have often been characterized as proxy wars between Saudi Arabia and Iran, with each country supporting opposing sides.

7. Arab-Israeli Conflict:

Support for Palestinian Cause: Saudi Arabia has historically supported the Palestinian cause and the establishment of a Palestinian state. The kingdom has advocated for a two-state solution to the Israeli-Palestinian conflict.

Peace Initiatives: Saudi Arabia has been involved in various peace initiatives and diplomatic efforts aimed at resolving the Arab-Israeli conflict.

Saudi Arabia's involvement in regional conflicts and alliances reflects its pursuit of security and geopolitical interests in the Middle East. The kingdom seeks to protect its borders, counter perceived threats, and promote its vision of regional stability. However, these involvements have also exposed Saudi Arabia to complex regional dynamics and challenges.

Chapter 4: The Arab Spring and Unrest: Saudi Arabia's Response to Regional Upheavals (2010s)

The Arab Spring movements and regional unrest had a profound impact on Saudi Arabia and the broader Middle East. These uprisings, which began in late 2010, were characterized by popular protests, demands for political change, and challenges to authoritarian regimes across the Arab world. Here's an overview of how the Arab Spring and regional unrest affected Saudi Arabia:

1. Domestic Response:

Security Measures: Saudi Arabia closely monitored the developments of the Arab Spring and took stringent security measures to prevent similar protests within its borders. The government was determined to avoid the spread of unrest to the kingdom.

Economic Measures: To address some of the socioeconomic grievances that were catalysts for the Arab Spring, Saudi Arabia announced various economic measures, including increased government spending and job creation initiatives.

Political Reforms: While Saudi Arabia did not undergo significant political changes as a result of the Arab Spring, it made some modest reforms, such as municipal elections and limited women's rights reforms.

2. Support for Regional Allies:

Gulf Cooperation Council (GCC) Intervention: Saudi Arabia, along with other GCC states, intervened in Bahrain in 2011 to support the Bahraini government in suppressing protests. This intervention was seen as an effort to prevent the spread of unrest in the Gulf.

Financial Assistance: The kingdom provided financial aid to other regional allies, such as Jordan and Egypt, to help stabilize their economies and governments during times of unrest.

3. Sectarian Dynamics:

Sectarian Tensions: The Arab Spring and subsequent regional conflicts heightened sectarian tensions in the Middle East, particularly between Sunni-majority Saudi Arabia and Shia-majority Iran. Saudi Arabia was concerned about the influence of Iran and Shia groups in countries undergoing political change.

4. Regional Conflicts:

Syrian Civil War: Saudi Arabia was actively involved in supporting Syrian opposition groups during the early years of the Syrian civil war. It sought the ouster of Syrian President Bashar al-Assad, who had Iranian support.

Yemen Conflict: The Yemeni civil war, which escalated during the Arab Spring, posed significant security challenges for Saudi Arabia. The kingdom led a coalition of Arab states in support of the Yemeni government against Houthi rebels, who were allegedly backed by Iran.

5. Impact on Regional Alliances:

Reevaluation of Alliances: The Arab Spring prompted Saudi Arabia to reevaluate its alliances in the region. The kingdom was particularly critical of the U.S. response to the uprisings, viewing it as insufficient support for traditional allies.

6. Regional Diplomacy:

Mediation Efforts: Saudi Arabia engaged in regional diplomacy to mediate and resolve conflicts in the aftermath of the Arab Spring. It played a role in diplomatic efforts related to Yemen, Lebanon, and other regional hotspots.

7. Ongoing Impact:

Long-Term Regional Instability: The Arab Spring and its aftermath contributed to long-term instability in the Middle

East. Conflicts, political transitions, and humanitarian crises continue to affect the region.

Shift in Regional Power Dynamics: The Arab Spring and subsequent developments have reshaped regional power dynamics, with Saudi Arabia and Iran vying for influence and countries in the region facing significant challenges.

Saudi Arabia's response to the Arab Spring was influenced by its desire to maintain stability, protect its interests, and manage regional dynamics. While the kingdom was largely successful in preventing widespread protests within its borders, the broader impact of the Arab Spring on the region has been profound and ongoing.

Saudi Arabia's approach to the Arab Spring was characterized by a combination of domestic and regional strategies aimed at preserving stability, safeguarding its interests, and preventing the spread of unrest within the kingdom. Here's an overview of how Saudi Arabia responded to the Arab Spring:

1. Domestic Measures:

Security Crackdown: Saudi Arabia took swift and decisive security measures to quell any signs of domestic unrest. It increased its security presence in major cities and used a combination of police, military forces, and intelligence agencies to suppress protests.

Preemptive Actions: The government also engaged in preemptive actions, arresting activists and dissidents before they could organize protests. This included monitoring and cracking down on social media activism.

Economic Initiatives: Recognizing that economic grievances were one of the driving forces behind the Arab Spring, Saudi Arabia announced various economic initiatives to address unemployment and improve living standards. These initiatives included job creation programs and increased public spending.

Political Reforms: While Saudi Arabia did not undertake significant political reforms in response to the Arab Spring, it did make some limited changes. In 2011, the king announced that women would be allowed to vote and run for municipal elections, a small step toward political participation.

2. Support for Regional Allies:

Bahrain Intervention: Saudi Arabia played a leading role in the Gulf Cooperation Council (GCC) intervention in Bahrain in 2011. The intervention aimed to support the Bahraini government in suppressing protests and preventing the spread of unrest in the Gulf region.

Financial Assistance: The kingdom provided financial aid to regional allies, particularly Egypt and Jordan, to help stabilize their economies and governments during times of unrest. This support was seen as a way to counter potential political changes in these countries.

3. Diplomatic and Regional Efforts:

Mediation and Diplomacy: Saudi Arabia engaged in regional diplomacy to mediate and resolve conflicts in the aftermath of the Arab Spring. It played a role in diplomatic efforts related to Yemen, Lebanon, and other regional hotspots.

Critique of Western Response: Saudi Arabia was critical of what it perceived as a lack of support from Western countries during the Arab Spring. The kingdom believed that Western powers were too quick to abandon longtime allies and not doing enough to stabilize the region.

4. Sectarian Considerations:

Sectarian Concerns: Saudi Arabia viewed the Arab Spring through the lens of its rivalry with Iran, a Shia-majority country. The kingdom was concerned that political changes in certain countries might empower Shia groups or align them with Iran's interests.

5. Long-Term Impact:

Regional Instability: The Arab Spring and its aftermath contributed to long-term instability in the Middle East. Conflicts, political transitions, and humanitarian crises continue to affect the region.

Shifted Regional Dynamics: The Arab Spring shifted regional power dynamics, with Saudi Arabia and Iran vying for influence and countries in the region facing significant challenges.

Saudi Arabia's response to the Arab Spring was primarily focused on preserving its domestic stability and regional influence. While the kingdom was largely successful in preventing large-scale protests within its borders, the broader impact of the Arab Spring on the region has been profound and continues to shape regional dynamics.

Chapter 5: The Reformist Wave: Intellectuals, Activists, and Calls for Change (21st Century)

During and after the Arab Spring, several intellectual voices and advocates for reform emerged in Saudi Arabia, contributing to public discourse and pushing for political, social, and economic changes. These individuals played a significant role in raising awareness about various issues and advocating for greater openness and reform in the kingdom. Here are some notable figures:

1. Jamal Khashoggi (1958-2018):

Background: Jamal Khashoggi was a prominent Saudi journalist and columnist known for his critical views on the Saudi government.

Role: He used his platform to advocate for press freedom, human rights, and political reforms in Saudi Arabia. His writing and commentary in international publications brought attention to Saudi issues.

Tragic Fate: Khashoggi's brutal murder inside the Saudi consulate in Istanbul in 2018 drew worldwide condemnation and intensified scrutiny of Saudi Arabia's human rights record.

2. Waleed Abulkhair:

Background: Waleed Abulkhair is a Saudi human rights lawyer and activist.

Role: He founded the organization Monitor of Human Rights in Saudi Arabia (MHRSA) and used his legal expertise to defend activists and promote human rights in the kingdom.

Imprisonment: Abulkhair was arrested and imprisoned for his activism and legal work, becoming a symbol of the struggle for human rights in Saudi Arabia.

3. Abdullah Al-Hamid (1950-2020):

Background: Abdullah Al-Hamid was a Saudi academic and activist.
Role: He co-founded the Saudi Civil and Political Rights Association (ACPRA), an organization that advocated for political and civil liberties in Saudi Arabia.
Imprisonment: Al-Hamid was imprisoned for his activism and passed away in prison in 2020, but his work continues to inspire other activists.

4. Hatoon Al-Fassi:
Background: Hatoon Al-Fassi is a Saudi academic, historian, and women's rights advocate.
Role: She has been a vocal advocate for women's rights and gender equality in Saudi Arabia. Al-Fassi has also highlighted historical contributions of Saudi women.
Women's Driving Campaign: Al-Fassi supported the campaign to lift the ban on women driving in Saudi Arabia, which was eventually successful.

5. Ali Al-Ahmed:
Background: Ali Al-Ahmed is a Saudi dissident and the founder of the Institute for Gulf Affairs.
Role: He has been a critic of the Saudi government and has worked to shed light on human rights abuses and political repression in the kingdom. Al-Ahmed has also highlighted the situation of religious minorities in Saudi Arabia.

6. Essam Al-Zamil:
Background: Essam Al-Zamil is a Saudi economist and businessman.
Role: He has been an advocate for economic reform in Saudi Arabia, particularly in the areas of privatization, diversification, and reducing the country's dependence on oil.

7. Raif Badawi:
Background: Raif Badawi is a Saudi writer and activist.

Role: He founded the Free Saudi Liberals blog, where he wrote about liberalism, secularism, and human rights in Saudi Arabia. Badawi was sentenced to a lengthy prison term and received public attention for his case.

These individuals, among others, have made significant contributions to the discourse on reform and human rights in Saudi Arabia. They have faced various challenges, including imprisonment and persecution, for their advocacy efforts. While the Saudi government has taken steps toward limited reforms in recent years, the work of these intellectuals and advocates has played a role in raising awareness about the need for broader change in the kingdom.

Activism and the use of social media have played a significant role in shaping public discourse and advocating for change in Saudi Arabia. The combination of a young and tech-savvy population, restrictions on traditional forms of activism, and the desire for greater social and political openness has led to the emergence of online activism as a powerful force for reform in the kingdom. Here's how activism and social media have influenced Saudi society:

1. Raising Awareness:

Highlighting Human Rights Abuses: Activists and individuals on social media platforms have used their voices to shed light on human rights abuses, political repression, and other issues in Saudi Arabia. They have shared stories, images, and videos to draw international attention to these concerns.

Advocating for Reform: Activists have used social media to advocate for various reforms, including women's rights, freedom of expression, and political change. Hashtags and online campaigns have been used to promote these causes.

2. Mobilization and Organizing:

Coordination of Protests: Social media platforms have been used to coordinate protests, gatherings, and demonstrations, allowing activists to come together and voice their demands.

Building Networks: Activists have built networks and alliances online, connecting with like-minded individuals and organizations both within Saudi Arabia and internationally.

3. Challenging Traditional Norms:

Debates on Social Issues: Social media has provided a platform for open discussions on social issues that were previously considered taboo in Saudi society, including women's rights, religious freedom, and gender equality.

Promoting Liberal Ideas: Some activists and individuals have used social media to promote liberal and progressive ideas, challenging conservative norms and advocating for a more open and inclusive society.

4. Amplifying Voices:

Circumventing Censorship: Social media has allowed activists to circumvent government censorship and restrictions on traditional media outlets. This has enabled them to reach a wider audience both within and outside the kingdom.

International Support: The use of social media has facilitated connections with international human rights organizations, journalists, and policymakers who can amplify the voices of Saudi activists.

5. Challenges and Risks:

Government Crackdown: The Saudi government has cracked down on online activism and dissent, arresting individuals for their social media posts and monitoring online activities.

Risk to Activists: Online activism comes with risks, as individuals who criticize the government or advocate for reform are vulnerable to harassment, imprisonment, or even violence.

Social Media Surveillance: The government has invested in advanced surveillance technologies to monitor social media platforms, making it challenging for activists to operate safely and anonymously.

6. Impact on Change:

Incremental Reforms: While social media activism has contributed to incremental reforms, such as women being allowed to drive and some relaxation of social restrictions, broader political change remains a significant challenge.

International Pressure: The international community, including human rights organizations and foreign governments, has taken notice of Saudi activism on social media, leading to increased pressure on the Saudi government to address human rights concerns.

Chapter 6: The Role of the Shia Minority: Marginalization and Discontent (21st Century)

The historical background of the Shia minority in Saudi Arabia is complex and has its roots in early Islamic history. Understanding the history of the Shia minority in Saudi Arabia requires exploring the broader context of Islamic schisms and the development of different sects within Islam. Here is an overview of the historical background:

1. Early Islamic Schism:

The division between Sunni and Shia Muslims originated in the early days of Islam following the death of the Prophet Muhammad in 632 CE.

The schism was rooted in a disagreement over the rightful succession of leadership. Sunnis believed that leadership should be based on consensus, while Shias believed that leadership should be through a bloodline, with Ali, the cousin and son-in-law of Muhammad, as the rightful leader (Imam).

2. Emergence of Shia Islam:

After the assassination of Ali in 661 CE, the Shia community continued to believe in the leadership of the Imams from the bloodline of Ali. This belief led to the development of various Shia sects, the largest of which are the Twelvers (Ithna Ashariyya) and the Ismailis.

3. Historical Presence in the Arabian Peninsula:

The Arabian Peninsula, including the region that is now Saudi Arabia, has a historical presence of Shia communities, particularly in the eastern and southern regions.

These communities have often faced challenges and occasional persecution, as they hold religious beliefs distinct from the Sunni majority in the region.

4. Eastern Province:
The Eastern Province of Saudi Arabia, known for its significant oil reserves, has a notable Shia population, particularly in cities like Qatif, Dammam, and Al-Hasa.
The Eastern Province's Shia communities have faced social, economic, and political challenges, including discrimination and restrictions on religious practices.

5. Sectarian Tensions:
Sectarian tensions between the Sunni majority and the Shia minority have existed in the Arabian Peninsula for centuries, occasionally flaring into conflicts and disputes.
These tensions have been exacerbated by regional geopolitical rivalries, including the broader Sunni-Shia divide in the Muslim world, with Saudi Arabia often representing Sunni interests.

6. Contemporary Issues:
In recent decades, there have been incidents of violence and unrest in the Eastern Province, often fueled by grievances related to discrimination, political representation, and economic disparities.
The Saudi government has made efforts to address some of these issues, including limited reforms and economic development initiatives in the region.

7. Impact of Regional Conflicts:
Regional conflicts, such as the sectarian tensions in Iraq and the civil war in Yemen, have further complicated the situation for the Shia minority in Saudi Arabia. These conflicts have sometimes spilled over into sectarian tensions within the kingdom.
The historical background of the Shia minority in Saudi Arabia is intertwined with broader Sunni-Shia divisions within Islam and the complex dynamics of the Arabian Peninsula. The situation remains a sensitive and evolving issue, influenced by both local and regional factors. Efforts to

address the concerns of the Shia minority continue to be a part of the broader socio-political landscape in Saudi Arabia. Marginalization and discontent among Shia communities in Saudi Arabia, particularly in the Eastern Province, have been longstanding issues with deep historical and socio-political roots. This discontent stems from various factors:

1. Religious and Sectarian Discrimination:
The Shia minority in Saudi Arabia has historically faced religious discrimination. They have often been marginalized in religious matters, as the official interpretation of Islam in Saudi Arabia follows the Sunni tradition.

Shia practices, rituals, and religious gatherings have been restricted or monitored, leading to feelings of marginalization and alienation.

2. Economic Disparities:
Despite the presence of significant oil resources in the Eastern Province, Shia-majority areas have faced economic disparities. Many Shia communities believe that their regions have not received an equitable share of the wealth generated from oil resources.

Unemployment and underdevelopment in these areas have contributed to economic discontent.

3. Political Representation:
Shia communities have expressed dissatisfaction with their level of political representation in the Saudi government. They argue that they are underrepresented in key government positions and decision-making bodies.

Calls for greater political inclusion and participation have been met with resistance from the government.

4. Socio-Political Tensions:
The Eastern Province has experienced periodic outbreaks of violence and protests, driven by grievances related to discrimination, economic hardships, and political marginalization.

These tensions have occasionally escalated into confrontations between Shia protesters and security forces.

5. Regional Factors:

The influence of regional conflicts, such as the sectarian strife in Iraq and the conflict in Yemen, has contributed to increased sectarian tensions in the region.

Saudi Arabia's rivalry with Iran, which is predominantly Shia, has also amplified regional tensions, affecting relations with its own Shia population.

6. Government Responses:

The Saudi government has implemented limited reforms and development projects in the Eastern Province to address some of the grievances. However, many Shia activists and leaders argue that these measures fall short of their demands for equality and inclusion.

The government has also conducted security crackdowns in response to protests and unrest, leading to arrests and imprisonment of activists.

7. International Scrutiny:

The treatment of the Shia minority in Saudi Arabia has drawn international attention and criticism from human rights organizations and foreign governments, adding to the pressure on the Saudi government to address these issues.

8. Impact on Regional Stability:

Discontent among Shia communities in Saudi Arabia has implications for regional stability, as it is linked to broader regional conflicts and sectarian tensions in the Middle East.

The marginalization and discontent among Shia communities in Saudi Arabia remain complex and sensitive issues with both local and regional dimensions. Addressing these grievances requires a multi-faceted approach that includes political, economic, and social reforms, as well as efforts to foster greater inclusivity and dialogue within the kingdom.

Chapter 7: International Criticism and Human Rights: Saudi Arabia in the Global Spotlight (21st Century)

Human rights concerns in Saudi Arabia have garnered significant international scrutiny due to a range of issues, including restrictions on freedom of expression, suppression of political dissent, harsh punishments, and violations of women's rights. These concerns have drawn attention from human rights organizations, foreign governments, and the global community. Here are some key human rights issues and the international response:

1. Freedom of Expression and Dissent:
Saudi Arabia has a record of suppressing freedom of expression, both online and offline. Journalists, activists, and bloggers who criticize the government or advocate for reform have been arrested, imprisoned, or even disappeared.
International Response: Human rights organizations and governments have condemned the crackdown on freedom of expression and called for the release of detained individuals.

2. Women's Rights:
While Saudi Arabia has made some progress in women's rights, such as allowing women to drive and attend sporting events, significant challenges remain. Women are still subject to male guardianship laws, and activists advocating for further reforms have faced arrest and imprisonment.
International Response: Women's rights activists have received widespread support from the international community, with calls for their release and the removal of gender-based restrictions.

3. Capital Punishment and Criminal Justice:

Saudi Arabia has one of the highest rates of execution in the world. The country's legal system has been criticized for lack of transparency, inadequate legal representation, and allegations of torture.

International Response: Many countries and human rights organizations have condemned Saudi Arabia's use of the death penalty and called for reforms in its criminal justice system.

4. Treatment of Migrant Workers:

Saudi Arabia hosts a significant migrant worker population, many of whom face exploitation, abuse, and poor working conditions. Concerns have been raised about the rights and treatment of these workers.

International Response: Various organizations, including the International Labor Organization (ILO), have called for improved conditions and protections for migrant workers in Saudi Arabia.

5. Execution of Dissidents and Critics:

High-profile cases, such as the murder of journalist Jamal Khashoggi inside the Saudi consulate in Istanbul, have highlighted the Saudi government's actions against its critics, both inside and outside the country.

International Response: The Khashoggi case led to widespread international condemnation and calls for accountability. Sanctions and travel restrictions were imposed on Saudi officials involved in the murder.

6. International Pressure and Sanctions:

Several Western countries have imposed sanctions and export restrictions on Saudi Arabia in response to human rights abuses and controversial foreign policies, such as the war in Yemen.

International Response: Sanctions and diplomatic pressure are part of international efforts to encourage Saudi Arabia to address human rights concerns.

7. Mixed Reforms:
The Saudi government has initiated some reforms in recent years, including Vision 2030, which aims to diversify the economy and promote a more open society. However, progress on human rights issues remains uneven.

International Response: Foreign governments and organizations have acknowledged and encouraged these reforms while also stressing the need for further improvements in human rights.

The human rights situation in Saudi Arabia continues to be a subject of international concern and scrutiny. While there have been some positive steps toward reform, significant challenges remain, and international pressure and advocacy play a crucial role in addressing these concerns and advocating for greater respect for human rights in the kingdom.

Criticism of Saudi Arabia's human rights record and other controversial policies has had significant diplomatic and economic implications. These criticisms have come from various quarters, including human rights organizations, foreign governments, international institutions, and the global public. Here are some of the key diplomatic and economic implications:

Diplomatic Implications:

Strained Diplomatic Relations:
Criticism of Saudi Arabia's human rights abuses and other contentious actions has strained diplomatic relations between the kingdom and other countries, particularly Western nations.

Instances such as the murder of journalist Jamal Khashoggi and the war in Yemen have led to diplomatic tensions, with some countries imposing sanctions or restrictions on Saudi officials.

Shifts in Alliances:
Criticism has prompted some countries to reconsider their alliances with Saudi Arabia. Western nations have faced pressure to reassess their relationships with the kingdom in light of human rights concerns.
Countries have sought to balance their interests in maintaining diplomatic relations with Saudi Arabia while addressing human rights issues.

International Isolation:
Saudi Arabia's international standing has been negatively affected by criticism and condemnation. The kingdom has faced isolation on certain issues in international forums and organizations.
This isolation can limit the kingdom's ability to influence global decisions and policies.

Economic Implications:

Impact on Investment and Trade:
Criticism of Saudi Arabia's human rights record has raised concerns among investors and businesses. Some companies have reconsidered their involvement in the Saudi market or scaled back their operations.
Foreign direct investment and trade agreements may be affected by reputational risks associated with doing business with the kingdom.

Economic Diversification Efforts:
Saudi Arabia's Vision 2030, a plan to diversify its economy away from oil dependence, relies on attracting foreign investment and partnerships. Negative perceptions resulting from criticism can hinder these efforts.
The kingdom's goal of becoming a global investment destination may face challenges if human rights concerns persist.

Energy Markets and Geopolitics:

Saudi Arabia's position as a major player in global energy markets and its role in OPEC make it a key player in global geopolitics. Diplomatic tensions and criticism can have ripple effects in energy markets.

Disruptions or instability in energy markets due to political factors can impact global economic stability and energy prices.

Tourism Industry:

Saudi Arabia has been working to develop its tourism industry as part of economic diversification efforts. Negative perceptions resulting from criticism can affect the kingdom's ability to attract tourists and investors in the sector.

Foreign Aid and Investment:

Saudi Arabia provides foreign aid and investment to other countries in the region. Criticism of its actions, such as the war in Yemen, has led to calls for reducing arms sales and reconsidering foreign aid relationships.

Economic ties and investments in other countries can be influenced by Saudi Arabia's reputation and actions.

In summary, criticism of Saudi Arabia's human rights record and foreign policies has had a range of diplomatic and economic implications. It has strained diplomatic relations, prompted shifts in alliances, and affected the kingdom's economic diversification efforts. These implications underscore the complex interplay between diplomatic and economic factors in the international response to human rights concerns in Saudi Arabia.

Chapter 8: The Khashoggi Affair: Murder and International Fallout (2018)

Jamal Khashoggi was a prominent Saudi Arabian journalist and writer known for his critical views on the Saudi government and his contributions to various media outlets. His background and subsequent disappearance in 2018 garnered international attention and controversy. Here is an overview of Jamal Khashoggi's background and the events surrounding his disappearance:

Background:

Early Life: Jamal Khashoggi was born on October 13, 1958, in Medina, Saudi Arabia. He came from a prominent Saudi family and was well-educated, studying journalism at Indiana State University in the United States.

Journalistic Career: Khashoggi had a long and distinguished career as a journalist in Saudi Arabia and beyond. He worked for various Saudi newspapers and held editorial positions at publications like Al-Watan and Al-Hayat.

Government Relations: Throughout his career, Khashoggi maintained close ties to Saudi officials and the royal family, which allowed him access to high-level sources and insight into the Saudi government.

Critical Journalism: Over time, Khashoggi's journalism took a more critical turn, and he began to write articles and give interviews that openly criticized Saudi policies, including its stance on freedom of the press and its involvement in the Yemeni civil war.

Disappearance:

Visit to the Saudi Consulate: On October 2, 2018, Jamal Khashoggi entered the Saudi Arabian consulate in Istanbul, Turkey, to obtain documents related to his upcoming marriage to his Turkish fiancée, Hatice Cengiz. He had expressed concerns about his safety but proceeded with the visit.

Failure to Exit: Khashoggi did not exit the consulate, prompting concerns about his well-being. Turkish authorities, as well as his fiancée, raised alarms about his disappearance.

International Outcry: News of Khashoggi's disappearance led to international outrage and condemnation. Many governments and human rights organizations demanded answers from Saudi Arabia.

Saudi Explanation: Initially, Saudi officials denied any involvement in Khashoggi's disappearance, claiming that he had left the consulate. However, as evidence mounted, they eventually acknowledged that he had been killed inside the consulate.

Investigation and Findings: Turkish authorities conducted an investigation and alleged that Khashoggi was murdered by a team of Saudi agents who had traveled to Istanbul specifically for that purpose. His body was reportedly dismembered.

International Response: The murder of Jamal Khashoggi led to international condemnation of Saudi Arabia. Many countries, including the United States, imposed sanctions on Saudi officials believed to be involved in the killing.

Impact on Saudi Arabia: The Khashoggi case had a significant impact on Saudi Arabia's international reputation, straining its relations with Western countries and prompting a reevaluation of its human rights record.

Ongoing Investigations: Investigations into the murder, accountability, and justice for Jamal Khashoggi continue to be topics of international concern and diplomatic discussion.

The disappearance and murder of Jamal Khashoggi brought global attention to the issue of press freedom and the treatment of dissidents in Saudi Arabia. It remains a deeply controversial and politically sensitive case that has had far-reaching diplomatic and human rights implications.

The international outcry and political fallout following the murder of Jamal Khashoggi were significant and had wide-ranging implications for Saudi Arabia and its relations with other countries. The events that transpired in the aftermath of Khashoggi's killing highlighted the global response to this high-profile incident:

Global Condemnation: The murder of Jamal Khashoggi sparked widespread condemnation from governments, human rights organizations, and the international community. Leaders and officials from various countries expressed shock and outrage over the killing.

Sanctions and Diplomatic Measures:

Several countries, including the United States, imposed sanctions on Saudi officials believed to be involved in the murder. These sanctions targeted individuals' assets and restricted their ability to travel.

Some countries, such as Germany, suspended arms sales to Saudi Arabia in response to the Khashoggi case.

Diplomatic ties between Saudi Arabia and certain Western countries, including Canada, experienced strain as a result of the incident.

International Investigations:

Calls for an independent and international investigation into the murder grew louder. Many countries and organizations demanded a transparent and impartial inquiry to uncover the truth behind Khashoggi's killing.

The United Nations and its special rapporteur on extrajudicial executions conducted investigations and called for accountability.

Media and Advocacy Campaigns:

The Khashoggi case brought heightened attention to the issue of press freedom and the safety of journalists worldwide. Media outlets and advocacy groups launched campaigns to raise awareness about threats to journalism and the need to protect journalists' rights.

Economic and Business Impact:
The controversy surrounding the murder led to concerns among businesses and investors. Some companies reconsidered their involvement in Saudi Arabia, affecting economic partnerships and investments.
Major international business leaders withdrew from the Saudi government's flagship investment conference, the Future Investment Initiative, in response to the Khashoggi case.

Diplomatic Pressures and Reassessments:
The Khashoggi case prompted a reassessment of diplomatic relations with Saudi Arabia. Countries faced difficult decisions about how to balance their economic interests with human rights concerns.
Some countries demanded transparency, accountability, and a full investigation from Saudi Arabia.

Impact on Saudi Arabia's Reputation:
The international fallout from the Khashoggi murder damaged Saudi Arabia's reputation on the global stage. The kingdom faced increased scrutiny and skepticism from the international community regarding its commitment to human rights and the rule of law.

Long-Term Repercussions:
The Khashoggi case had a lasting impact on Saudi Arabia's foreign relations and diplomacy. It also influenced perceptions of the kingdom and its leadership.

Ongoing Repercussions: Despite initial condemnations and sanctions, the Khashoggi case remains a topic of ongoing international discussion and concern. Calls for accountability and justice continue to be raised by governments, human rights organizations, and advocates.

In sum, the murder of Jamal Khashoggi generated a global response characterized by condemnation, sanctions, and diplomatic pressures on Saudi Arabia. It underscored the complexities of balancing economic and political interests with human rights considerations in international relations. The case also had lasting implications for Saudi Arabia's reputation on the world stage and its relations with other countries.

Chapter 9: Online Dissent and Social Media: Challenges to State Control (21st Century)

The rise of online dissent and activism has had a profound impact on Saudi Arabia, particularly in the context of the kingdom's restrictive environment for freedom of expression and political dissent. Online platforms and social media have become important tools for Saudis and activists to voice their opinions, advocate for change, and raise awareness about various issues. Here are key aspects of this phenomenon:

1. Digital Communication as an Outlet:
Saudi Arabia has a relatively young population, and a significant portion of it is tech-savvy. The internet and social media have provided a platform for Saudis to communicate and organize beyond traditional government-controlled media.

2. Social Media Platforms:
Platforms like Twitter, Instagram, Snapchat, and YouTube are widely used by Saudis to express their views and connect with like-minded individuals. Twitter, in particular, has been a prominent platform for political and social discourse.

3. Advocacy for Social Issues:
Saudis have used online platforms to advocate for social issues, including women's rights, labor rights, and religious freedom. Activists have initiated campaigns and shared personal stories to shed light on these issues.

4. Political Activism:
Online spaces have allowed Saudis to engage in political activism and express dissenting views on government policies and actions. This has included criticism of

government decisions, human rights abuses, and calls for political reforms.

5. Challenges and Risks:
Despite the opportunities for free expression online, Saudi authorities have monitored, censored, and cracked down on online dissent. Activists, bloggers, and social media users have faced arrest and prosecution for their online activities.

6. Global Reach and Solidarity:
Online dissent in Saudi Arabia has gained international attention, with global human rights organizations and foreign governments expressing concern about the treatment of activists. Online campaigns have also sought to build solidarity with international counterparts.

7. Platforms for Women's Rights:
Women's rights activists have utilized social media to campaign against the male guardianship system, promote gender equality, and document cases of discrimination. The #Women2Drive campaign, for example, garnered significant international support.

8. Role of Diaspora:
Saudi activists in exile have played a key role in online dissent, as they can speak more freely from abroad. They use social media to maintain connections with those inside Saudi Arabia and amplify their messages globally.

9. Government Response:
Saudi authorities have taken measures to monitor and control online dissent, including the implementation of cybercrime laws and surveillance. They have arrested and imprisoned individuals for their online activities.

10. Evolving Landscape:
The landscape of online dissent in Saudi Arabia is continually evolving. Activists adapt to government crackdowns, find new ways to communicate securely, and leverage social media to draw attention to issues.

Online dissent and activism in Saudi Arabia are part of a larger global trend where digital platforms have empowered individuals to engage in public discourse and advocate for change. However, the Saudi government's response has demonstrated its determination to maintain control over online spaces, resulting in a challenging environment for activists and online dissenters.

Social media platforms have had a significant impact on Saudi Arabian society and politics, shaping the way people communicate, share information, and engage in public discourse. Here are key aspects of the impact of social media platforms in Saudi Arabia:

Freedom of Expression: Social media platforms provide a relatively open space for Saudis to express their views and opinions on various topics, including politics, religion, and social issues. This has allowed for a degree of freedom of expression that was previously restricted in traditional media.

Political Activism: Twitter, in particular, has become a prominent platform for political activism and dissent. Saudis use hashtags to discuss and critique government policies, voice their political opinions, and rally support for various causes.

Censorship and Surveillance: While social media platforms offer a platform for free expression, Saudi authorities have also increased online censorship and surveillance efforts. Websites and content deemed critical of the government or religious authorities are often blocked, and individuals engaged in online dissent may face monitoring and legal repercussions.

Women's Rights Advocacy: Saudi women have used social media to advocate for their rights, particularly in campaigns against the male guardianship system and for the right to drive. Activists and ordinary women have shared their stories and experiences, raising awareness and garnering international support.

Global Reach: Social media platforms have allowed Saudi activists to reach a global audience and raise awareness about human rights issues in the kingdom. Campaigns initiated by Saudi activists have received attention and support from international human rights organizations.

Youth Engagement: Saudi Arabia has a large youth population, and social media platforms have played a crucial role in engaging young people in political and social discussions. It has also been a tool for political mobilization, including during the Arab Spring.

Religious Discourse: Social media has influenced religious discourse in Saudi Arabia. While some use it to promote conservative interpretations of Islam, others use it to discuss more progressive and reformist interpretations, sparking debates about religious and social norms.

Economic Opportunities: Social media has also opened up economic opportunities for Saudis, with many entrepreneurs using platforms like Instagram to start businesses and sell products. Influencer marketing has become a significant industry in the country.

Government Engagement: The Saudi government recognizes the importance of social media and has established official social media accounts to engage with citizens and convey its messages. These accounts provide a channel for government announcements and responses to public concerns.

Challenges and Risks: Despite the opportunities, online activism and dissent in Saudi Arabia come with risks. Individuals who express dissenting views or criticize the government can face legal consequences, including arrest and imprisonment.

Changing Media Landscape: Social media has disrupted the traditional media landscape in Saudi Arabia, with many citizens turning to digital platforms for news and information rather than relying solely on state-controlled media.

In summary, social media platforms have played a transformative role in Saudi Arabian society by providing a space for free expression, political activism, and advocacy for various causes. However, they also pose challenges, as the Saudi government seeks to maintain control over online discourse and dissent. The impact of social media continues to evolve as the digital landscape evolves and as Saudi activists adapt to changing circumstances.

Chapter 10: The Future of Dissidence: Prospects for Change and Stability (Present and Beyond)

As of my last knowledge update in September 2021, the dissidence landscape in Saudi Arabia was characterized by a complex mix of challenges, including government crackdowns on dissent, online activism, human rights concerns, and the Saudi government's efforts to control and manage opposition. It's important to note that the situation can change rapidly, and developments may have occurred since that time. Here is an overview of the key aspects of the dissidence landscape in Saudi Arabia as of that period:

1. Crackdown on Dissent:
The Saudi government, led by Crown Prince Mohammed bin Salman, had undertaken a significant crackdown on dissent, targeting activists, journalists, academics, and religious clerics critical of the regime. This included mass arrests and detentions.

2. Online Activism and Social Media:
Despite government restrictions, social media remained a critical platform for activists to voice their concerns and engage in political and social discussions. Twitter, in particular, continued to be a space for political discourse and criticism.

3. Women's Rights Activism:
Women's rights activists, both inside and outside Saudi Arabia, continued to campaign for gender equality and an end to the male guardianship system. Several activists had been arrested and detained for their advocacy efforts.

4. International Advocacy:
Human rights organizations, foreign governments, and international activists had been vocal in raising concerns

about human rights abuses and the treatment of dissidents in Saudi Arabia. The Jamal Khashoggi case had also heightened international scrutiny of Saudi Arabia's actions.

5. Online Surveillance and Censorship:
The Saudi government had increased efforts to monitor and control online dissent, implementing strict cybersecurity laws and blocking websites and content deemed critical or inappropriate.

6. Shia Minority Dissent:
Dissent and protests within the Shia minority in Eastern Province had continued, with some Shia activists expressing grievances related to discrimination, religious freedoms, and social and economic inequalities.

7. Economic and Social Changes:
The government had initiated economic and social reforms under the Vision 2030 plan, which included diversifying the economy and introducing cultural and entertainment reforms. While some welcomed these changes, others remained critical of the pace and extent of reforms.

8. Challenges to the Saudi Government:
Dissent had also manifested in challenges to the Saudi government's policies, including its involvement in the war in Yemen, its regional policies, and its diplomatic disputes with neighboring countries like Qatar.

9. Expatriate Dissidence:
Saudi dissidents living in exile had played a significant role in criticizing the government and advocating for change from abroad. These individuals often used social media and international platforms to amplify their voices.

10. Legal Reforms:
The Saudi government had announced legal reforms, including changes to the legal system and the introduction of new laws aimed at improving human rights. However, many

remained skeptical of the government's commitment to implementing these reforms effectively.

Please note that the situation in Saudi Arabia is subject to change, and it is advisable to consult current news sources and reports from human rights organizations for the latest developments and insights into the dissidence landscape in the country.

Predicting the future of dissidence in Saudi Arabia is challenging due to the evolving nature of political, social, and technological factors. However, we can make some general observations and predictions based on historical trends and ongoing developments. Keep in mind that these predictions are speculative and subject to change based on various factors:

1. Continued Online Activism: Online activism and dissent are likely to persist as a prominent form of expression in Saudi Arabia. Social media platforms will remain crucial for citizens to voice their opinions, advocate for change, and discuss political and social issues.

2. Government Crackdowns: The Saudi government is likely to continue its efforts to monitor and control online dissent. Cybersecurity measures and censorship may become more sophisticated as authorities seek to prevent the spread of critical content.

3. Persistence of Women's Rights Activism: Women's rights activists are expected to continue their campaigns for gender equality, the abolition of the male guardianship system, and broader women's rights reforms. The government may make limited concessions while maintaining control over the pace and scope of reforms.

4. International Advocacy: International human rights organizations, foreign governments, and advocacy groups are likely to continue pressuring Saudi Arabia over its human rights record and treatment of dissidents. High-profile cases, such as that of Jamal Khashoggi, will remain focal points for international scrutiny.

5. Exile Activism: Saudi dissidents living in exile are expected to play an increasingly significant role in criticizing the government and advocating for change from abroad. They will continue to use international platforms to amplify their voices and collaborate with global human rights organizations.

6. Shia Minority Dissent: Dissent within the Shia minority is likely to persist, with some activists continuing to raise concerns related to religious freedoms, discrimination, and socioeconomic disparities. The government may respond with a combination of repression and limited concessions.

7. Economic and Social Reforms: The government's Vision 2030 economic and social reforms may generate a mix of support and criticism. While some may see these reforms as positive steps, others may view them as insufficient or as attempts to distract from human rights concerns.

8. Legal Reforms: Legal reforms may continue to be announced, but their effectiveness and implementation will be closely scrutinized. The government may use legal reforms to improve its international image while maintaining strict control over dissent.

9. Changing Regional Dynamics: Regional developments, including conflicts and alliances, can impact the Saudi government's approach to dissent and its relations with regional actors. Shifts in regional politics may influence Saudi Arabia's domestic policies and its response to dissidence.

10. Unpredictable Events: As history has shown, unexpected events and developments can significantly impact the dissidence landscape. High-profile incidents or crises could lead to shifts in government policies or public sentiment.

In summary, the future of dissidence in Saudi Arabia will be influenced by a dynamic interplay of political, social, and technological factors. While certain trends are likely to continue, the specific outcomes and trajectories of dissent in the kingdom will depend on how these factors evolve and interact in the years to come.

Conclusion

In the pages of "House of Saud: Saudi Arabia's Royal Dynasty - Thrones, Oil, and Vision 2030," readers have embarked on an extraordinary journey through the complex and multifaceted history of the House of Saud and the Kingdom of Saudi Arabia. This four-book bundle has delved into the heart of a royal lineage that evolved from desert chieftains to formidable monarchs, shaping the destiny of a nation and impacting the world in profound ways.

In Book 1, "The Rise of the House of Saud: From Desert Chieftains to Saudi Monarchs (1700s-1900s)," we unveiled the nomadic roots of the Saudi family, tracing their remarkable journey from humble beginnings to the establishment of the First Saudi State. The enduring Bedouin traditions and tribal alliances laid the foundation for their rise to prominence.

Book 2, "Oil, Power, and Influence: House of Saud in the 20th Century (1900s-2000s)," navigated through the tumultuous 20th century, where the discovery of oil catapulted Saudi Arabia into the global spotlight. We witnessed how the Kingdom leveraged its oil wealth to become a major player on the world stage, while also experiencing internal transformations and challenges.

The third installment, "Modernization and Tradition: House of Saud's Vision 2030 (2000s-Present)," transported us into the 21st century, where the ambitious Vision 2030 plan aimed to diversify the Saudi economy and usher in a new era of social and cultural change. We explored the challenges and opportunities presented by this transformative vision.

Finally, Book 4, "Dissidence and the House of Saud: A History of Opposition (20th-21st Century)," delved into the voices of dissent that have echoed throughout the House of Saud's history. From religious clerics to women's rights activists, we examined the opposition movements that emerged and the government's responses, shedding light on the complexities of dissent in Saudi Arabia.

As we conclude this compelling narrative, it is evident that the House of Saud's legacy is one of resilience, adaptability, and enduring significance. Their journey from the arid sands of the Arabian Desert to the modern corridors of power is a testament to the ever-evolving nature of leadership and governance. The discovery of oil, the pursuit of modernization, and the challenges of dissent have all left an indelible mark on Saudi Arabia's past and present.

In an era defined by global interconnectedness and shifting paradigms, Saudi Arabia's role in the Middle East and the world remains pivotal. As Vision 2030 continues to unfold and as the Kingdom grapples with the complexities of dissent and societal change, the House of Saud faces both opportunities and challenges on the path ahead.

"House of Saud: Saudi Arabia's Royal Dynasty - Thrones, Oil, and Vision 2030" has aimed to provide a comprehensive and insightful exploration of these intricate facets. It is our hope that this bundle has enriched your understanding of Saudi Arabia's past, present, and the intriguing possibilities that lie on the horizon. As the House of Saud continues to navigate the currents of history, its story remains one of enduring significance in the tapestry of our world's political and cultural landscape.

About A. J. Kingston

A. J. Kingston is a writer, historian, and lover of all things historical. Born and raised in a small town in the United States, A. J. developed a deep appreciation for the past from an early age. She studied history at the university, earning her degree with honors, and went on to write a series of acclaimed books about different periods and topics in history.

A. J.'s writing is characterized by its clarity, evocative language, and meticulous research. She has a particular talent for bringing the lives of ordinary people in the past to life, drawing on diaries, letters, and other documents to create rich and nuanced portraits of people from all walks of life. Her work has been praised for its deep empathy, its attention to detail, and its ability to make history come alive for readers.

In addition to her writing, A. J. is a sought-after speaker and commentator on historical topics. She has given talks and presentations at universities, museums, and other venues, sharing her passion for history with audiences around the world. Her ability to connect with people and make history relevant to their lives has earned her a devoted following and a reputation as one of the most engaging and insightful historical writers of her generation.

A. J.'s writing has been recognized with numerous awards and honors. She lives in California with her family, and continues to write and speak on historical topics.